P9-ART-013

Also by Gary Hart

Right From the Start
A New Democracy
America Can Win (with William S. Lind)
The Double Man (with William S. Cohen)
The Strategies of Zeus
Russia Shakes the World

THE GOOD FIGHT

Random House New York

THE
GOOD
FIGHT

The Education of
an American
Reformer

GARY
HART

Library of Congress Cataloging-in-Publication Data

Hart, Gary.
The good fight: the education of an American
reformer/Gary Hart.
p. cm.
Includes index.
1. Hart, Gary.   2. Legislators—United States—
Biography.   3. United States. Congress. Senate—Biography.
I. Title.
E840.8.H285A3   1993
328.73′092—dc20   92-56817
[B]

Manufactured in the United States of America

9 8 7 6 5 4 3 2

First Edition

Book design by Lilly Langotsky

For
A. L. H.
and
J. W. H.

No man is so much raised on high by any of his acts as are those who have reformed republics and kingdoms with new laws and institutions. . . . After those who have been gods, such men get the first praises.

NICCOLÒ MACHIAVELLI

The Discourses

(Discourse on Reforming the

Government of Florence)

Foreword

A VOICE OF RETICENCE

This is a book about reform—more specifically, about why it is so difficult to bring about change in a country that claims to believe in change. Some of the barriers to reform in America are cultural, and one of the more intrusive is our society's present egocentricity.

The author's only qualification to write on this theme of reform is a quarter century of personal experience, experience in trying to bring about major progressive changes in a variety of arenas. The question is, How can this experience be used to identify the barriers to reform and yet avoid the prevalent malady of egocentricity? It is, stylistically at least, a problem of voice. In relying on personal experiences while minimizing ego, the author sought guidance from Henry Adams, who addressed the same problem, albeit on a much larger and a more important scale, by using the third person. In his classic autobiography, the story of his own "education," his voice is that of detached observer of himself and his life. Few today would quarrel with the assertion that this approach succeeded: the reader readily appreciates Adams's remote reports of his thoughts and experiences.

Adams was clearly reticent about the abundance of ego in his own age. Jean-Jacques Rousseau was a great educator of the eighteenth century, Adams noted, and the first to "erect a monument of warning against the Ego." Like Adams, the author would use the ego only "for purposes of model, to become a manikin on which the toilet of education is to be draped in order to show the fit or misfit of the clothes. The object of the study is the garment, not the figure." The objects of the study of this book are the ideas that formed the education of a reformer in the good fight for progressive change.

In an age festooned with ego, the author's use of the third-person narrator is a small form of protest. Today's cult of narcissism demands that all reality be personalized, all truth revealed through the eyes and experience of a personality. Validation of the personality, through focus on his or her story, takes precedence over ideas. Instead of understanding the idea, we try in every way possible to know the personality that may (or may not) have produced the idea. Ego and personality become barriers to progress; they obscure the larger goal: the search for cause, mission, and the ideal. By seeking to diminish the author's role and by focusing on the worthy lives of great reformers, it is hoped the reader can clearly focus on the idea and the ideal of reform in America.

Contrary to the conservative's bias, the instinct for reform does not exist for its own sake. A reformer does not seek change out of boredom with the status quo. Reform is dedicated to notions of progress and justice, to the notion of society's improvability. It is based on concrete ideas and proposals for achieving them. In this book, the author will sketch the lives and passions of his teachers—great individuals who have challenged orthodoxy, including Thomas Jefferson, Leo Tolstoy, Mikhail Gorbachev, and Vaclav Havel—as a kind of mosaic backdrop against which the good fight is waged.

In order to illustrate and dramatize the cause of reform, both concretely and philosophically, the author has drawn on his immediate experiences—as an activist, senator, and presidential candidate—on the front lines of the struggle. These clashes and struggles make greater sense if seen in the historic context of the reform impulse, whether exhibited by Søren Kierkegaard challenging the Danish Church or by John Wesley fighting for social justice in eighteenth-century England. The vision of these and other reformers is worth explication and appreciation as we wage our own good fights.

Thus, the first part of the book is devoted to the inspiration provided by reform heroes of the past—an unlikely quartet composed of Wesley, Kierkegaard, Tolstoy, and Jefferson. The second part tells of the author's own experiences as a reformer and his education in the struggles to reform the CIA, the Pentagon, the energy industry, and our national economic agenda. The final part concerns the hope for future reform and is set in the context of reform heroes at home and abroad.

Reformers challenge the conventional wisdom. They are at best troublesome and at worst provocateurs. They almost never succeed in their own lifetime. But often their ideas are adopted by more conventional leaders and thus given acceptance. Being singular and sometimes idiosyncratic, a reformer offers his inevitable enemies much by way of ammunition. The nineteenth-century Irish patriot Charles Stewart Parnell is one of the more notable examples of those whose personal struggles are used to obscure their public, political ones.

The author, likewise, had the misfortune to become a pioneer of sorts in a late-twentieth-century test by the American media of the outer limits of its authority to inquire into the private lives of public figures, if need be by surreptitious surveillance. Happily for those who follow, there are positive indications that those limits are being restored to a saner, more humane perimeter. In the meantime, the author fervently hopes that his effort to provide a guided tour through the late-twentieth-century reform battlefields of America can be seen apart from a single sensationalized incident, now years old, that was viewed as comic by some, as tragic by a few, and with indifference by most who care for America's future. This book has been written as a brief against those who sought to trivialize the ideal of democratic reform by trivializing the author's life.

The voice of the reformer in this book is a voice of reticence, reticence occasioned by a lifetime of little success in battles for reform, by personal and political failures, and mostly, by an age of ego. This book is written in a kind of refined Tolstoyan belief that ideas, in the long run, are more important than personalities and politicians. The voice of the reticent reformer is meant to focus the reader's attention on ideas for progressive change and not on the one who wages the good fight to carry them out.

GARY HART

KITTREDGE, COLORADO

Acknowledgments

This book owes its existence to Mr. Jonathan Karp, of Random House, who is its editor. He is not to be blamed for its shortcomings, because it is not exactly the book he originally imagined. Out of great respect for him, the author should also write that book someday. In any case, Jonathan deserves the credit for whatever this book adds to the good fight. Ms. Philippa Brophy, of Sterling Lord Literistic, once again deserves much appreciation for her patience and long-suffering in the role of mediator between author and publisher. The author extends particular thanks also to Bill Shore and Rick Allen for valuable editorial assistance, encouragement, and friendship. Mostly, all who believe in progressive change must acknowledge the continuing contribution of the heroes of reform, great and small. They deserve the greatest praise.

Contents

Introduction

REFLECTIONS OF A FAILED
REFORMER

Much of this book was written in the darkest hour of
the morning, when mortality pulls a chair close to the
bedside and whispers her inescapable reminder into a
troubled and wakeful ear, a reminder seldom delivered
and almost never heard by a reformer swept up in the
dust, heat, and combat of public life. Moments—or
years—for reflection, however granted, demand response to mortality's reminder. And for those inclined
toward political reflection, quadrennial national elections provide the occasion to ponder our country's future in the context of its complex past.

The 1992 presidential election represented the decline of an era of economic royalism and social Dar-
winism. It does not necessarily, however, signal the
advent of a new era of reform. The Democratic ascen-
dancy and the Clinton administration arrived on a
platform of change but also on a platform of modera-

tion. President Clinton's position on any spectrum of historic reform will probably be determined less by what policy initiatives he chooses to undertake and more by the boldness of his reaction and response to unpredictable challenges. Franklin Roosevelt did not arrive on earth burdened with the natural reformer's soul, but his response to fate and crisis made him twentieth-century America's great reformer.

The real prospect for a late-twentieth-century reform era will be taken up in this book's afterword in light of a quarter century of reform's frustration by "gravity, custom and fear," by materialism and greed, and by cultural trivialization.

But there are other profound barriers to reform. A nation founded in revolution has adopted political structures so inherently conservative as virtually to guarantee against any replication of its birth throes. To the degree that the tides of history finally require change in America, often after years or decades of lethargic status quo, reform is the American alternative to revolution. Structures and institutions, policies and programs are altered or experimented with to answer changed circumstances and, more important, to prevent social chaos and upheaval. The most vivid illustration of this phenomenon is the New Deal response to the Great Depression.

Change in the context of politics is a debased term, routinely raised as the rallying cry of the opposition party, the party out of power. But it is a freighted word, a word with significance, because it is the catalyst of reform. Reform of political, social, and economic institutions rarely occurs when things are calm, when all is well. Reform is the orderly but still controversial response to the geological plate shifts of history. In 1992, few would contemplate revolution, but many would vote for a Democratic presidential candidate who promised change. If they voted for him in large enough numbers, and if circumstances turned out to be as dire once in office as he described them to be in seeking the office, then he might even find it a necessity to venture beyond marginal change to undertake fundamental institutional and structural reforms.

It all depends, as it always has, on how bad most Americans really think things are. The operative word here is "really," for it is fashionable for Americans to decry the state of the nation on the one hand but shrink with apprehension from genuine new ideas and approaches when proposed. We are more courageous in our analyses than we are in our prescriptions. Even in periods when our problems seem to lend themselves to easy solutions and quick fixes, however, it is important to study and understand the elements and theory of reform. For we may discover that, beneath the surface, those same problems have roots so deep and grotesquely intertwined that traditional remedies and superficial fixes will not suffice. The only answer under such conditions, whether we like it or not, is fundamental change: reform.

An illustration exposing the difference between traditional and reform thinking is in order. In the 1970s, America faced an energy crisis that threatened to damage the nation's economy severely and permanently. Public outcry springing from widespread fear led the institutions of government to struggle to devise a national energy policy. These institutions—the White House and Congress in particular—performed admirably in fashioning a reform energy program out of a tangled thicket of interests. Then two things happened: a laissez-faire president who did not believe in such things entered office, and as if to demonstrate his life-long good fortune, world oil prices fell through the floor. All likelihood of major reforms in energy policy disappeared. Has the dragon been dispatched? Of course not. It is merely lying in wait for the coming of another likely hour in which to strike, an hour when the nation is again asleep. Drift and good fortune will defeat anticipation and reform every day of the week.

One fact remains inescapable: the day will come when circumstances will require an era of American reform. This book represents an effort to discover and disclose the reform ideal, its nature, texture, roots, and —for some—its peculiar attractions. After a confused quarter century of reformist activism, there is a wry satisfaction in being given a kind of permanent sabbatical in which to try to sum up a lifetime of reform, the movements and their motives, the Dionysian, psychedelic sixties, the Machiavellian seventies, the narcissistic, materialistic eighties (the rich man's sixties), the sober nineties. Most understand when the Grateful Dead sing, "What a long, strange trip it's been."

Even accepting that each generation believes its time to be unique, little in the American experience— except for the revolutionary and Civil War periods— compares with the past three decades in terms of social oscillation. Over the past thirty years, Americans have experimented with virtually every extreme of personal gratification—as if in an effort to evade the draft of civic duty—and have charged about in a complex variety of reform and counterreform skirmishes, all of which seem to have left them more confused than ever.

This reformer was of the tranquil Eisenhower happy-days generation, in whom the bright star-burst promise of Kennedy and Camelot ignited the spark of idealism and produced the ultimate empowerment of "one person can make a difference, and every person should try." Of those to whom much is given, much is required. This was the light that fired the torch of our idealism and thrust a student of philosophy and religion, rather listlessly and unconvincingly inclined toward academia, into the more secular cause of public service, the cause of social justice and economic equity, of helping to improve his nation's well-being here and now. This is what persuaded him to exchange the abstract world of knowledge for the fiercely political world of public service.

By way of contrast, two decades later "leaders" of the eighties told Americans they were responsible only to and for themselves, and devil take the hindmost. Admittedly, there were those in the sanctuaries of official and corporate America who professed belief that all boats—supposedly including even the tiniest leaky skiff—would be lifted by what they saluted in the glib rhetoric of the day as a "rising tide." Society's mood at the time was very much inclined toward these dreamy beliefs in notions of utopian wealth. But very quickly, a preponderance of bitter evidence uncloaked this halcyon metaphor to reveal a stiff financial breeze filling the sails only of the gilded yachts.

Missing during the heyday of rampant individualism was any sense of the virtue of idealism—the notion that one ought to live for something larger than oneself—that had characterized the advent of this reformer's era. The eighties, by contrast, were a great lottery featuring many financial winners, society's heroes who suddenly became famous and ended up merely notorious. An impressive number of these winners are now in jail, mostly for manipulations of securities laws that even the most sympathetic (de)regulator could not forever ignore, especially when aroused from bureaucratic slumber by deceived investors and irate taxpayers. But his fellow citizens still honor the leader who bankrupted the nation, apparently because he managed it all with an amiable grin.

Americans found it convenient to believe that the antique notion of social progress was but a mirage, a snare, and a delusion, and the only worthy pursuit was a return to the latent values of the buccaneer, values never far below the surface of the American imagination. So the eighties produced a class of buccaneers so egregiously greedy that it would have brought a blush of shame to the countenance of Commodore Vanderbilt in his prime.

This age of acquisitiveness bordering on plunder salved its social conscience by restoring the doctrine of personal charity, the ancient alternative to collective responsibility through social reform. Like a prim Anglican bishop delicately stepping over the bodies of the hungry and the homeless, Reagan's successor cynically put forward the homily of something called a thousand points of light. Presumably, this was meant to suggest that the human detritus of rampant laissez-faire could be accounted for if only each buccaneer would put just a farthing more in the Sabbath collection box. By the time Mr. Bush reached the front of the long queue for power, it had become necessary to erect a patently fraudulent belief such as this as a façade for morality, because even the most ardent Reaganite no longer clung to the popular but cruel notion that the poor remain so by choice.

The points-of-light philosophy, if it could be dignified as such, had got White House occupants through the eighties and early nineties by somehow managing to convince middle-class Americans that more serious efforts at social and economic reform were unnecessary at best and hopeless at worst. Americans have exhibited a healthy skepticism toward political reforms except in the most desperate of times, preferring to believe, with some cause, that the reformer is simply a kind of cranky misfit congenitally disposed to disturb the status quo. And America has had more than its share of these. The watchword, chanted like a mantra during the reformer's Senate years, was "If it ain't broke, don't fix it." Mostly this came from politicians who were still willing to debate whether the Great Depression qualified as "broke."

This reformer, looking back over a quarter century, is clearly tempted to settle scores with political administrations that gave a new meaning to the words *callousness* and *insensitivity*. Critics might wish to write this off as petty partisanship—except for this: history repeats itself, and it repeats itself in direct proportion to the public's ability to forget. The sooner we dismiss the Reagan-Bush era from our memory, the sooner it will return in some new form. The grievance here is less with Reagan and Bush and more with the mentality that brought them to power. Selfish leaders with no sense of social justice are promoted by voters who share those values. Times change, and the writing hand, having writ, will move on. But the memory of injustice must remain if injustice is not to conquer once more.

Even so temperate a social critic as Emerson thought "the key to all ages is—imbecility," by which he meant that almost all men, including heroes, at almost all times are "victims of gravity, custom and fear." Applying Emerson to the prospect for ongoing American political reform, the historian Arthur Schlesinger, Jr., wrote, "Given the power of gravity, custom and fear, the dead weight of inertia, of orthodoxy and of complacency, the tasks of persuading majorities to accept innovations remain forever formidable. What counts in the end is the subversion of old ideas by the changing environment."

As the twentieth century draws to a close in America, it is eminently clear that the political establishment's old ideas and dead weight of inertia are being subverted by a changing environment. All that popular majorities lack is a giant reform hero of Rooseveltian proportions (either Theodore or Franklin) who will challenge them to cross the static barricades of the status quo.

But foot soldiers of reform forever face deeply entrenched economic and political fortifications. Even though the Founders feared the instability that may result from mobocracy, the government institutions they created to disperse power, when coupled with innate American individualism and skepticism, encourage instead power structures dedicated to the preservation of economic royalism and corporate conservatism. "What struck me in the United States was the difficulty of shaking the majority in an opinion once conceived," wrote Tocqueville. Absent mass depressions, revolts of workers, or the immediate drama of burning cities, the reformer faces established power networks unfriendly to any idea pregnant with change. According to Machiavelli, "The reformer has enemies in all those who would profit by the older order, and only lukewarm defenders in all those who would profit by the new order; this luke-warmness arising partly from fear of their adversaries . . . and partly from the incredulity of mankind who do not believe in anything new until they have had actual experience of it."

Perhaps when all is said and done, the reformer is a mere crank, a perennial discontent, if not malcontent, one who is simply incapable of accepting and enjoying things as he finds them. This view of the American reformer as misfit explains much. It boxes the compass of unorthodox thought and behavior and makes the reformer an outsider, an émigré in a self-imposed internal exile from a society that refuses to meet his seemingly impossible standard of social perfection.

One would like to believe, however, that there is more to it than that. First of all, the American reformer is practically unique in the world of modern Western democracy. He has no real counterpart in sister industrialized cultures. He is, in his own ponderous way, as sui generis as the American bison, and with many similar characteristics—stubbornness, implacability, anachronicity, and humorlessness. His like is not to be found, for example, among late-twentieth-century European socialists, for he rejects the confines of doctrine and ideological orthodoxy. He does not want to move left; he wants to move forward. He is not a rigid ideologue; he is a pragmatic progressive.

The great question—to go forward or remain still—has found itself near the center of the age-old debate regarding the nature of government and has much to reveal concerning the complex motives of the American reformer. Jefferson and Emerson, among many others, found it persuasive to argue that virtually all democratic societies arrange themselves into two political parties, one of the status quo and one of change. Parties of change are brought into existence for any one of several reasons: the need to achieve a greater degree of social equity, the advent of eras of technological or economic upheaval, the occurrence of dramatic events in world affairs, or simply and most profoundly, the fear of revolution.

As the principal political instrument of cultural and ethnic assimilation, social innovation and experimentation, and correction of the maldistribution of wealth, the Democratic party can on most occasions—certainly throughout most of the twentieth century—lay fair claim to being the legitimate party of reform in America. The qualifier is important for two reasons: first, the early-twentieth-century tide of reform, the Progressive era, was led by Theodore Roosevelt, who established himself in the leadership of his own party as a reformer; and second, the Democratic party demonstrates a periodic tendency—most evident in the mid-nineteenth century—to conserve its own bastions of power rather than challenge the status quo. This latter point is crucial, for when the Democratic party has become conservative, has resisted reform and hidden from change, it has withered and failed. American voters sense intuitively and powerfully when the Democratic party betrays its beliefs, its historic role and mission, and its soul, and they turn it out of power and keep it out.

In this respect, the Democratic party shares a burden with America itself. Both hold themselves to very high standards, to historic missions not shared by their competitors, and therefore are judged harshly when they fail to uphold those standards. People demonstrate frustration with the Democratic party by denying it power when it betrays its true nature.

The reform impulse is based on an ironic gamble: to preserve is to risk; to conserve, one must change; for society to save its most treasured values, it must confront and constantly challenge a world that refuses to remain static. This truth is central to the American experience and thus to the American character. It is the reason America will sacrifice both leadership and uniqueness when it decides to stop, to stay, to refuse to embrace change. This is why, again intuitively, Americans want a Democratic party that is true to its Jeffersonian heritage and is a true reform party.

But Americans are profoundly uncomfortable with a Democratic party either too cautious or too confused to innovate when change demands it. A Democratic party that is not a reform party—one that is a toothless lion—is an increasingly disgusting thing. Americans do not need a neo-protectionist party desperate to preserve outdated, noncompetitive industries. They do not respect a party concerned with indexing old entitlement programs at the cost of affordable health protection for all. They will not embrace a putative reform party more concerned with preserving internal power-sharing arrangements than with challenging the status quo.

This is the epicenter of the reform dilemma. Those who share in power, those who by traditional position, negotiation, or election mandate participate in the governing process—and this includes opposition parties, established constituencies, the press and the broadcast media, and sources of political financing (among them lobbyists who double as advisers)—all define the boundaries of acceptable behavior and debate. Rules, both explicit and implicit, govern the terms for acceptable participation in the formulation of public policy. To participate, one must negotiate or win admission to the established arena through one of these means or institutions. Among themselves, these institutions and leaders constantly negotiate and renegotiate power-sharing arrangements. Manifestly, average people and so-called ordinary citizens have only limited access to these arrangements. Their best chance of making their views known is through their elected representatives, and even this small claim is usually handled by the multitudinous organizations to which most citizens belong.

This political process will instantly be recognized by a student of elementary civics as classic republican theory. And it works well in times of progress, expansion, and growth. An electorate whose standard of living is expanding complains only marginally. "Men," said Emerson, ". . . are conservatives after dinner."

But this is a beautiful theory being murdered by a gang of brutal facts, including the current facts of social stress and civil unrest, urban riots, racial strife and rising unemployment, and most of all, stagnant or falling net family incomes. One muscular fact leads this brutal gang: Americans are increasingly angry with traditional power structures and their arrangements for sharing power that now compose their government. They believe, with a great degree of accuracy, that their government operates in a world separate from them. The link of legitimacy perpetually being granted by the people to the governing power structure is seriously weakening. There are strong but still benign signs of this—at least as it applies to the two traditional political parties—in the nearly 20-percent vote for Ross Perot in the 1992 election.

As it has for the past several elections, the Democratic party has asked in 1992 to be given primary leadership within the established power structure. But

Americans do not particularly like the established political power arrangement and resent their historic reform party being co-opted by it. How can the Democratic party change things, they ask, when it is already so much part of things?

Sadly, the Democratic party became part of things largely during the radical antireform years of the 1980s. It did so because it did not have a Big Idea of its own, a new central organizing principle with which to govern in a rapidly changing world—a world seeking a new center of gravity after the collapse of communism —and because the president was believed to have a mandate, a mandate never meant to be used as he used it. The Reagan program was profoundly antireform, antiprogressive, and antidemocratic. It is now widely perceived to be so. But a decade ago many Democratic officials went along or kept quiet, intimidated into silence by the Great Communicator (a fiction) even as he ridiculed every traditional belief they and their party professed to have. The banner of reform, and the rhetoric attendant on it, were claimed in the name of antireform while Democrats permitted themselves to be herded into a pen called liberalism and cowed into silence.

This reformer participated in Senate Democratic caucuses in the crucial years of the early 1980s, when the prevailing sentiment was to acknowledge President Reagan's popularity, profess the belief that his policies were potentially disastrously wrong, but counsel giving him sufficient rope with which to hang himself and his party. There is much to be considered here concerning cynicism and want of courage on the part of party "leaders." Suffice it to say, however, that Reagan took the rope of debt that many Democrats helped provide and used it to hang the American economy.

During this dark period, when America's future was being mortgaged, when the middle class saw wealth evaporate upward and young people were seduced by chimeras created out of nothing more than debt and deficit, borrowing and buyout, Democrats could have reclaimed the strong convictions of their founder, Thomas Jefferson. Jefferson would have reminded us that he and his colleagues created a *democratic* republic, and he would have restated his conviction that laws and institutions must go hand in hand with the progress of the human mind; that is, they must evolve through reform. The Jeffersonian party of the late twentieth century could have used a reminder that it represents real people in more than just rhetorical ways. For this party had become as republican as the Republicans, preferring in important ways to share its opposition power among its constituencies rather than engage real citizens, meaningfully and consistently, in the administration of their own affairs. It is no accident that President Clinton's victory had much to do with his persistent promise to "stay in touch" with real people outside Washington.

It was Jefferson, not Hamilton, after all, who advocated self-government through ward-republics, a system of government analogous to that of our New England townships. These ward-republics had as their purpose the prevention of the centralization of power and the institutionalization of civic duty. Most important, however, was the sense of participation: "A government is republican in proportion as every member composing it has his equal voice in the direction of its concerns." "Every day," Jefferson argued, one must be a "participator in the government of affairs." This must be read as an instruction not only to the participator but also to the government that must assure participation.

It is much too easy today to dismiss democratic republicanism as some kind of anachronistic Jeffersonian sentimentality. Whatever other faults Jefferson may have had, sentimentality was not one of them. In fact,

Jefferson saw intuitively and clearheadedly that regardless of party or faction, the Hamiltonian formulation would prevail unless all citizens had a real opportunity to participate in the making of decisions that affect their lives and their progeny's future.

Even more important was Jefferson's belief that only the "common sense of the American people" could guarantee the country's adaptability. Reformers, he knew, would come from the ranks of wage earners, toilers, people of the soil, those with little stake in preserving the status quo and the existing power structures. Two hundred years later an American reformer would come to see that the enemy of reform—conservatism—is the natural by-product of concentrated wealth and power, just as manure is the natural by-product of cattle. For Jefferson, the idea of progress was associated with the "improvability" of the human mind, his assurance of which was central to his understanding of human nature. But to keep pace with a changing world, the progress of the human mind requires the constant reformation of human, political institutions, a notion anathema to the forces of conservative, centralized power.

In an 1813 letter to John Adams, he said it this way:

> One of the questions . . . on which our parties took different sides, was on the improvability of the human mind, in science, in ethics, in government, etc. Those who advocated reformation of institutions, pari passu, with the progress of science, maintained that no definite limits could be assigned to that progress. The enemies of reform, on the other hand, denied improvement, and advocated steady adherence to the principles, practices and institutions of our fathers, which they represented to us as the consummation of wisdom, and akme of excellence, beyond which the human mind could never advance.

Not only do certain individuals and classes separate on the issue of progress and reform versus conservatism and resistance to change, but political parties and the philosophies they represent also divide along these lines. Using Emerson's famous description, there will always be parties of memory and parties of hope. "Conservatism makes no poetry, breathes no prayer, has not invention," he wrote; "it is all memory."

So to believe that knowledge expands and improves, one must believe that the human mind is capable of expanding and improving with it. And to encourage—even to permit—the improvement of the human mind, and to keep pace with the progress of knowledge, human institutions and laws must be reformed. To Jefferson's regret, this even required a political party to champion the cause of reform against the conservative forces of concentrated power and wealth. Such a cause was not and is not liberalism, as partisan Republican campaign consultants have pejoratively defined it. It is reform progressivism.

No more singular, powerful argument can be made for the necessity of reform than this. Indeed, the lonely reformer would belong to the Democratic party not because his forefathers did but because it still offers the promise of becoming once again what Jefferson wished it to be: the party that truly distributes power instead of hoarding it in the salons of Washington, the party of participation, progress, and reform, the party of hope.

The hope for the Democratic party and for America rests in an ability and a willingness to exchange encrusted power-sharing arrangements, cordial and comfortable for those involved, for genuine democratic republicanism and truly broad-based civic involvement. And, too, it rests in a willingness to select leaders committed to the Jeffersonian notion of reform—a notion that encompasses the reform of party structures, political rules, and comfortable personal arrangements, the reform of political and government institutions, and the reform of the fundamental policies that guide the nation.

Fate in the form of yet another Russian revolution has given us a unique opportunity to restructure our practices and priorities for a new century. The question is whether America will prove worthy of this opportunity, whether it will remain still or go forward.

The creed of the American reformer is a simple one: times change; therefore, we must change. This proposition is essentially biological—perhaps even Darwinian—in derivation. "Adapt or die" is the way it is taught to schoolchildren, some of whom go on to become sufficiently successful that, predictably, they dedicate themselves to the total frustration of this natural law.

Even in the best of times—and the late twentieth century was by no means such a time—the reformer's lot is less than enviable. To the European, the reformer is but an exotic, a creature to be humorously observed and possibly given dinner. But to the American of means or consequence, the reformer has about him the smell of gunpowder. Disgust is the wealthy man's best response, fear and loathing his worst. "Conservatism, being an upper-class characteristic, is decorous," wrote Thorstein Veblen, "and, conversely, innovation, being a lower-class phenomenon, is vulgar." To the person of property, power, or position, heavily invested in things-as-they-are, there is but a distinction without a difference between a reformer and an outright revolutionary.

But the reformer's most dangerous enemy is not the person on the right, the orthodox conservative. The reformer's real enemy is the establishment center, the clubby pragmatist, the person to whom fortune has granted that most admirable of qualities, absolute certainty. Certainty has enormous seductive charm. It qualifies one to govern and to lead. To have a sense of certainty is to belong to the ultimate secret society: the elect who have been granted divinity's greatest boon—security. Certainty by definition knows no doubt.

To believe in progress and improvement in the human condition is to harbor the most perilous doubt of all, the doubt that the status quo truly offers security. Furthermore, the person of certainty is a person of calculation, whereas the reformer is a person of passion. Certainty is greatly afraid of the passionate pilgrim, the quixotic Jeremiah crying doom upon a society that will neither change nor doubt, a society certain of its status and its security.

Jefferson may or may not have anticipated the dilemma of the American reformer at the twilight of the twentieth century. His eighteenth-century empiricism led him to believe that advances in scientific discovery would direct the forward march of human wisdom and that the conservative laws and institutions structured by forces of concentrated wealth and power would be brought along in the wake. Science, broadly defined to include all knowledge, would bring along politics.

But the latter-day American reformer finds new and difficult twists that amount to virtual frustration of political progress. Jefferson, optimist that he was, thought science to be benign. He would doubtless have been dismayed to see its most extravagant manifestations two hundred years later dedicated to fantastic engines of destruction. The worst of these engines were never used for their designated purposes (thanks to God), but they were destructive to reform and reformers nonetheless. Science in the service of the cold war came to be the enemy of reform. Science as applied to the methods of war came to be the principal instrument of antireform.

America was largely ignorant of this development. And of reformers who could warn of its dangers, there were few. Public revenues of enormous proportions that might otherwise have been dedicated to the genuine progress of the human mind and spirit instead found their way into the laboratories of science, which brought forth guidance systems for nuclear missiles of such astonishing accuracy at such incredible distances that even this American reformer could not fail to be impressed. Here was science, as applied to war, literally extracting the breath—and life—from social progress and reform.

There developed, especially within the party of reform, a conspiracy of silence. Laws and institutions were not keeping pace with the progress of the human mind simply because this particular form of progress took much of the public's money in a cause with which none dared quarrel, the defense of our way of life, our values, and our very liberties. Or so we quickly came to believe, under a heavy barrage of self-generated propaganda. Reform in the shape of laws and institutions adapted to the progress of the human mind took second place or worse. Arguably, the human mind was not making much progress during the cold war.

So the American reformer found himself hostage to a scientific preoccupation with missile guidance systems and their political applications. Beyond the diversion and co-optation of science by the military-industrial complex, two other phenomena bracketed the reformer's brief activist career. Though now flawed in skeptical retrospect and seemingly so brief in memory as to suggest it possibly never even happened, there once arose a new time of idealism and optimism, and then it fell prey to a plague of assassins. Camelot might have swept up many a young reformer into its unlimited promise of progress and hope, but fate, meanwhile, was in the shadows, slipping lead into the boxing gloves. Sane people thought then—and a few still do—that it all happened in a nightmare. Others, almost by anticipation, had entered their own nightmare world so deeply that serial assassinations came to seem probable and even predictable. This slightly mad point of view gained more adherents as time went on, and existence became increasingly surreal. There's nothing particularly astonishing, the disciples of mad, random history would say, about presidents and presidential candidates being shot dead practically in midsentence. Life, they would say, is like that—just one damned thing after another.

Like medieval sorcerers, however, the assassins unleashed an ever-grander sequence of events in the form of political scandals, each of which rivaled its predecessor for outright strangeness. To rescue society from its own self-destruction there arose not the reforms so many desperately longed for but deliverance in the form of a new generation of media heroes. Exposé was the order of the day. And genuine professional fervor quickly gave way to excesses of triviality positively comic in their grandeur. Seen as a whole, the pattern of assassination-scandal-trivialization was not one to offer encouragement to a reformer or to the cause of reform, particularly when played out during the frightening cold war era of mad science driving even madder politics.

The decade of the 1980s was not a pretty sight for a reformer or for anyone else with even the vaguest memory of a better time or true style in the nation's capital. Of courage there was none, except if one is to count the occasional political resignation; and too many of those quickly came to be seen—often rightly but still cynically—as flight from the hangman. Any truly grand gesture of protest would have been greeted with utmost scorn and contempt, so much had cynicism come to be the common sauce on every Washington dinner table. It took official (that is to say, permanent) Washington about three hours—not counting the inaugural ball—to size up the new Reagan administration and find it pathetically wanting in all the categories that really mattered: cleverness, style, and wit. Thereafter, the relationship between official Washington and the Reagan "team" was the same as that between Rome and the Visigoths: respect —respect bordering on fear that the new, rough conquerors might parade social Washington through the streets in chains; respect for the big battalions, something the ever-flourishing industry of cliché makers called "an election mandate." Soon the new team, as it called itself and insisted on others calling it, solidified its hold on policy by systematically and expeditiously dismantling as much of the New Deal and the Great Society as it felt it could safely get away with but offered little else by way of entertainment. For Washington, entertainment is usually measured in scandals. But such scandals as there were—and they came to be monumental—involved only gross violations of the public trust and the squandering of public resources and thus failed to meet the new standard of salaciousness then being erected in and around Washington by the eager and growing army of muckrakers. Sadly, the nouveau muckrakers were left to write pathetic stories about the lamentations of the angry and unhappy children of a muddled president.

History will search in vain for even the slightest glimmer of reform in the Washington of the eighties. While the ruling Visigoths plundered the great palaces, warmed their daily kill before the public hearth, and toasted the destruction of the last monuments of civilization, beneath the Capitol in the catacombs long hidden for such an hour a tiny and ever-shifting band of reformers met to mumble prayers for deliverance. Terror—fear of public exposure and ridicule—haunted their every move and their every dream. One or two might find solace in a dim remembrance of the spirit of Jefferson. But few found courage. All in all, it was not a good time for the progress of the human mind.

Pausing at the close of a quarter century of activism, of pushing and hauling the Sisyphean rock of progressive reform up a steep, unforgiving, and treacherous hill, a reformer might have cause to reflect on the symbols used to characterize his age: "public service is the noblest profession" began it, and "parliament of whores" would bring it to its cynical close.

Taken all together—the misdirection of scientific genius, laws and institutions defending society's ramparts rather than expanding its boundaries, the stealthy assassin replacing the public mandate, levels of public and private corruption to make even Warren G. Harding cringe, the information industry's total loss of distinction between news and entertainment—all might make even the heartiest reformer wish for a more likely hour to occupy his lonely missionary station on progress's furthest outpost.

Lonely outposts have been known on some occasions as venues for the construction of signposts for those who may follow on reform's never-ending pilgrimage. Random ruminations on struggles and failures—not even deserving the description of diary—may offer guidance on trails marked by treacherous pitfalls. Failure inevitably awaits the reformer's search for the grail of the social ideal. But from the failure of others, each generation can learn to fail better. The reform quest, like life itself, represents a series of unexpected trials—battles sometimes sought by the reformer and sometimes seeking him—all elements of a mosaic whose common theme is the uses of the forces of change to replace an unacceptable present with a more ideal future.

These stories of struggle and failure are the evidence of a genuine reform impulse, an impulse whose authenticity can be verified only by exposure of its roots. The roots of one lone reformer are of consequence in the great scheme of the human struggle toward progress only to show the richness of the historic soil that gave them life and purpose. This diary of one reformer, notes on the roots of the reform impulse and the failed struggles with reaction and the status quo, itself is but the signpost of a life, a signpost others may see and take encouragement from on the long, unfinished road toward social justice and human happiness. For reform is nothing but the American ideal: the pursuit of happiness.

The 1992 election may represent a turning point for America—a crossroads where the road less traveled, the road of reform, will prove to be the path toward a just and prosperous future. It is devoutly to be wished. But a better, more humane nation will be realized only through a fundamental departure from the values of the 1980s and the restoration of the values of reform and renewal that have been the hallmark of our past greatness.

PART I

Lives of Instruction in Reform

I

THE SEARCH
FOR THE JUST

According to ancient Jewish tradition, there are always among the children of God a very small number of chosen men who must keep alive the ideal of true justice. This burden is heavy both because the Just, as they are called, are not endowed by nature or divinity with any special equipment to carry it—they are not, in other words, especially holy or just themselves— and because they must represent the ideal of justice, usually in an imperfect way, to the community and the nation at large. They must try to embody the ideal, represent it, and speak for it when the community and the nation behave unjustly or fall short of the ideal.

The grief of the whole world is said to repose upon these thirty-six just men, known as the Lamed Vov. André Schwarz-Bart's novel *The Last of the Just* describes how the Lamed Vov are "the hearts of the world multiplied, and into them, as into one receptacle, pour all our griefs." "When an unknown Just rises to Heaven," as Schwarz-Bart relates an Hasidic story, "he is so frozen that God must warm him for a thousand years between His fingers before his soul can open itself to Paradise. And it is known that some remain forever inconsolable at human woe, so that God Himself cannot warm them." In the novel, Mordecai of Zemyock, himself one of the Just, explains his predicament to his puzzled wife, Judith: "When a Lamed-Vovnik weeps, or whatever he does, even when he's in bed as I am, with the wife he loves, he takes upon himself a thirty-sixth part of all the suffering on earth. But he doesn't know it, and his wife doesn't know it, and half his heart cries out while the other half sings."

Injustice has been rampant throughout human history, but to a reformer never more so than in the late twentieth century. Both within America and between America and much of the third world, the gap between haves and have-nots seems to grow daily and palpably. It isn't just staggering discrepancies in standards of living between rich and poor. It is the overabundance, surplus, and wasteful consumption on the one hand and the resolvable need on the other. Nothing would more characterize this than the fantastic growth of wealth among the top 1 or 2 percent of Americans while one in five children in America lived in poverty during the Reagan-Bush years.

During this same period, justice has increasingly come to be defined with parsimonious narrowness as the dispensing of punishment to those accused of violating society's laws. But the justice of the Just of Jewish tradition is a much nobler thing. Justice means fairness, equity, a charitable nature, and humanity itself, and it relates to the standard of performance of the whole community, the whole nation. A just society is not simply a stern, law-and-order hierarchy; it is a humane, caring, inclusive society. Justice is not only punishment for lawbreakers; it is the concern of the community for those outside the gates, for those left behind in progress's turbulent wake, for those to whom fortune has paid no visit.

But even to speak of misfortune or the unfortunate is to perpetuate the ancient mythology of a personified Fortune, who smiles on the prosperous and frowns on the poor, a mythology that gives credence to the comforting but damnable heresy that the poor are poor because they drew losing numbers in the lottery of life, a lottery whose dictates are neither alterable nor subject to question. Fortune's lottery aside, if the few have much and the many have little, a just society will find democratic ways to create a more tolerable balance.

Humane justice operates on the moral and ethical plane and often has to do with sins of omission, whereas narrow justice operates on the legalistic plane and has to do with sins of commission against the person or property of another. One's view of the standard of justice for a society will necessarily condition one's view of the role of that society's government. For if a society also believes itself to be a community or a commonwealth—that is, a people bound together by common interests and values beyond the accident of geographic space—then that society acting through its government will have a positive duty to achieve and ensure the highest level of political, economic, and social, as well as legal, justice. On the other hand, a society or nation may have perfected a legal justice system and still fall short of community, of having achieved an equitable and humane society for all its people, of standing for social justice.

This perplexed reformer, reflecting on the strangely nonjust and curiously non-American decade of the eighties, would come to conclude that the conservative aristocracy had somehow slyly managed to convince many of his fellow citizens that America had reached such a strait that it had to sacrifice social justice to ensure legal justice. How else could one account for the harsh symbols of the age—the bellicose rhetoric, the leaders' bullyboy swagger and amateurish, tough-guy John Wayne imitations, the chip on the shoulder, the rise of the oddly non-American icons played by Arnold Schwarzenegger, Sylvester Stallone, Charles Bronson, and Chuck Norris, the renegade cops of Clint Eastwood (originally a likable, harmless cowboy), the nearly desperate search for new villains—Noriega, Saddam Hussein, Qaddafi, and some ineffectual and long-since forgotten Grenadan—against whom to dispense our wrath? It was as if we had to find opportunities to enforce legal justice abroad in order to avoid confronting the shortage of social justice at home.

This also had much to do with one's view of the role of government. This reformer who somehow found himself—by fate? by accident?—in the big bore Senate of the seventies and the considerably smaller bore Senate of the eighties would be endlessly perplexed by a conservative logic that could find no fault in a government's conduct of military operations abroad and no good in that same government's conduct of humane operations at home. Legal justice, law and order at home and abroad, was something government was good at; social justice—construction of a ladder of opportunity and caring assistance for those who couldn't climb it—was something the very same government was not good at.

Besieged bands of reformers, constitutionally incapable of sharing this logic emotionally and never capable of reconciling it intellectually, came to believe the Faustian trade of social justice for legal justice could be understood as non-American only in that it strayed so far from what family, church, synagogues, and schools —the entire community—had taught that America believed in and stood for. This reformer could not practice McCarthyism in reverse; so for him, this odd circumstance would be non-American rather than un-American.

The point was tellingly made early in this reformer's Senate term. Attending his first formal Armed Services Committee presentations by senior military and civilian Defense Department officials and other expert witnesses, he sat on the dais next to a good friend and new colleague, John Culver, Democratic senator from Iowa, who could best be imagined as a kind of liberal Wrath of God. After almost a day of testimony unrelenting in its concern for the dire weakness and pathetic, abject helplessness of America's defenses, a surprising amount of which was delivered by official and unofficial witnesses of Eastern and Central European heritage, Senator Culver was moved to remark, in a stage whisper clearly audible throughout the large room, "Did you ever wonder why the people who seem most concerned about America's security all speak with an accent?"

There was no suggestion in this that some right-wing, foreign cabal had hijacked American security policy, especially in the era of Gerald Ford—benign by comparison with that of the next Republican president. Rather, it was representative of one of many similar indicators of a national policy tilted strongly in some non-American ways against social justice and in favor of a narrow, rigid, orthodox form of legal justice. Such a tilt could not help but color a nation's view of the world, the world's view of the nation, and the nation's view of itself.

During a period of such restrictive, almost authoritarian understanding of the meaning of justice, were voices heard to the contrary? Yes—but sadly only occasionally, spasmodically, and unevenly, for the party of reform—by implication and modern American performance, also the party of social justice—was not always there to hold the mirror of justice up to the face of American society. And of the Just there were few.

According to the Jewish legend, the tiny band of the Just will, whether its numbers especially want to or not, stand up against injustice when it appears before them. Unlike the latter-day reformer, the Just are not pesky, cranky, unassimilated misfits. They are ordinary men without any other special mission, conformists with no extraordinary need to be nonconformists, intent only on going about their lives—but with an inner compulsion for justice so strong that they have no choice but to stand up, to say no, to reject cruelty, inhumanity, and injustice. They have no choice; they have no control. They are possessed by the justice dybbuk. Once provoked by profound injustice, they will not accede and they cannot sleep.

Why has God withdrawn the Just from the world? How have we all become so callous that we can step over the homeless on our way to the office? What kind of modern, industrial, advanced-technology, superpower country can sit complacently by while the number of children in poverty regularly increases? What kind of leaders do we have? What kind of president did we elect? What kind of justice is this?

An angry reformer might come to wonder, in his late middle years, what has happened to his nation, to his society. He would desperately wish to know when our values changed, when our beliefs changed, when we changed. He would seek to compare, with considerable unhappiness, the idealist nation of hope and promise introduced to him in his unsophisticated youth with the selfish, self-righteous, self-absorbed nation desperately in search of entertainment known to him in his mature years. He would find no answers. He would continue to search for the last of the Just.

When the wily assassins fired their bullets, were we killing ourselves? When like the prodigal son we went, figuratively, to a foreign land to seek ease and comfort, were we forfeiting our birthright and our inheritance? Have we, by neglecting the poor in body and the poor in spirit, so angered the Almighty that He has turned his face away from a society lacking in mercy, humanity, and compassion? When we dispossessed the natives by force and farmed their lands with slaves, did we sacrifice our sense of justice?

It would require an Isaiah to know. But neither he nor the Just could be heard for the MTV, the sitcom static, and *Entertainment Tonight* tomorrow and forever. In olden days, a just man might be stoned or put to the torch for his impertinence in calling into question the adequacy of authority's justice. Today he would simply be ignored or treated with contempt for distracting us from the scandal-obsessed talk show.

The just man or woman is the personification of society's conscience and therefore an awful nuisance. He or she cannot be tolerated. Even worse, in an age in which ego, "success," and self-aggrandizement are the norm, the just person is the most detestable of social outcasts—a bore. Tirades against social injustice would be increasingly irresistible to a reformer, and the more genteel, conservative antireformers would have to remind him sternly of America's relatively high position on any international scale of justice. This message is therapeutic, but it would not do for a reformer who holds his or her country to a very high standard, as much as anything else because his country, through its orators, rhetoricians, and politicians, claims to hold itself to the same high standard. A notable exception to this high level of rhetorical performance on the scale of justice would be, perhaps predictably, the reformer's master, Jefferson, who had occasion to render a judgment so startling in its harshness and clarity that it demanded carving in the marble of his monument, to the confusion if not consternation of generations of schoolchildren: "I tremble for my country when I contemplate that God is just."

A notably imperfect and unfinished reformer would nonetheless long for a certain striving for the perfection of justice in his nation. It wasn't so much attaining the ideal as striving for it—never being satisfied, never being comfortable—that was his preoccupation. Any tendency toward smugness, especially where the plight of the poor was concerned, would be seen as America's worst characteristic. From a religious point of view, the reformer would come by this striving for perfection honestly. For both his family and his early church believed in the doctrine of holiness, that a kind of spiritual perfection could be achieved here on earth. Needless to say, this doctrine represents a distinctly minority point of view in the general Christian church. But it was there nonetheless throughout his impressionable youth, and a young boy had the great misfortune of being born a kind of literalist, of taking not only his nation's Founders but also his spiritual leaders at their word.

From his earliest days, the young reformer's mother and father implanted in him the ideal of social justice in immensely practical ways. The lesson was both spiritual and immediate. God has neither time nor tolerance for anyone base or cowardly enough to diminish the status of a fellow human being in any form. In terms of family values (the watchword of 1990s Republicans), it was considered thoroughly reprehensible and unacceptable to hold in contempt any classmate or family because of race, religion, or social class. The last category was the easiest to observe, since with the exception of a small but distinct country club set and the truly poor, all Franklin County Kansans in the 1940s and '50s were securely fastened in the socioeconomic bracket of the lower-middle income.

Callous schoolboy expressions of bias, prejudice, or bigotry were early cause for vigorous chastisement. A schoolboy would be made to feel mean and despicable for repeating even a casual school-yard joke. All fellow human beings were to be treated with respect, and those "down on their luck" deserved whatever assistance one could offer. The adolescent reformer sought heroes of these ideals—over time, Wesley, Kierkegaard, Tolstoy, and Jefferson, among others—less as intellectual instructors and more as living, practicing embodiments of justice, spirituality, progressive reform, and civic virtue. These and many other sources of inspiration would be looked to for the content of their lives as much as for the intellectual impact of their ideas.

Much later, in the brief years of national politics and then beyond, some would find it odd that a politician might have been inspired by these kinds of lives, rather than, say, Roosevelt, Truman, and Johnson. But it had little to do with politics or intellect; it had much to do with the future reformer's family and spiritual roots. And more than anything else, it accounted for the overwhelming sense, later in life, that politics is not a way of life but a means to an end; it is not a career but a way to achieve justice, equality, and social reform, the ideals from earliest life.

It was, in fact, the search for social justice that would create the instinct for reform in this young church boy, propel him from the search for personal perfection in the spiritual realm to the search for social perfection in the temporal realm, carry him from seminary to law school, thence to social activism, thence to public service. The constant beacons on this winding road would be service and justice. Indeed, throughout his life, he would seek the just person to follow.

Early on the historic figure closest to this ideal of justice whom he could find to guide him was the great eighteenth-century English Methodist reformer John Wesley. Wesley's teachings were propounded in the Kansas boy's own church for their emphasis on spiritual perfection. But, predictably, the boy would find himself attracted by a somewhat different theme: the Wesleyan mandate to reform secular, social, and economic institutions with the specific mission of alleviating the awful plight of the poor. John Wesley and his hymn-writing brother, Charles, could not dissociate the mandate of Jesus' teaching, particularly the disquieting Sermon on the Mount, from the search for social justice. The Wesleys were the Just of their time and place.

John Wesley's message, often delivered outdoors to crowds large and small in the unorthodox manner then called field preaching, was that salvation comes through faith and good works, acts of social reform and social justice; this message ran contrary to what had become the stale routine and ecclesiastical orthodoxy of the Church of England. Wesley contributed all income from his several books to the poor, organized weaving activities for poor London women who had no other means of support, and set up free medical clinics, where electricity and electrical machines were put to the not entirely scientific use of treating various ailments.

During the 1760s and '70s, a time when the nation was being transformed from an agrarian to an industrial society, England suffered a number of failed harvests. Mass social dislocations occurred, and the existing gulf between rich and poor widened further. In his sermons and letters to the press, Wesley argued against the widespread practice of distilling grain into alcohol, which contributed not only to the dramatic rise in drunkenness and violence but also to the increase in the price of bread. He also pleaded with the nobility and the gentry not to waste so much precious meat and other scarce food in their luxurious kitchens. In a citizens' effort to alleviate the worst forms of poverty, he organized what were to become Methodists into a corps of volunteers known well into the nineteenth century as the Christian Community.

One Wesley biographer wrote: "Wesley and the early evangelicals had begun the slow process of bringing the rich and powerful to a more just and compassionate approach to the problems of poverty. The change in the national conscience of Britain between the mid-eighteenth century and the Victorian age, at all social levels, owed much to Wesley." Some historians went as far as to credit Wesley with saving Britain from bloody rebellion during the tense days of the American revolutionary war and the French Revolution. Furthermore, Wesley was a pioneering opponent of slavery and the slave trade. From an early visit to the colonies, especially South Carolina, in 1736, Wesley denounced the enslavement of man by man. "This equally concerns every gentleman that has an estate in our American plantations; yea, all slave-holders, of whatever rank and degree; seeing men-buyers are exactly on a level with men-stealers. Give liberty to whom liberty is due, that is, to every child of man, to every partaker of human nature. Let none serve you but by his own act and deed, by his own voluntary action. Away with all whips, all chains, all compulsion!"

At his death, in 1791, all England mourned, and a journal noted for its bitter criticism of John Wesley wrote this: "He directed his labors towards those who had no instructor; to the highways and hedges; to the miners in Cornwall and the colliers in Kingswood. . . . By the humane and active endeavors of him and his brother Charles, a sense of decency, morals, and religion, was introduced into the lowest classes of mankind; the ignorant were instructed; the wretched relieved; and the abandoned reclaimed."

For the Wesleys, then and now, there will always be a profound difference between the private charity of a thousand points of light and the practices of a just society. The Benefactors' philosophy assumes the poor are always with us and fine gentlemen and ladies will distribute tokens of charity by the way. The Just challenge this assumption, demand institutions that address the conditions creating poverty, and call for an equitable society that offers opportunity and humane conditions for all. The Benefactors find their roots in Calvin, aristocracies, class societies, and paternalistic condescension. The Just are the natural, inevitable product of revolutionary democracy kept alive through constant progressive reform.

Hannah Arendt found the political basis of progressive reform in the founding of America:

> The social question began to play a revolutionary role only when, in the modern age and not before, men began to doubt that poverty was inherent in the human condition, to doubt that the distinction between the few, who through circumstances or strength or fraud had succeeded in liberating themselves from the shackles of poverty, and the laboring, poverty-stricken multitude was inevitable and eternal. This doubt, or rather the conviction that life on earth might be blessed with abundance rather than cursed by scarcity, was prerevolutionary and American in origin; it grew directly out of the American colonial experience.

In the ongoing, divisive, unproductive debate over welfare in America, the silent conservative premise is ever thus: there have always been poor people, and there always will be, and society's government should not tax wealth in a futile effort to alter nature's laws. In a lifelong struggle to appreciate monolithic resistance to reform, a reformer would conclude that the simple notion of social justice is a profoundly heretical one to established elites and present-day aristocracies, that, indeed, the very speculation that democracy has a social as well as a political component contains for some a heresy of terrifying proportions.

There is something almost sinister about parents, teachers, and politicians fostering idealistic beliefs in the young, knowing they are untrue. It is beyond cynicism. It is cowardly. If society will always be unfair and unjust, this should be revealed to the child as clearly, coldly, and early as possible. Otherwise, the life of one's nation becomes a fairy tale ritually repeated with the sure knowledge that someday the child will come to place the idealistic democratic myth in the same category as Santa Claus and other sentimental poppycock. The grown-up child can then live life for himself and placate that lingering memory-dream by voting for national leaders who prattle about "a thousand points of light."

In such times as these, voices are heard to complain that we have no strong leaders. Perhaps what is meant is that we cannot find the Just. Perhaps an inner, innocent voice is saying that justice, not strength, is wanting. Having been so constantly preoccupied with the need for strength during the desperately wasteful decades of the cold war, we forgot about the search for justice.

Americans are notoriously softhearted, sentimental people, even in ages of materialism and consumption. It is not uncommon, even today, for grown men to weep at idealistic Frank Capra movies or tales of bravery, sacrifice, and courage or stories of those who acted on a higher, better plane. Even dismissing such behavior for its most tear-jerking, sentimental content, a reformer could believe there is something more here. It could be the lingering childhood memory of a better society that does its best to achieve the dream of both liberty and justice for all, or it could be the lingering belief that we might actually become the people we told our children we truly are.

Before his death in a minor German extermination camp called Drancy, Ernie Levy, the last descendant in the line of the *lamedvovnik* Mordecai of Zemyock, is recognized by an old rabbi who identifies him as one who would be called to the destiny of a just man, "Not a Just Man of the Levys, but a true Unknown Just, an Inconsolable—one of those whom God dares not even caress with his little finger." The old rabbi is correct, for shortly thereafter Ernie Levy dies in a Nazi gas chamber, clutching young children to him while reciting ancient Jewish legends. The author of *The Last of the Just* concludes the novel with this: "At times one's heart could break in sorrow. But often too, preferably in the evening, I can't help thinking that Ernie Levy, dead six million times, is still alive somewhere, I don't know where. . . . Yesterday, as I stood in the street trembling in despair, rooted to the spot, a drop of pity fell from above upon my face. But there was no breeze in the air, no cloud in the sky. . . . There was only a presence."

A sentimental reformer who never accepted the notion that the democratic ideal of equality and justice was a myth would come to believe that late-twentieth-century America was less in search of new and stronger political leadership and more in search of the Just.

2

TO WILL ONE THING

The young midwestern man, making his troubled odyssey from acolyte theologian to activist reformer,
would search for intellectual signposts and find them
in unlikely places—in nineteenth-century Denmark
and Russia.

The student reformer encountered a number of spir-
itual-intellectual influences as he moved his quest
from a small Kansas town to an equally small Oklahoma town, which harbored a struggling church college, where circumstance and the most meager of
scholarships would draw him. There, thanks to his
own Socratic lamplighter, he would be introduced to
Søren Kierkegaard. Leo Tolstoy he would find pretty
much on his own.

There is nothing more dangerous than a person who
takes a profound idea seriously. Powerful monarchies
and empires have been destroyed by people, like Jef-

ferson, who took the radical idea of democracy seriously. Long before, Jesus changed human history with the singular ideal of loving God above all else and loving one's neighbor as oneself. Thereafter, in the case of both Jesus and Jefferson, tradition, authority, and orthodoxy in the form of established institutions predictably moved in to convert simple but radical ideas and ideals to orthodoxies that were threatening only to those who would not bend a knee to institutionalized doctrines and priesthoods.

As George III would have his Jefferson, so Pope Leo X would have his Martin Luther. Entrenched power structures supported by pillars of custom, gravity, and fear would inevitably give way to the forces of liberation, democracy, and reformation. But then no sooner would old orthodoxies be breached than the perverse human need for certainty and security would require new structures to contain the spirit of freedom, organize its cause, house its doctrines, train its missionaries, propagate its truths, set its standards, and establish its orthodoxies. It would not be long before the protest of the Reformation would become Protestantism and would find itself not much better off than the Church of Rome with which it had broken in the late sixteenth century.

In the case of Danish Lutheranism, that time of institutional rigidity and regimentation would be the first half of the eighteenth century, and its Luther would be a marginally ostracized, piercingly brilliant philosopher who would radically and disruptively take Jesus at his word—much to the consternation of the established state church. For Kierkegaard, the truth of Christianity was as singular as the truth of democracy was for Jefferson.

In the 1950s, Kierkegaard was not readily available, especially not to a young prereform philosophy student in Oklahoma, struggling most of the time to fathom why he was studying philosophy in the first place. For Kierkegaard, one needed an introduction, and in the student's case the introduction came soon after the introduction to philosophy itself and from the same source: Professor J. Prescott Johnson. What struck the befuddled student right off about Johnson was not just his high-voltage intellectual and physical energy but also his curious and his vague resemblance to the student's father. Both were men of humble but not mean circumstances, had affinities, born of necessity, for machines and the outdoors, and possessed a fine combination of humility, humor, and genuine humanity. The student's father would introduce him to the streams and fields of Kansas by way of affirming an instinct for nature and the outdoors. Johnson would introduce him to Plato and Kierkegaard by way of affirming an instinct for books and learning.

Johnson's philosophical roots were classical. His methods were Socratic. Knowledge was not to be dispensed quantitatively in memorizable thoughtlets; it was to be extracted qualitatively by bringing the student to comprehend inherent truths such as the Platonic Ideals: the True, the Good, and the Beautiful. But Johnson also labored on the two-thousand-year-old frontier between classical philosophical truths and the truth of Christianity. He would strain to synthesize them, but he would not find the resolution of his search in the comforting systems of orthodoxy. Observing Johnson's struggle, on more than one occasion this confused and malleable student would have recourse to the lines of Tennyson:

> Our little systems have their day,
> They have their day and cease to be.
> They are but broken lights of Thee.
> And Thou art greater still than they.

Human systems, perhaps especially religious ones, do not like the suggestion, whether made by Kierkegaard, Tennyson, Johnson, or even a questioning student, that they may be historically dispensable. So, predictably, Johnson became the subject of recurring, annoying, and usually pathetic little inquiries that never managed to deserve the description witch hunt but shared the same premises as the Athenian persecution of Socrates. It was widely believed by the college administration that the professor of philosophy was manipulating the obscure Dane to corrupt the faith of his students, not, heaven knows, by advocating heresy outright, but by that more classic and sinister practice of encouraging students to ask questions—about traditions, about orthodox doctrines, about systems and institutions themselves. From this struggle between college and professor, the student got his first practical lesson in reform, a lesson he would have occasion to contemplate often a quarter century later in the vastly different arena of high politics: human institutions do not appreciate being questioned or challenged.

Kierkegaard had his lifelong quarrel with the established Church of Denmark, and his unlikely introduction into the complex academic and theological environment of Bethany Nazarene College in the 1950s was similarly volatile. The guardians of the orthodox faith—several times pruned from its original trunk and replanted—saw him and Johnson as troublemakers at best and heretics at worst. They were, part and parcel, challengers of the system. Johnson, precariously queued for tenure, walked a constant tightrope. Not always his own best ally, he could exacerbate the situation with perverse glee. Seeing the academic dean approach one day, Johnson crossed to the far side of the wide hallway, holding his briefcase at arm's length and shouting, "I have Kierkegaard in here. Unclean! Unclean!" The best of Johnson's critics would struggle with Kierkegaard's complex and elaborate ironies, seeking a clue to Johnson. The worst could not take the trouble and simply assumed Johnson and his cabal of students conducted black masses in the dormitory boiler room in the small hours. They would happily have offered Johnson hemlock, and they would have found no irony in doing so.

Johnson's confused critics were right about him and about Kierkegaard but, predictably, for the wrong reasons. Both men threatened orthodox systems, but out of conviction and belief, not out of disbelief and doubt. They did not wish to destroy the system; they wished to reform it. Kierkegaard held the mirror of the Ideal up to the Church's face, and it was forced to see the difference, the distance between promise and performance, ideal and real, profession and practice.

Authority demands obedience and conformity in direct proportion to its insecurity and fear, its fear that it has not been faithful to the Ideal. For Kierkegaard, the Danish Church had replaced spirit, meaning, and message with form, ritual, and appearance. It was frightened by the implication of its own revolutionary message, and therefore it sought to deradicalize the message. Preaching charity, love, and social justice is always more comfortable than actually practicing them. The literal practice of a revolutionary gospel usually requires a radical change in human behavior. So piety is always preferable to true discipleship.

Kierkegaard did not believe that individual salvation rested in the reform of the institution of the Danish Church. At its best, the institution could only be the vehicle, the medium through which the individual's search for "purity of heart" could be worked out with "fear and trembling." He wished the Church to reform itself, to shed its hypocrisy so that it could better perform this ultimately serious mission.

During the impressionable early years of the student's college education, Kierkegaard, the reclusive, melancholy Dane, would leave a profound impression on the tabula rasa of the student's mind and spirit. Kierkegaard, through his philosophical meditations, would confirm the student's preintellectual suspicion that his own spiritual quest was meant to be a lonely one. Through his critical "attack upon Christendom," he would implant in the student a philosophy of reform. Defenders of orthodoxy, whether religious or political, often wrongly see their greatest threat from other institutions. In fact, the greatest threat to orthodoxy is from a lone, usually lonely, individual who, through single-minded dedication to the Ideal, possesses "purity of heart."

Purity of heart, says Kierkegaard, is "to will one thing." In the case of faith, that one thing is a personal relationship with God, a relationship unadorned by ritual and ceremony, unencumbered by dogma and catechism. When such an existentialist (one who relates reality and truth immediately to his own personal existence) comes along, he or she threatens institutional orthodoxy in two ways. First, the institution, whether church or party, becomes superfluous as an intermediary institution. And second, the pure of heart contrast dramatically with the halfhearted, the compromisers, the game players, and the cynical.

Professor Johnson's introduction of the student-reformer to Kierkegaard—as well as to other existentialists, such as Marcel, Berdyayev, Jaspers, and Miguel de Unamuno—had a profound effect spiritually and politically. Kierkegaard taught this reformer the necessity of conviction, fierce commitment to an eternal truth, and the single-minded dedication to "willing one thing." All men and women are human, yet none, especially not the reformer, would possess the purity of heart Kierkegaard placed central to human spirituality. But like justice itself, it represented an ideal toward which to strive. Later, pursuing that ideal would become more important to the reformer than would the assurance of a career and political acceptance.

Humans, by nature and instinct, seem to be creatures of organization. Let a revolutionary come along, preaching insurrection and overthrow of a corrupt system, and they will often happily risk fortune and sacred honor for the cause of freedom. Revolutionary muskets and rhetoric will scarcely be cold, however, before the struggle for power to govern in the postrevolutionary arena will have broken out, often with equal or greater deadly force. Parties are formed, leaders chosen, titles dispensed, regulations drafted, headquarters rented, letterheads printed, accounts opened, lines of authority drawn, doctrines engraved, membership limited. The important thing is to establish the creed; this determines membership. To participate, an oath must be sworn. The creed and the oath become crucial. How else to distinguish believer from nonbeliever, faithful from heathen, chosen from damned? Deviation is not permitted. Questions cannot be raised. Authority will be shared only among members.

Postrevolutionary orthodoxy quickly sets in. Orthodox systems become closed. Dissent will not be heard. Unorthodox thought, especially if it challenges the new orthodox creed, is not permitted. Curiously enough, images of plumbing immediately arise. The Nixon White House created teams of plumbers to prevent leaks (that is, disclosures damaging to authority). Writing prophetically well before Watergate and about the space program of the sixties, Norman Mailer equated the new priesthood of rocket scientists with plumbers; the job of both, he said, was "the prevention of treachery in closed systems."

The job of the reformer is the reverse of that of the plumber; it is to introduce treachery into closed systems. Closed systems may be required for the elimination of waste, but they are anathema to the ongoing, ever-changing, experimental search for truth and justice. The Church of Rome of Luther's day, the Church of England of Wesley's day, the English monarchy of Jefferson's day, the Danish Church of Kierkegaard's day, the Nazarene Church of Johnson's day—all were orthodoxies, closed systems with established creeds, resistant to new ideas and regenerating reform. All feared change.

Political parties, being intensely human institutions, share many of these same fears, this mature reformer would come to understand. A few years later he would watch with expectation and excitement as a young Massachusetts senator breached the walls of a dormant Democratic party to wrest power from a recalcitrant old guard. Then he would participate marginally in that president's brother's tragic assault on an entrenched administration caught up in war. Then four more years of the reformer's life would be dedicated to Democratic party reforms, culminating in the Pyrrhic capture of the party's presidential nomination for George McGovern. And thence to elective office, and the struggle to change national policy would begin.

The embryonic reformer would learn from Kierkegaard and Johnson the constant human tension between the desire for security and the instinct for change, between stability and experimentation, between authority and participation, between orthodoxy and reform. Of pain there would be much, and of learning there was little, in his lifelong quarrel with authority. In moments of weakness throughout, he would often envy the comfortable insider. In the United States Senate, he would often hear, with mixed emotions, the single central truth of all orthodox institutions from the earliest dawn: "If you want to get along, you have to go along."

To get along, he understood; to go along, he never could. Ease in life is to be achieved by compromise, but compromise is a reformer's hemlock. Therefore, life would not be easy. Principles and convictions, for this reformer, possess sharp edges. The art of survival in the world of compromise requires the constant definition and redefinition of what is principle, what is really important, what is worth fighting for. Whether leading a filibuster in 1983 against the MX missile, a weapon whose prime contractor was headquartered in his home state of Colorado, opposing the popular Reagan tax cuts in 1981, or becoming the first national candidate to refuse political-action-committee contributions, the reformer would not lack for occasions to test the borderline between pragmatism and principle.

Age curtails the opportunities to put principles to the test, even though it may not dull the edges of those principles. Kierkegaard, and his disciple Johnson, would remain clear beacons on dark nights at sea for their constant focus on the Ideal. Tempted to fight every battle along the way, this reformer would be called on to keep the true end in focus. The trick of it all was to resist despair, the despair of cumulative injustices, defeats, untruths, and inequities, to know that sieges against inert authority demand supreme patience, and to search constantly in unlikely places for the small bits of courage necessary to challenge established orthodoxies.

Kierkegaard compared the constant harassment he received from the faithful to being trampled to death by geese. There is that to it.

3

A BEAR IN
THE DEN WITH GOD

"With God he has a very suspicious relation; they sometimes remind me of the relations of two bears in one den." This was Maxim Gorky's judgment of Leo Tolstoy, one of the greatest religious and social reformers of the nineteenth century, who also happened to be its greatest novelist.

As Wesley would form Methodism out of the Church of England and Kierkegaard would form existentialism in part out of his quarrel with the established Church of Denmark, so Tolstoy would be excommunicated by the Russian Orthodox Church for his insistence on social justice and social reform and his advocacy of passive, nonviolent resistance to the cruel repressions of established authority.

It was perhaps inevitable that a reformer with a certain instinct for religious reform would eventually find a lifelong pilgrimage through literature bringing him to the awesome doorstep of Leo Tolstoy. Even today the very name conjures up a certain majestic mystery that has its source in words, words on pages of books, books that from earliest memory seemed to a Kansas boy to hold the answers to life and the universe, books that told stories, revealed amazing new pieces of information, depicted the endless facets of the human character and the countless new circumstances and relationships into which his fellow creatures might wander, books that had the power to cause laughter and tears and make him think, books most of all that like experience itself were "an arch wherethro' gleams that untravell'd world, whose margin fades for ever and for ever when I move"—and when the boy read. The boy was still very young when he came to realize that if he never went beyond Ottawa, Kansas, the whole world would still be his in those words, on those pages, in those books.

The boy read books compulsively and obsessively; that is, he read all the time and everything any newfound author had written. Throughout his early years, he read authors serially, and later he would read several authors simultaneously. In his early grade school years, the first victim of this serial-reading obsession would be L. Frank Baum, producer of genial fantasies. Then he devoured all of the western romances of Zane Grey. Then there came the science fiction period of Robert Heinlein and others, but all of Robert Heinlein. Other series came and went. Then, in adolescence, the boy found John Steinbeck. He had faint memories of the last years of the Great Depression, but the experiences of the Joad family were fresh in the experience of his parents and family. *The Grapes of Wrath*, with its earthy power, would be the first occasion on which fiction could be related to his own life. He reacted emotionally to the shattering theme of social injustice, a theme that would resonate throughout his life. Villainous banks and faceless, inhumane oligarchies became a sober reality. After reading all the Steinbeck the Carnegie Public Library (to the boy, an immense, cathedrallike place) could then afford, he found his way with ease to Hemingway—of course, all of Hemingway. If *The Grapes of Wrath* showed the injustice and the inhumanity concentrated wealth was capable of, *A Farewell to Arms* suggested that duty and honor might transcend political and military authority. It was but a short step from terse Hemingway to ineluctable Faulkner. *As I Lay Dying* and *Absalom, Absalom!* would plumb some psychological cellars the young man might not then be equipped to understand. But *Light in August* proved, as Faulkner said at the close of his Nobel laureate speech, that man would not just endure; he would prevail.

Literature lightened the load of the classical philosophers at Bethany College. But having reached, at least symbolically, fictional contemporaneity, the red-eyed student wandered back into the nineteenth century and found, in a fresh way, the Americans Melville, Poe, and Hawthorne. He had come by now to appreciate, at least rustically, symbolism and metaphor. So great whales, scarlet letters, talking ravens, and swinging pendulums took on richer meaning than when they had been taught in earlier years. But great nineteenth-century American writers pursuing powerful themes of good and evil, justice and injustice, war and peace were not operating alone. On his 1831–32 visit to the United States, Tocqueville made his famous observation and prediction: "There are at the present time two great nations in the world, which started from different points, but seem to tend towards the same end. I allude to the Russians and the Americans. . . . Their starting point is different and their courses are not the same; yet each seems marked out by the will of Heaven to sway the destinies of half the globe."

The Great Russians of the time were, like their American counterparts, exploring the interior universe of the human mind and spirit and the historic exterior world of war and peace. Tolstoy, who began publishing his works some thirty years after Tocqueville's pronouncements, was mesmerizing. How could one human mind capture so much of history and experience in words? Tolstoy himself provided a great library in which a lifetime of reading, exploring, learning, feeling, and imagining could be invested. And in a nineteenth-century explosion of cultural genius, there were also Pushkin, Lermontov, Chekhov, Gogol, and of course, the incomparable Fyodor Dostoyevsky.

Still pursuing his odyssey of professional career and personal salvation through the philosophical and theological groves of academe, the reformer-as-young-man now moved from Oklahoma college to Connecticut seminary. He took his friends the Russians with him. It was by then becoming clear to him that theological academics would neither provide him an acceptable career nor save his soul and that the right side of his brain required constant nourishment from literary sources. Thus, he lived a complex dual life, a Jekyll-and-Hyde existence within the cloistered seminary walls: inky-fingered theological note taker by day, literary vampire by night. It was enough to make a confused young man hunger for the comparative clarity to be found at the barricades of political reform. Tolstoy was shortly to play a significant role in guiding this transition.

Happily for the student, other lamplighters, both intellectual and spiritual, would appear on the scene to carry on Johnson's Socratic role. One appeared in the person of a brilliant young European intellectual named George Steiner. Still in his prolific twenties and lecturing at Princeton, he had by then produced, inter alia, a work entitled *Tolstoy or Dostoevsky*. Steiner readily acknowledged his debt to Sir Isaiah Berlin, whose classic essay "The Hedgehog and the Fox" was built on a theme from Archelochus: "The fox knows many things, but the hedgehog knows one big thing." Using the categories of hedgehog and fox, Steiner established historic categories not only for the two Russian literary giants but also for historians, philosophers, and political leaders. Thereafter, this reformer would repeatedly have occasion to use these categories in better appreciating the leadership styles of Senate colleagues and presidents. If Reagan was a hedgehog, Mikhail Gorbachev was the classic fox.

Tolstoy himself managed the unique feat of living a life as big as his monumental literature. He was a walking, acting epic. According to Professor Berlin, "He was by nature a fox but believed in being a hedgehog." Tolstoy's obsession with social justice, especially in his later years, led him to undertake often extraordinary experiments in a search for the causes and effects of poverty, social caste, and discrimination. Increasingly made desperate by cankerous urban poverty, Tolstoy came to believe he could isolate its causes, organize prosperous, gentrified society to combat it, and bring justice—if not also utopia—to the world. He was fifty-five years of age and, after a lifetime packed with experience, fame, and literary success, was beginning a struggle to define the meaning of his life in spiritual terms.

Relativism, compromise, and accommodation came to be anathema to him. From the basic instructions of Jesus, he forged moral principles like iron absolutes within the smithy of his soul. In his later years, he came to see even the happiness of family life as a distraction from his search for meaning and truth. "The new conditions of happy family life," he had written some years earlier, "completely diverted me from all search for the general meaning of life." Materialism, including even the basic need to provide for his family, would forever represent for Tolstoy the relativist barrier to spiritual perfection. Besides, time spent on the daily cares of the household operations is not time spent wrestling with the God-bear in the den of eternity.

Increasingly, Tolstoy found faith and life-meaning among simple, working people—"unlettered folk: pilgrims, monks, sectarians and peasants"—and saw only hypocrisy among those in his own social circles, the landed gentry and the titled wealthy. "The whole of life of believers in our circle was a contradiction of their faith, but the whole life of the working-folk believers was a confirmation of the meaning of life which their faith gave them." He saw his society of aristocratic wealth and power to be pervaded by idleness, amusement, vanity, and selfishness, all in the name of avoiding sorrow, suffering, and death, life's three realities. By contrast, the humble working folk—"endlessly different in their manners, minds, education, and position, as they were—all alike, in complete contrast to my ignorance, knew the meaning of life and death, labored quietly, endured deprivation and sufferings, and lived and died seeing therein not vanity but good." And, Tolstoy concludes, "I learnt to love these people." Faulkner would reach many of the same conclusions decades later.

Loving them turned out to be considerably easier than serving them. Turning his monumental energies to this task in his late fifties, Tolstoy would ask—as others had asked before and have asked since—"What then must we do?" He had gone to live in Moscow in 1881, had discovered "town poverty" characterized by a kind of evil, crime, and debauchery unknown in his home province of Tula, and had promptly devised a plan of philanthropic activity with which to "demonstrate his goodness." He would identify areas of need by accompanying census takers then beginning their periodic rounds, organize his affluent social circle into a permanent philanthropic clearinghouse that would eradicate depredation on a case-by-case basis, and prevent poverty from breeding and ever taking root again.

It was utopian to a fault, "a thousand points of light" a hundred years before the American invention, and ultimately futile.

Tolstoy was among the first of his age to link industrialization to the urbanization of poverty and thus to sharpened class disparities, conflict, and eventual revolution. A vast industrialized working class would toil on behalf of a tiny ownership class. Towns, places where "nothing is grown but everything is consumed," would increasingly become magnets for those seeking to escape an industrious life and discover the "magic inexhaustible purse" possessed by Tolstoy and others in his social and financial circles. Not finding it, more and more formerly simple working folk would become poor, nonworking people dependent on the charity of the few working people. Tolstoy saw the institutions of society—industries, the wealthy class, powerful governments supported by the Church, the army, and the police—as the perpetuators of this hopeless poverty. He and others like him, he thought, were the problem that no amount of organized charity could solve. If an unjust system made people poor and kept them in poverty to maintain itself, private or public handouts could not correct it. Money per se was only the symbol of the true evil it represented, power over people: "In plain Russian it results that those who have money can twist those who have none into ropes." This is a proposition difficult to refute.

Reaching what are generally considered radical conclusions in his mature years, for almost three decades Tolstoy went on to apply them to the society in which he found himself: a dying monarchy. Needless to say, there were those of importance in that society who were not delighted to find themselves exposed by the great bear's spotlight of hypocrisy. He did not wait for polite society to ostracize him; he ostracized himself, living and working with the Tula peasants. The Russian Orthodox Church excommunicated him, suffering the condemnation of masses of peasants whose souls it claimed to care for and earning Tolstoy's disdain. Already in a den with God, he would not require the Church's introduction.

Tolstoy's many critics have argued for a century that he talked a better game than he played. Pledges to divide up his properties among serfs and peasants and to live and work among them were constantly frustrated by his fierce, fractious, suicidal wife. But he could, and did, eliminate dependence on servants for the performance of daily tasks. He expanded his personal assaults on class-based injustice with a voluminous collection of books, essays, tracts, and correspondence, to the great irritation of Church and State. And he increasingly adopted peasant life, values, and practices. From 1881 to 1883, he worked exhaustively to organize relief to alleviate yet another of Russia's recurrent famines. And throughout the eighties, nineties, and beyond, he repeated and intensified his warnings to his "circle," the governing elites, of a massive revolt looming and brewing across the vast land.

In Tolstoy's nineteenth-century Russia, the czarist state, perfecting centuries of practice, maintained authority with brutality. Revolutionaries, political and religious dissenters, or simply a worn-down serfdom seeking to protest being crushed beyond human endurance invited the lash, the gun butt, or worse. Unjust trials, inhumane imprisonments, torturous punishments, summary executions—all taxed even the legendary patience of the Russian serfs. Revolt was brewing, and Tolstoy knew it. His rival and contemporary, Dostoyevsky, had faced a mock firing squad for alleged sedition. Lenin, becoming active at the very end of the century, was drawn to extremism and jail early, like many of his age. Anarchy, not democracy, was the preferred alternative to monarchy. Czar Alexander II became the victim of the anarchist's bomb. Warnings of the coming storm abounded.

Throughout the first half of his turbulent life, Tolstoy had not been unfamiliar with the violent culture of his time. He would recount at length the abuse of unlucky servants by drunken noblemen, the gross mistreatment of street women, the casual destitution of families, the brutality and inhumanity just beneath the thin veneer of polite society. Indeed, his persistent feelings of guilt for the existence of this behavior and his inability to reconcile the teachings of the Russian Orthodox Church with the practices of its clergy and faithful led him to what he believed to be the central truth of Jesus' teachings and the revolutionary paradox that would come to transform his life and condition the course of political action down to the present day: "resist not evil," do not repay violence with violence, endure the unjust blows of fate and your fellow man, the meek (that is, the nonviolent) will inherit the earth. All this formed the core of Tolstoyan belief in the late nineteenth and early twentieth centuries.

The core of that belief came to be the sanctity of human life. "Resist not evil" represented such a sweeping pacifism that it prevented the wronged man from retaliating against his oppressor. In "The Kingdom of God Is Within You," Tolstoy wrote: "There may be a semblance of mathematics admitting that two is equal to three, but there can be no real science of mathematics [based on this notion]. And there can only be a semblance of ethics in which murder in the shape of war and the execution of criminals is allowed, but no true ethics. The recognition of the life of every man as sacred is the first and only basis of ethics." Furthermore, he believed that complex, layered society and government permit all involved in the brutality of war and executions to escape personal, immediate accountability: "So many instigate, assist or sanction the commission of every one of these actions that no one who has a hand in them feels himself morally responsible for it."

Tolstoy saw clearly the wars of the twentieth century that would result from the crumbling of cruel, unjust empires constructed over previous centuries. He believed that the radical restructuring of society around principles of justice and equality would prevent wholesale bloodshed:

It is clear now from the very simplest, most commonplace point of view, that it is madness to remain under the roof of a building which cannot support its weight, and that we must leave it. And indeed it is difficult to imagine a position more wretched than that of the Christian world today, with its nations armed against one another, with its constantly increasing taxation to maintain its armies, with the hatred of the working class for the rich ever growing more intense, with the Damocles sword of war forever hanging over the heads of all, ready every instant to fall, certain to fall sooner or later. Hardly could any revolution be more disastrous for the great mass of the population than the present order or rather disorder of our life, with its daily sacrifices to exhausting and unnatural toil, to poverty, drunkenness, and profligacy, with all the horrors of the war that is at hand, which will swallow up in one year more victims than all the revolutions of the century.

Through his increasingly eschatological vision of a Civitas Dei and his call for the radical reform of a corrupt and corrupting social order, Tolstoy became the prophet of a new century. Much of the impending struggle between an open but often unjust capitalist system and the Marxist totalitarian utopia is foretold in Tolstoyan fiction and hortatory literature. It is by no means an accident of history that a young Indian lawyer living in late-nineteenth-century South Africa found in the teachings of Tolstoy the germ of the idea of freedom, justice, and social revolution. A correspondence began—including one of the last letters Tolstoy was to write—and the idea of passive, nonviolent resistance as carried forward by Mohandas Gandhi was to liberate India, shatter the British Empire, and forever change the post–World War II world. It is safe to conclude that at the very least, Tolstoy was the prophet of twentieth-century nonalignment, which had its roots in Indian self-liberation.

Ironically, a young, black American preacher, jailed for his advocacy of civil rights in the 1950s, would find occasion to read and be powerfully influenced by the teachings of Mahatma Gandhi while in jail. From Gandhi, he learned the lessons of passive nonviolent resistance, and the modern American civil rights movement began. From this reformer's point of view, the name of Martin Luther King, Jr., would be especially appropriate to his mission.

On August 19, 1991, a military coup was mounted against the reformist government of Mikhail Gorbachev. Resistance, centered on President Boris Yeltsin and the Russian White House, was passive and nonviolent. Students and other democrats peacefully persuaded young soldiers to come over to their side. Resistance leaders recalled the civil rights movement led by Martin Luther King a quarter century before in the United States. The ideas and spirit of Leo Tolstoy lived again on the barricades around the Russian White House.

Maxim Gorky imagined Tolstoy as one of "those pilgrims who all their life long, stick in hand, walk the earth, travelling thousands of miles from one monastery to another, from one saint's relic to another, terribly homeless and alien to all men and things. The world is not for them, nor God either. They pray to Him from habit, and in their secret soul they hate Him —why does he drive them over the earth, from one end to the other?" The critic George Steiner accounted for Tolstoy's demand that God's kingdom be created here on earth in this way: "If this could be accomplished, God might be tempted into walking once again in the garden. There Tolstoy would await Him in an ambush of desire. The two bears would be at last in the same den."

4

JEFFERSONIAN
REVOLUTION

Thomas Jefferson believed there should be an American revolution every nineteen years. Presuming he had not paid a visit to George Washington's extensive stock of Madeira wine just before writing this—an unlikely possibility since he was a man of almost infinite sobriety—a twentieth-century reformer can take him at his word. Jefferson, this reformer's mentor and secular master, was not given even to short flights of hyperbole. Besides, this reformer had been taught in the very heartland of America's public school system to treat the words of the Founding Fathers with the utmost seriousness, if not reverence.

What could he possibly have meant by this radical idea? The implications are overwhelming—blood in the streets, chaos, permanent instability, the utmost kind of social and political unpredictability: anarchy. The possibilities for mischief are practically endless.

No sanctity of contract, no full faith and credit of the United States, no dependability in foreign treaty arrangements, no infinite life for political parties, not even lifetime careers for politicians. Surely Jefferson could not have been serious.

A Kansas boy, even before he knew enough to identify himself as a reformer, was known to have quietly and politely raised this question when the Jeffersonian notion of perpetual, generational revolution first emerged from some otherwise mundane supplementary reading assignment. The confusion and vague uneasiness in the voice and demeanor of that and subsequent teachers would cause a young reformer to believe something here deserved further investigation.

Why, to start with, nineteen years? Because this represented the length of a generation in Jefferson's day, and he was, if anything, a precise man. For today's purposes, one could as easily say twenty or twenty-five or almost any other reasonable number of years, and the point would not be lost. For the point was to place each generation within a bracket of time, to institutionalize a kind of judgment day for civic accountability. And revolution—did he seriously mean bloody revolution? Having just come through the ultimate social upheaval of revolution, he knew clearly what that involved; he did not mean, quite obviously, that bloodshed was a prerequisite.

What he did intend—and he intended it with deadly seriousness—was that every two decades or so a new generation should be required collectively to define its values or redefine those of its forebears and undertake the arduous but constructive duty of deciding for itself the kind of political and social system it wished for itself. It should not be burdened by the dead hand of the past, the anchor of tradition, or the smothering comfort of custom.

Democracy, like liberty itself, is a treasure. It has to be taken out periodically, inspected, examined in the harsh light of a new day, and then shined up before being bequeathed to progeny, who themselves would repeat not a ritual but a divine duty and honor. Thus would it remain fresh and new and worthy of respect. Jefferson believed the diamond of democracy could withstand such scrutiny and examination as any future generation might devise. And if it couldn't, then some other, better gem of a system must be found that could better guarantee life, liberty, and the pursuit of happiness, form a more perfect union, and promote the general welfare.

Thomas Jefferson thus became a kind of Isaac Newton of government, not only creating a new system but also insisting that each future generation test its viability. This consummate audacity flowed immutably from a cosmology based on change. As Heracleitus twenty-three hundred years before might confidently state that one could not step into the same river twice, Jefferson would state with equal confidence that we could not live in the same world twice.

To the antireformer, this is but relativism's ugliest façade, an open invitation to question, and most probably reject, society's oldest and most treasured values. If society's laws and institutions are not permanent, says the conservative, then nothing can remain sacred for long. Mere anarchy is loosed upon the world. The center will not hold. And besides, who will invest with any confidence in the stock market?

But this neurotic lack of confidence misunderstands the tensile strength of the structures and beliefs that bind society to democracy. A reformer entering elective politics for the first time in the mid-1970s would notice almost immediately the impact of ideas on so-called ordinary people. Indeed, the connection between reformer as idea producer and citizens as idea consumers was immediate and electric and would remain so throughout the reformer's brief life in office, which itself was not long enough, thanks to God, to qualify as a career. In fact, this connectedness was so powerful and so sustaining that it quickly doubled back on itself, so that once challenged, the idea consumers themselves became the most creative of idea producers. It was nothing but the purest Jefferson. Citizens had more and better ideas about how to govern themselves than did all their elected representatives rolled into one.

Starting in the late 1970s and continuing for a decade, this reformer championed the cause of military reform across America in the widest possible variety of venues. In Washington, the notion of military reform was considered arcane and complex. In the rest of America, an amazing range of people would understand and readily respond to the notion that our military forces required restructuring. Veterans and many active-duty personnel in particular responded with agreement and ideas of their own on the elimination of redundancies, the modernization of force structures, and reforms in doctrines and strategies.

The ability of citizens to understand, appreciate, generate, and be empowered by ideas is strong evidence of the benign quality of Jefferson's notion of generational revolution—or perhaps one could as easily say it is strong evidence of his notion of revolutionary regeneration. Every citizen with even a spark of reformer in his soul—and that is many more citizens than most political pundits would even hazard to guess—would also understand the paradigm on which the wisdom of the perpetual revolution of generations is founded. It is simply this: values produce beliefs; beliefs are the source of principles; principles are the basis of ideology; ideology produces policies; policies are the foundation of programs. There is, in other words, a logic to the development of ideas that govern our lives. Policies and programs do not materialize out of thin air. Ideas matter, and the ideas that have the greatest impact are those that result from this logic that links values to programs. In a society that values its children, a fundamental belief in and respect for the future of children becomes a matter of social principle. The principle of the rights of children then becomes a basic element of the ideology of a political party. This ideology necessarily requires the party to develop a policy around children's interests, and this, in turn, results in specific programs, such as better-quality education, day care, health care, and social protections.

In the best of times, and these days do not by any means qualify for that distinction, policies and the programs that follow from them are the grist of the American political mill. Rarely does debate rise to the exotic philosophical level of ideology, let alone to that of principles, beliefs, and values. In this era of trivialization, it is difficult to sustain even the most modest level of debate. Any message for mankind left in the hollow log of the commercial media has to be pithy, cute, and not very challenging. In an atmosphere of trash-compacted messages ricocheting wildly through a media vacuum, supply-side economics was a made-for-TV overnight sensation. Serious debate about the rights and interests of children was avoided entirely, and more than a million American children were added to poverty's rolls in the 1980s.

Never mind that it managed to be both wrong and wrongheaded and that it wrapped itself tightly in a false flag of reform. Supply-side economics could be—and was—diagramed on a cocktail napkin and explained by even the densest congressperson or TV anchorperson (often indistinguishable both in appearance and intellect) in no more than eight seconds. Thus, it was the perfect idea for the high-speed eighties—it was economic junk food. The ease of this supremely dubious notion's acceptability in a not very sober period would make a reformer, the American bison of politics, ponder whether his country would ever return to an age in which it would seriously discuss its future.

The ramifications for the American body politic were enormous. If the majority of voters and the majority of elected representatives could believe supply-side economics, they were capable of believing almost anything. And sure enough, the military equivalent of supply-side economics swiftly appeared from the ever-fertile mind of our president Reagan (with considerable thermonuclear assistance from Dr. Edward Teller) in the form of Star Wars. Those who found it both easy and convenient to believe that balanced budgets would necessarily result from massive tax cuts for Wall Street barons would not have to invest even one watt of intellectual energy in believing that we could knock down thousands of Soviet missiles with thousands of American missiles and that we could carry out this spectacular enterprise at such distances in deep space as to make World War III no more hazardous than the annual Fourth of July fireworks exhibit in Forest Park, Ottawa, Kansas.

Such ideas, plus others equally ludicrous, were to demonstrate powerfully the dangers created by the reform party's stagnation. A discouraged reformer would be brought to propound a kind of Gresham's law of politics—bad ideas drive out good ones—as well as its more important corollary—in a political vacuum, bad ideas will multiply like mink in desperate heat.

Alas, an alert critic will surely say, this is precisely the reason Jefferson's notion of generational revolution is profoundly dangerous: one simply cannot trust the next generation not to go off miscocked. On the contrary, a reform disciple of Jefferson would be called on to respond, simply calling a wacky notion reform doesn't make it reform. Reform can be borne as a false flag as easily as it can be borne as a true one. Jefferson was not advocating revolution for revolution's sake; he was advocating it for progress's sake. And progress possesses certain immutable characteristics, tax cuts for the rich not being among them.

The supply-side idea did not spring full blown from any political brow of Zeus. It had a parentage, albeit one more of artificial insemination than of natural intellectual reproduction; it was enough of a policy cyborg to flourish in the nonreform vacuum. It reportedly was produced in some petri dish in the economic laboratories of *The Wall Street Journal* by mixing certain vital fluids from Keynesianism with counterpart cells produced by an ideology conservative in character and notable for its consistency, simplicity, and lack of relevance to reality. Thereafter, the lineage is clearer, if not more legitimate, for modern conservative ideology is founded on ancient notions of laissez-faire, which in turn flow from strong beliefs in the destructive intervention of governments and the ultimate value of self-reliance, a value with strong resonance in American culture—thus, values (self-reliance), belief (antigovernment), principle (laissez-faire), ideology (conservatism), policy (supply-side), and program (tax cut).

In only one significant respect does all this have to do with what late-twentieth-century America would see as radical Jeffersonian notions of recurring revolution. Occasional reform, prompted by eras of great internal stress, has been the principal means by which this great conservative nation has avoided, if not evaded, more drastic social and political remedies. The paradigm for the party of reform might follow thus: values (communitarian), belief (equity), principle (social justice), ideology (reform), policy (progressive), and program (experimental). There are precious few progressive policies or truly experimental programs at century's close because this great causal chain has separated. And the separation has occurred where imagination and courage are most wanting. At some time— when exactly is not important—the links of principle and ideology pulled apart.

Jefferson believed the periodic reform of laws and institutions was required to realize values such as commonwealth and community, beliefs in equity, and principles of social justice. Periodic revolution or reform was both the centerpiece of a progressive ideology and a practical prescription for responding to, and positively channeling, change. Institutional reforms had an even more fundamental purpose: to secure the blessings of liberty for each generation. To stand still, only to conserve, was a prescription for the erosion of political values and the ultimate loss of liberty due to the battering power of chaotic change. A democratic society has no choice but to risk inventing new institutions, imagining new policies, and adapting courageously to a world in flux if it wishes to preserve its democratic ideals. The ideology of reform is necessary to keep hope alive, to affirm progressive change.

As minister to France in 1789, Jefferson addressed a letter to Madison, as he often did simply "because a subject came into [his] head" and "without knowing by what occasion" he was writing. This particular letter raised a unique and profound issue:

> The question Whether one generation . . . has a right to bind another, seems never to have been started either on this or our side of the water. Yet it is a question of such consequences as not only to merit decision, but place also, among the fundamental principles of every government. . . . I set out on this ground which I suppose to be self evident, 'that the earth belongs in usufruct to the living,' that the dead have neither powers nor right over it.

So strongly did he feel that one generation could not burden another with debt or encumbrance on land that he wrote, "By the law of nature, one generation is to another as one independent nation to another." He wanted the Constitution to contain a declaration that no national debts could be contracted that could not be repaid within a generation's nineteen-year span. His logic would find resonance today: "By reducing too the faculty of borrowing within its natural limits, it would bridle the spirit of war." Prescient Jefferson somehow knew that the new nation would experience its strongest appetite for credit when the dogs of war were loosed. Late-twentieth-century conservatives, so anxious about debt, so bellicose about diplomacy, might more soberly contemplate a constitutional balanced-budget amendment knowing that it would doubtless fatally constrain the willy-nilly dispatch of American military forces.

Now from the ineluctably logical mind of Jefferson comes the really dramatic part: "On similar ground it may be proved that no society can make a perpetual constitution, or even a perpetual law." This is quite simply a stunning declaration. "The earth," he continued, "belongs always to the living generation. They may manage it then, and what proceeds from it, as they please, during their usufruct. . . . Every constitution . . . and every law, naturally expires at the end of 19 years. If it be enforced longer, it is an act of force and not of right." This is not a proposal, nor is it simply an idea to be rehearsed in university debate forums or kicked around by scholarly gentlemen in their clubs or in the Senate reading room; it is as concrete a philosophical conclusion as a genius human mind can have. And the implications for traditionalism and conservative orthodoxy are awesome.

Do not dismiss Jefferson's position as the musings of an unfinished radical. For some thirty-five years later Jefferson had this to say in a letter to Major John Cartwright, an English reformer:

But can [constitutions] be made unchangeable? Can one generation bind another, and all others, in succession forever? I think not. The Creator has made the earth for the living, not the dead. Rights and powers can only belong to persons, not to things, not to mere matter, unendowed with will. . . . A generation may bind itself as long as its majority continues in life; when that has disappeared, another majority is in place, holds all the rights and powers their predecessors once held, and may change their laws and institutions to suit themselves. Nothing then is unchangeable but the inherent and unalienable rights of man.

One must presume that by *nothing*, he means *nothing*.

Basing his conclusions on a lifetime of belief, Jefferson wished to thwart any kind of permanent aristocracy—the predictable social and political aristocracies of wealth and power—by institutionalizing reform, by keeping alive the spirit of revolution in the hearts of future generations of Americans. For him there were only two realities: change and the inalienable rights of man. To respond progressively and creatively to the former was the best assurance of the preservation of the latter. His most famous statement of this truth came in an 1816 letter to Samuel Kercheval:

I know also, that laws and institutions must go hand in hand with the progress of the human mind. As that becomes more developed, more enlightened, as new discoveries are made, new truths disclosed, and manners and opinions change with the change of circumstances, institutions must advance also, and keep pace with the times. We might as well require a man to wear still the coat which fitted him when a boy, as civilized society to remain ever under the regimen of their barbarous ancestors.

Of barbarity, Jefferson perhaps knew less than the late-twentieth-century reformer. Happily, he would never know the barbarities of modern warfare and weaponry, the barbarities of crime, homelessness, and hunger in America's great cities, the barbarities of modern political finance in the name of democracy, the barbarities of poverty among America's children, the barbarities of "technopoly," even the barbarities of entertainment. Were he to see such things today, it is more than possible he might wish to shorten the time span for generational revolution to five years or as often as required. Careerism and courtierlike behavior among late-twentieth-century politicians alone would surely have driven him into a rage at the perversion of the citizens' democracy he envisioned for the new nation. Simply to document the gap between promise and performance, between ideal and real, in present-day democratic practice is to make the most powerful case for generational revolution and institutionalized reform.

After intense resistance, a reformer today, instinctively suspicious of all those who seek to amend the Constitution to solve some temporal economic or political grievance, would begin to appreciate the notion of constitutional limits for members of Congress and the widespread public outrage underlying it. For in late-twentieth-century America, such social underpinnings as party loyalty, trust in government, confidence in the future, optimism about opportunity for one's progeny—all would be in sharp descent among the vast majority of citizens. Against the backdrop of the successful—some would dare to say victorious—outcome of the cold war, unprecedented economic prosperity by historical standards, and international security on a scale unknown for a half century or more, historians will study with wonder at the breadth and depth of discontent in the America of the period. Even a cranky, frustrated reformer might find it difficult to divine the true sweep of this discontent.

There could be only one explanation, and it should have been clear all along: in an era of great change,

America felt stagnant. The country was ripe for reform, yet reform was not occurring. Indeed, it has been decades since a new generation has assumed responsibility for itself by imposing its own stamp of authority and priority on its government and on its society. Psychologically, the price of weakness and lack of courage is shame. The rodent of fate that gnaws most tellingly is not the rodent of failure but that of never having tried, of never having assumed responsibility. Several generations have failed collectively to grasp the reins of social responsibility that would have allowed them to guide the nation toward a better destiny. We worship our bold and brave frontier ancestors for their endurance, sacrifice, and courage, yet we see all around us the results of our failure to challenge our own frontiers.

As Newton's second law of motion is a law of nature, so is change. The forces of the status quo, tradition, and, inertia are powerful indeed. For every argument for progressive change, there are ten against it. It may be that late-twentieth-century America as a nation and a society simply isn't in the mood for reform. This has happened before, with the consequence that—as with slavery—some price had to be paid. Though difficult to calculate, the price of inertia today is potentially infinite. One can only guess that it will be tallied in lost lives, decayed cities, a polluted environment, misallocated resources, and public discontent, none of which, at least for now, is irredeemable. But for how long can a revolutionary country go without revolution? For how long can a democracy founded on the ideal of adaptability refuse to adapt?

Both political parties have sins to be forgiven. Democrats must account for their failing to attend to the flame of idealism, reform, and progress. Some of the party's leaders must account for placing their career over the interests of the party and the commonwealth. Some of its constituent groups must account for their insistence on the preservation of a full share of a diminishing economic pie. All, including this failed reformer, have much to account for.

But the party of memory, responsible for the administrations of the eighties, has, if anything, an even greater burden. For its members are the people who may or may not have negotiated delays in the release of American-embassy hostages in Tehran to rig an election but who most certainly produced a massive illegal Iran-Contra fiasco, who searched for every opportunity to enervate measures protecting environmental quality, who gleefully cooperated with the opposition party in the wanton mismanagement and destruction of the savings-and-loan industry, and who—most of all—fostered a stranglehold on the nation's economy and policy-making machinery. Presuming there is some sort of political judgment day, however, there will be no more serious charge brought than that young people were actively and systematically discouraged from public service and every effort possible was made to stamp out the last ounce of idealism or sense of a better society through collective action. For a reformer, there can be no more serious political sin.

Sooner or later a thoughtful person, reformer or not, would come to ask himself an obvious question: what is a conservative doing in government in the first place? There could have been no fewer than several hundred occasions throughout the seventies and eighties when this reformer was startled to hear conservative senators-for-life damning their own government, even during periods when their own kind was in the White House. It did not require great intelligence on such occasions to ask oneself, If he hates the government so much, what is he doing here? Under these circumstances there could be only one plausible answer: this great patriot is sacrificing most of his adult life, at the cost of great personal anguish, pain, and misery, in an occupation he detests, for one reason and one reason only—to protect America from me. Yes. He was there, serving in a government he hated, to make sure this lonely reformer did not subvert democracy on some dark night, did not try some dastardly sneak attack on orthodoxy, traditional values, and the so-called American way of life—to make sure, in short, that he did not successfully carry out some reform, some change in the status quo. After all, a conservative, as it has been said, is but the worshiper of dead radicals. The emphasis here is on *dead*.

What would a radical conservative—and this is not a contradiction in terms—possibly have done with Jefferson? What would he do with Jefferson today? Have him locked up? Have him deported? Put him on some government blacklist? Most certainly, Jefferson would never receive a security clearance in today's climate and therefore, ipso facto, would be disqualified from any but the most menial public service. I know little of Jefferson, even after a lifetime of study, but I do suspect, with a kind of small-bore reformer's instinct, that Jefferson would not be especially keen on public service in late-twentieth-century America.

He wasn't particularly keen on public service in his own lifetime, which was, by comparison, positively Olympian. Is it conceivable that Jefferson would have shaken his political tin cup for campaign contributions at political rallies and fund-raisers? Not a chance. Would he implore lobbyists for donations with the implication that he would look with considerable favor on that forthcoming little amendment before the Finance Committee? Be serious. Would he carefully craft his letters and speeches to avoid offense to even the most obscure but angry interest group? Not in a lifetime. Would he be inclined to wrap together some strands of grapevine from Monticello and stride with purposeful anger through the corridors of the White House and the halls of Congress, driving out the craven money changers, political pack rats, and assorted pollsters, consultants, and political junkies? In a heart-beat.

How have we drifted so far from the spirit of '76? Why have we so totally dismissed a notion as grave and powerful as that of perennial reform or generational renewal? Why have the great majority, who profit by progressive change, surrendered their "unalienable rights" of self-government to an established aristocracy, an aristocracy not of heredity and title but of institutionalized conservative political power? In a functioning democracy, rights cannot be forcibly taken away; they can, however, be abandoned. A vast number of American citizens have effectively ceded their constitutionally guaranteed natural rights to self-government, and more are joining them daily. Yet at the same time, they find themselves angered by the quite-predictable results: corrupt campaign-finance practices, gross official abuses of power, manipulation of the legislative and regulatory processes, the alienation of the people from their government.

At the close of his generation's period of contribution, a saddened reformer finds himself compelled to compare the age of the New Deal and its experimentation in pursuit of community with the Reagan revolution and its individualism in pursuit of material success. It was as if his own government had specifically invited his fellow citizens to partake of a modern-day Faustian bargain: you give us your vote and forget about civic duty, obligation, and social responsibility, and we will give you all the tax cuts you can swallow. Just leave all issues of public policy and our country's future to us. Only one thing, the antireform aristocracy would say, forget about progressive reform, and totally abandon even the most fleeting dream of generational renewal. The price of this bargain, of course, has been the subtle but inevitable loss of America's humanity.

Within one or two more generations, the memory of

the reform ideal, of social progress, will be greatly dimmed, perhaps even gone forever. And of reformers there will be none left. Our country, like Dr. Faustus, may then long for one single chance to reverse its bargain, to give back to the aristocrats some of the comforts of me-for-myself in exchange for we're-all-in-this-together, for a better chance for our children, for a noble ideal, for the elusive but constant dream of democratic revolution for every generation.

5

KENNEDY AND
THE NOBLE PROFESSION

Rarely do we escape the strong influences of our youth. If fortune has been kind and these influences are benign, rarely do we want to. But even benign influences can be troublesome to ease and comfort. "The Hound of Heaven" Francis Thompson would call his powerful poem. And well he might, for the Hound of the title is no less than the Eternal Himself, relentless in His pursuit of the poet's soul:

> I fled Him, down the nights and down the days;
> I fled Him, down the arches of the years;
> I fled Him, down the labyrinthine ways
>   Of my own mind. . . .

So it would be for a young Kansas boy who though healthy in every respect, would seem to family and friends more quiet than average, bookish and occasionally dreamy and distracted. Was that muffled, troubling sound the relentless Hound's heavy breathing?

Early preoccupation with doctrines of holiness, sanctification, and perfection, with avoidance of evil and even the appearance of evil, and—most of all—with the consuming notion of salvation itself, would never totally disappear. But time would reshape and redirect it, temporally and outwardly, under the serial influence of the unlikely quartet of Wesley, Kierkegaard, Tolstoy, and Jefferson. This prolegomenon to a reformer's life would weave together intricate and unpredictable themes of social justice, resistance to established power structures, a suspicion of authority bordering on genteel rebelliousness, dissatisfaction with traditional methods, a fascination with innovation, and—most of all—dedication to progressive reform.

Out of a religious environment laden with behavioral strictures, Wesley would emerge to remind one of a gospel originally dedicated to healing, caring, and serving. Out of an educational environment heavy in its undergraduate phase with strict doctrine and anti-intellectualism and (ironically) heavy in its graduate phase with intellectualism and little doctrine, Kierkegaard would emerge to focus attention on the individual's lonely relationship with God rather than his relationship with church liturgy and doctrine. Out of the later environment of law and policy, the spirit of Tolstoy as reformer would reemerge to remind him that a life in society carried a greater responsibility than just that of professional service to affluent interests and to remind him, too, that government policy must liberate, not enslave. It was left finally to Jefferson to provide the practical rationale for public service as civic virtue and a citizen's obligation.

But the politics of the 1950s offered little by way of inspiration or opportunity for the application of idealism. Save the aberrant excesses of Joseph McCarthy, the Torquemada of the cold war, the politics of the time were managed by sober men, caricatures of traditional politicians, and seemed largely unimportant to a young midwestern man struggling to find some meaning and purpose through education. These nostalgic happy days represented not only simpler times but they represented better times as well. We were in the process of forgetting Korea and had not yet heard of Vietnam. Looking back, it was a time of innocence. We were innocent of many things, including assassinations.

The first serious discussion about John Kennedy involving this reformer occurred in a social ethics class at the Yale Divinity School in early 1960. The question was whether a Catholic could even hope to become president. Although the topic was then beginning to be discussed as Kennedy was increasingly drawing public attention, the fact that he might actually be barred from national office by his religion came as a surprise. An even greater surprise was that serious classmates in a notoriously liberal school might believe so, as might a high percentage of one's family and friends in the less liberal Midwest. Families divided, often very sharply, over this question.

The growing intensity of the debate, especially in Protestant circles, caused Kennedy himself to become suddenly a figure of interest. A moment's inspection revealed him to be a political figure apart from the stereotype, not only in the overreported aspects of money, looks, wife, glamour, youth, hyperactive family, heroism, and so forth but much more important in that occasionally unconcealed sense of his that the whole political enterprise was a great escapade, a serious frolic whose failure would not be life threatening. Indeed, it was his success that proved to be life threatening. And here would be the ultimate irony for the man whose very specialty in twentieth-century American politics was irony. It was the unique application of the ironic quality of life to politics that made him so appealing, both to a reformer and to a reformer's generation. He represented a combination of purpose, intelligence, laughter, folly, and doom that has yet to be replaced. Perhaps it never will be.

Byronic Kennedy may have been, but of cynicism he would know something also. Even the politics of happy days would feature a cynical undercurrent, and he was, at least in part, his father's son. But the intelligence he brought to the task enabled him always to see, in that curious detached way, the distance between what was and what was meant to be. This, of course, is but irony's simplest definition, and thus his alternating amusement by and amazement at his real generational counterpart, Richard Nixon. Nixon, who would have had to have reached to the Pluto of his own personal solar system of emotions to see the dawn of an ironic thought, was a walking, talking bundle of ironies. Neither he nor anyone else could conceivably have been more single-minded about the ambition of politics. Kennedy had clearly said to himself, if not to his father, This far will I go in pursuit of the top job— and no further. Nixon, we now clearly know, was up for anything. In those days preceding and beyond the confrontation of 1960, one imagines Nixon in his darker hours maddened to the borderline of frenzy by a single thought: Kennedy makes it look so easy. Theodore White later wrote that Kennedy bore the same fascination for Nixon as the snake charmer has for the cobra.

Nixon aside, Kennedy bore a different fascination for a younger generation, one that had never heard— or certainly had never heard from a politician—a challenge to idealism that demanded, not suggested, a sense of civic duty, obligation, and responsibility as well as a concrete response to that demand. Both Adlai Stevenson and Hubert Humphrey, it must be said, were John the Baptists in this regard; but neither would achieve the presidential platform that Kennedy promoted and then used (and either might have used with equal effect) so effectively to motivate a generation to public service. "Politics is a noble profession" was the simple, liberating message, and some form of public service was open to all and was the responsibility of all who could make some contribution to their country or the world.

For a short time, the national government was to become the principal vehicle for service. After years of Wesley, Kierkegaard, Tolstoy, and Jefferson, as well as years of the country club atmosphere of the Eisenhower presidency, here was finally a message this reformer, as well as many others of his age, would greet with pleasure and purpose. Kennedy's challenge was subtle. It was not a wholesale endorsement of careerist politics. Rather, it was a challenge to public service. Until this time, to make a positive impact on society's public life, it was necessary to seek public office, to become a politician. But becoming a politician was not an attractive or available option. It required connections, money, access, position, an insider's entrée to a closed, secret society. To improve society, to make progress, to change things, one had to have some power. But, it seemed to a young man with a growing instinct for reform activism, to get power, one almost had to have it already, to be born or invited into the ultimate secret society, the political fraternity.

There was no way this could ever happen for a working-class young man from the Midwest, virtually none of whose very extended family had ever shaken hands with any politician above the rank of sheriff. There was simply no way onto the closed treadmill of political power. Besides, who would want on? Politics, everyone knew, was dirty, manipulative, corrupt, and corrupting. That is, even if one is introduced to the system innocent, clean, and idealistic, he will not remain so for long. It was a life of deals, trades, confusion of public and private interests, and ultimate cynicism carried out by politicos motivated primarily by self-interest, cartoon stereotypes who smoked cigars, slapped backs, laughed too loudly, lined their own pockets, and alone shared the secrets of power.

For idealism there was neither room nor opportunity. The idea of public service as a noble ideal was almost as foreign to the age of Eisenhower as it came to be in the age of Reagan. Under Eisenhower, the government was the arena in which power groups arbitrated their arrangements and divided up the pie provided by the taxpayers. During the Reagan years, the government was made the enemy of the people, an evil thing to be scorned, demeaned, and ultimately crushed. In between came a period—stunning when viewed in retrospect—in which everything in the way of true social progress was possible through a benign but activist government. It was not quite a utopian dream (Kennedy called himself an idealist without illusions), but it was close. The poor would be clothed, fed, and housed. The jobless would have work. American industry would flourish and support a strong but benevolent American presence in the world. Our art and culture would be the envy of the world. Our bounty would be shared with all—save the Kremlin strongmen—who shared our democratic ideals. It was nothing less than the dawn of a golden age.

A quarter century later it was clear that starry-eyed reformers such as this lonely one anticipated too much, expected too much, hoped for too much of any president or administration. No possible collection of humans could have sustained such a burden of idealism and optimism. The years that have passed since the early sixties seem now to make that period almost a dream of optimism whose passing marked the end of American innocence. The growing postwar economy and absence of serious international competitive challenge made everything seem possible. Resources for public as well as private endeavor seemed limitless. The decision to travel to the moon, so intriguing in its technology, so dreamy in its metaphor, was the perfect symbol of the age. Until it finally was achieved a decade later, it would continue to serve as a startling reminder of the unlimited possibilities this country offered. How often, a decade after that, would this reformer, then aspiring to national leadership, hear the rhetorical question "If we can send a man to the moon, why can't we . . . ?"

In effect, the Kennedy-inspired mission to the moon unwittingly put technology at the service of reform—and the servant soon became the master. The strong suggestion was to look for deus ex machina rather than *deus ex corde*. This was a historic detour of significant proportions. Wesley, Kierkegaard, Tolstoy, and Jefferson saw man as both the barrier to and agent of reform. The human propensity to seek comfort in the past could be overcome only by the selective human propensity to explore the potential of the future and by adapting human methods and institutions to facilitate the exploration. But the laboratory wizardry of the sixties held open the possibility of a technical fix for what were, or were soon to become, contradictions rooted in the human condition. The whole theory of America in Vietnam was based on American technological superiority. All the premises were correct—except that they overlooked the human factor. Technological superiority, particularly when applied in Vietnam so late in the day and so heavy-handedly, was no solution to decades of ideological polarization overlaid on more than a century of colonization. Democracy arrived in Vietnam on a gunship, and tragically it departed in the same way.

The same mentality, however, continued to pervade American thinking beyond the 1960s. As a young government lawyer, this reformer participated in a task force to carry out a Lyndon Johnson–inspired scheme to design a giant dam in the Mekong Delta that was meant to provide water for increased crop production and thus political stability in South Vietnam. In addition, it would demonstrate to North Vietnamese Communists the advantages of alliance with the West. It badly missed the point. The nationalist strain in Vietnamese communism cared more for independence and autonomy than for Western friendship. Soon thereafter, in anticipation of worsening urban congestion, crime, and deterioration, a team of young experts (and reformers) would study the notion of developing large-scale "new towns" on public lands in the West. It was then an exciting and bold idea, the creation of model communities. Resources for such a grand undertaking seemed readily at hand, but it was not the answer to looming urban blight.

The list of technological schemes to address humanity's problems was endless, and it was a monument to the misplaced age of reform-through-science: nuclear power plants that would produce energy "too cheap to meter"; giant desalination plants that would eliminate drought worldwide; atomic explosions that would liberate buried natural gas and oil shale deposits; a similar series of atomic detonations that would cut a new canal across the Isthmus of Panama; revolutionary portable communication systems; networks of battlefield sensors; spy planes that would fly beyond the limits of interception. There was no end to the possibilities of technological innovation and its application to human need. Nowhere was this more true than in the idea of security through strategic deterrence—the idea that the most lethal and accurate of nuclear missiles would constrain the behavior of our Communist adversaries. None of it ever really worked, of course, but we didn't know that at the time. For a reformer boundlessly optimistic about overcoming all hidebound resistance to progressive change, it seemed that science might truly become the handmaiden of politics, if not of philosophy as well.

A politics premised on the boundless promise of technology was not a politics inclined to perceive much need for institutional reform. The laboratory would provide solutions unavailable from governors and legislators. Relative to what preceded and succeeded it, the brief Kennedy era was a time of reform, a time when change was treated as a challenge and an opportunity and not as a threat. In some cases, optimism led to an enthusiasm for intelligence that came to be badly misplaced. Pentagon reforms based on new techniques of quantitative analysis laid the groundwork for serious errors of judgment regarding the application of these same techniques to battlefield management in Vietnam. An administration selected almost entirely on premises of scholarship and intellect let its collective self-confidence lead it to conclude that raw brainpower was more than a substitute for seasoned judgment. Yet whether in the Cuban missile crisis or the integration of southern universities, young men aged quickly, exercised reasoned judgment, and gained wisdom virtually overnight.

To a reformer, John Kennedy was the most compelling political leader of his time. He has now joined history, and his faults will be critiqued for as long as history is written. But about some leaders there is a dimension beyond the reach of conventional criticism. Either one senses it, or one does not. It is, in that respect, subjective. It is enough for some of us to say that he changed our lives, that he made public service both attractive and noble, that he caused us to aspire to the classic ideal of civic duty. Effort may and will be made to show that he was not worthy of respect, that his character was too deeply flawed to deserve admiration, that his life ended before his true role could be defined. None of this is true or important for those who redirected their lives because of the challenge he represented.

There is a traditional kind of leadership that achieves and wields power directly—the leadership of Lyndon Johnson and Richard Nixon, for example. There is also a nontraditional leadership, which empowers indirectly—that of John Kennedy and Ronald Reagan. Reagan empowered young people to seek wealth, success, prosperity. Kennedy empowered young people to serve their society, to contribute, to improve their nation and their world. Each generation, each society must constantly choose the values it will honor. If the Reagan values had in fact produced the society they promised—a society of prosperity, opportunity for all, and higher standards of living—then they would deserve respect and admiration for generations to come. But they did not.

The Kennedy values of service, duty, responsibility, and reform demand a more complex judgment. They are less quantifiable. They cannot be evaluated readily in numbers such as gross national product, net family income, rate of taxation. They can finally be appreciated only in the lives they changed and the contribution to a better society those lives represent. It is both easier and more exciting to analyze the way in which power is wielded in the traditional, direct sense. The politics of empowerment is more subtle and more difficult. The politics of empowerment says each person can make a difference for the better, and every person should try. The idea of empowerment does not guarantee civic virtue, but it does liberate that virtue where it already exists.

Idealism is an attribute virtually peculiar to youth. It is repeatedly explained that mature years bring realism, a sense of limits, personal and family obligations and preoccupations (as Tolstoy noted), and the need to lay aside reserves for the winter season. The limitless excitement of youth contains the sense that all is possible for oneself and, if one is so concerned, for one's society. That is why a leader has the greatest chance to change the direction of a nation by appealing to the enormous energy of youth. In Kennedy's case, it has been argued that having been jaded by a cynical father and a political career, the man was essentially fraudulent in his idealistic claims. But he was not that great an actor. It is difficult, if not impossible, to deceive an entire generation over several years. As if to authenticate his challenge, those who had responded to his admonition to ask what they could do for their country in many cases continued to ask that same question for years after his death.

The ideas and influences of Wesley, Kierkegaard, Tolstoy, and Jefferson had, by this proto-reformer's mid-twenties, formed a faculty within his mind, and without fully understanding what it meant, he had become a reformer. As disparate as these influences were, they had threads in common. Each had interests that were widely diverse, but each was passionate and single-minded. "Purity of heart," said Kierkegaard, "is to will one thing." Each pursued what was good and beautiful and true with passionate intensity. All were intellects; all, except perhaps for Wesley, were monumental intellects. Again except possibly for Wesley, all were men who stood alone. Kierkegaard and Jefferson had unfulfilled and unrequited affairs of the heart; Tolstoy perished in old age virtually alone at the Astapovo railroad station, either running away from or toward the Hound of heaven. Each was intensely but independently religious, preferring to be alone in a den with God than to rely on the comforting dogmas of the institutional church. One way or the other, all would be considered heretics. Wesley fought to break the liturgical shackles of the Church of England, to bring the gospel with immediacy to every man and woman. The immediacy of the gospel and the intensity of its message was similarly central to all Kierkegaard's belief. Tolstoy would struggle to hone the gospel to its immediate and central truth and would find "resist not evil." And like Tolstoy, Jefferson was so put out by the gothic theological constructs of the established church that over a weekend, he took scissors and paste to the New Testament and reduced it to the essence of Jesus' teachings, centered largely on the Sermon on the Mount. The parallels between Tolstoy and Jefferson in this regard are striking, but all four men shared the same intense, insistent need to reduce religious truth to its essence.

Perhaps these men imparted in the young reformer an understanding of the futility of a lifelong struggle with religious authority and led him to realize that a life devoted to saving one's soul was both selfish and unchristian, and so he came upon the Kennedy challenge at a time when a secular mission was called for. Partisanship had not been part of the reformer's life by his mid-twenties. But several summers' labor plus the day-to-day struggles of his own working-class family was enough to incline him viscerally and philosophically toward the party of the common man. He quickly became a more intense, uncritical, and passionate partisan than he might be in later life. Law school became the training ground for public service. The excitement of social reform in the early sixties began to focus on civil rights, the dominant social issue, which would finally give way to the Vietnam War.

At that time, a young man from the happy days of the midwestern 1950s would not begin to know of the deeply corrosive role that race had played, and would continue to play, in his nation's life. But it would not be long before police dogs and cruel batons, murdered children and burned buses would reveal the ugly truth. No conversion to the cause of justice and equality was necessary: it had been part of his upbringing. But he would be ashamed of himself for not understanding the harsh reality of racism sooner and ashamed of a nation that had quietly accepted an undemocratic society so hypocritically and for so long. The civil rights traumas of the sixties were yet another reason for commitment to a life of public service.

The reform impulse had taken the first twenty-five years of the young man's life to form fully. As much as one analyzes all the intellectual and even spiritual components of such an impulse, even the one who feels it can never fully account for it. Many times one might ask, Why this intense need to change things, to improve things, to try to make things better? No clear answer would ever come. In an age laden with amateur and popular psychology, the temptation to seek an explanation in some childhood trauma or family mystery always exists. Later a surprising number of journalists would try to do the same, with notable lack of success. The simplest explanation almost always being the correct one, the reformer would finally conclude that this is just the way things are.

The reform instinct is not necessarily more noble or more exceptional than any other benign instinct. Perversely, one might argue that Hitler, Genghis Khan, and Napoleon were reformers of a sort. But this argument, perverse or not, reveals the important distinction. True reform is not simply about taking one system and changing it into some other. Real reform is not value-neutral. Reform means to make better, to improve, to change for the sake of progress, not simply for the sake of change.

America in 1960 was ready for energy and vitality, although it is less clear that it was ready for structural change. Even the referendum on "getting the country moving again" proved barely favorable to Kennedy. The lassitude of the late Eisenhower years, featuring a nagging recession and a stagnant economy, called for vigorous experimentation. Kennedy responded with a Keynesian tax cut that produced economic growth— and the last balanced budget—well into the late sixties. (Thinking to repeat the experiment, but in vastly different circumstances, the Reagan supply-siders tried the same thing in 1981, but with tragic consequences for the federal budget deficit.)

Kennedy himself understood that the narrowness of his mandate prevented sweeping economic, political, or social reforms. He undoubtedly would have been astounded, and no doubt gratified, by the revolution soon to come in civil rights and race relations. But he never presumed to believe that the voters had authorized him to alter fundamentally the values or structures of the day. The post–Bay of Pigs, post–missile crisis Kennedy, however, unlike the "bear any burden" Kennedy of the inaugural, showed distinct signs, principally in the widely noted American University speech, of understanding deeply and intuitively the need for a profoundly different approach to U.S.-Soviet and East-West relations in order to avoid nuclear war.

The America of Kennedy's administration was a comfortable, conservative, but restless America. Like animals before an earthquake, Americans were restless and unaccountably disturbed. How could anyone know what waited just ahead—assassinations, Vietnam, Watergate, social revolution, trauma-induced loss of national confidence? But the uneasy sense of something uncontrollable about to happen existed vaguely nonetheless. Especially before the cultural revolution of the late sixties and seventies, this America was very much controlled by white male representatives of the business, government, press, and financial elites. What need they saw for reform was marginal at best.

It is eminently safe to believe that these governing elites had no affection for the Jeffersonian notion of generational revolution. Even the Democratic party—nominally, at least, the reform party—accepted John Kennedy as its leader reluctantly and only after having been dominated by him in the primary and convention season. There were other leaders, such as Stevenson and Humphrey, more liberal; some, such as Symington, more socially acceptable; others, such as Johnson, more politically established—but none threatened the status quo more than Kennedy. Indeed, it was Kennedy's outsider status, nontraditional politics, and potential for innovation that made him attractive to young reformers.

Thus, a generational change of leadership produced not reform but the opportunity for reform for yet another generation then in the making. Many who responded to the call to public service would make their presence felt for a quarter century or more to come. None could then know, but it was to be a period of cultural and political turmoil rivaling any in American history. For some, it would be their chance to bring about structural reform, if not generational revolution. It would be a period less full of happiness than of heartbreak and failure, a period characterized by reform deferred.

PART II

A Life in Pursuit of Reform

STUDENT
VOLUNTEER TO PRESIDENTIAL
CANDIDATE

6

A PLAGUE
OF ASSASSINS

Assassination is the ultimate act of revolution. Political murder, the most violent, vivid, and extreme form of political action, leaves no margin for response. Assassination became a metaphor for the 1960s and beyond. Assassination raped a generation politically, alienated it, and made it conspirational. For America of that time, assassination assumed a metaphysical dimension; it became a fatalistic prism through which life would be viewed. Young children in school on November 22, 1963, were heard to ask, "Will Daddy be killed, too?"

On that day, this reformer lost, or believed he lost, both desire for public service and the instinct for reform. Even though he might thereafter almost ritually serve out his anticipated term as a government lawyer, he would know that the excitement and the hope of helping to renew America were gone. This dream had been assassinated and, therefore, any subsequent dream might be annihilated as quickly. Assassination took on terrorism's most vivid mask: there were no defenses, it represented madness, and it could happen at any time. It diminished expectations, increased the stakes of randomness, promoted individual insularity, pierced the heart of optimistic reform, and colored all of life with fatalism. Assassination, especially as it assumed a pattern, killed even the incentive to dream.

The sudden shock of John Kennedy's death carried with it boundless lifelong lessons in the fickle and tenuous grip of Fortune. All the world, including the health and safety of one's family, became hostage to randomness, accident, and rabid treachery. Life as Murphy's law—if the worst possible thing can happen, it will—seemed less a joke and more a prophecy. No institution, office, or person—no president, pope, or prime minister—seemed secure. Order was shattered, continuity crushed. The smiling, wealthy, invulnerable leader of the world was snuffed out with as little energy as it took to pinch a candle flame. Indeed, "mere anarchy was loosed upon the world."

Sometime thereafter, a sad and fatalistic reformer would finish a dispirited term of service in the Justice and Interior departments of the national government and return with his family to their chosen home state of Colorado. As rich as one's private life might be made by the birth and flowering of one's children, so one's public life and the challenge of reform would now seem a hollow mockery. The great social and civil rights legislation of the early Johnson years would seem but a martyr's monument erected by an anguished populous, not the redemptive act of enlightened constituencies and congresspersons sobered to the need for a just and reformed republic.

Very soon the social progress of this time would blur and dissipate as the dogs of war, growing impatient at their leashes, would be loosed upon an obscure region of Southeast Asia. The chance for further victories in the age-old struggle against racism and poverty would be abandoned for a different conquest, an ideological conflict whose costs, causes, and consequences would only gradually be fully appreciated.

The Great Society period, from 1964 to 1967, now seems merely a time of recurring shock, numbness, and fatalism, its real progress in justice and equality an unappreciated memory. It seemed no more than a heartbeat from John Kennedy's death to Mylai, but during this traumatic time, due largely to Lyndon Johnson's legendary political skills and final conversion to social progressivism, the causes of the elderly, minorities, and the poor advanced demonstrably. It was a meaningful time for progressivism, if not also for reform, but much of its meaning was lost on a nation still sleepwalking through the fog of its loss. Optimism had become a fragile thing, and laughter was seldom heard. The Civil Rights Act of 1964, introduced by Kennedy a year earlier, and the Voting Rights Act of 1965, were landmarks on the road toward racial justice and equality. The War on Poverty legislation of 1965 and 1966, as well as Medicare and Medicaid, financed by the economic growth stimulated in the early sixties, represented a direct government assault on the causes and conditions of economic inequity.

Reformers could scarcely appreciate the importance of the early Johnson years because the agent and the leader of change was lost. For this reformer, all hope, all thought of future activism seemed futile and pointless. It was not, as Kennedy critics would later endlessly assert, a case of generational hero worship, of uncritical fascination with a magnetic personality at the cost of objectivity. Undoubtedly for many young Kennedy admirers there was some of that. But for those seriously drawn to public service and social change, Kennedy's death suggested something deeper and more sinister. It suggested the presence of ominous dark forces just beneath society's veneer, forces that if goaded by the threat of institutional change, could rise up to strike down anything or anyone—including an increasingly popular president of the United States—who might threaten the status quo, traditional power structures, ancient political arrangements. The first Kennedy assassination, soon to be punctuated and underscored by more assassinations, had about it a dark, mystical quality. It seemed a warning against straying too near the permissible boundaries of social change. It suggested the presence of forces threatened by Kennedy's potential, forces angered by his unpredictable energy. He seemed too independent of established power structures and too capable of rearranging networks and agreements carefully arbitrated over time by powerful interests.

Central to the Kennedy myth was the element of almost Dionysian unpredictability. As exciting as this might have been for those lacking power, it was just as threatening to many controlling power. He was criticized by political pundits and professionals for his lack of the insider's legislative skills. But our weaknesses almost always mask our strengths, and John Kennedy's unwillingness or inability to play backroom politics made him that much more appealing to a generation that did not respect worn-out politics. Contrary to the conservative leadership that would come to power in the eighties, Kennedy was not antipolitical or antigovernment; he was pro–new politics and pro–new government.

After many years' reflection, this reformer, brought to public service by Kennedy's proactive, progovernment admonitions, would come to wonder whether some perverse logic dictated that leaders skilled at politics could not inspire idealism and those who empowered people to participate in democratic governance seemed less capable of political manipulation. There have been notable exceptions—for example, Franklin Roosevelt—but they have been rare. Not only are the two sets of leadership qualities antithetical, but those who possess one set also seem to antagonize those who possess or support the other set, as illustrated most vividly by the Kennedy-Johnson relationship.

There is a worthwhile insight here concerning barriers to reform. In addition to the reform idea, progressive change in a parliamentary republic requires two things: broad-based public support for the reform measure and its institutionalization in statutory form. One kind of leadership, charismatic and apart from the political system, inspires the public to march. Another kind, convivial, manipulative, and nonthreatening to its insider peers, is normally required to maneuver the legislative process. The public is often suspicious of the leader who is an insider, and politicians are often distrustful of the leader who has charismatic appeal to a mass following. The extraordinary Franklin Roosevelt gained the latitude to become both charismatic outsider and cunning insider only by virtue of the deeply troubled times in which he governed. Few could have been Roosevelt in Roosevelt's times; virtually no one can be Roosevelt in relatively secure and stable times.

It is widely believed that the trauma of the first Kennedy assassination provided the public impetus hitherto lacking for the dramatic domestic reforms of the mid-sixties engineered by Lyndon Johnson. Assassination in the sixties produced the same extraordinary grant of executive authority that depression had produced thirty years earlier.

The Kennedy killed in November 1963 seemed a different man from the Kennedy who became president in January 1961. Whether this transformation was the result of the single epiphany of the 1962 missile crisis or a collection of sobering experiences beginning with the Bay of Pigs failure in April 1961, he seemed to become more sober and more reflective. Kennedy seemed to equate youth with life and life with youth; so aging, even mentally, was not a welcome phenomenon. But no amount of life experience, even for the wealthy and the well connected, can prepare one for the stark world of the American presidency, with its savage bureaucratic infighting, the government agencies' narrow self-protectionism, layers of courtiers' sycophancy, and the general inclination of most factions to put self-interest over national interest. Although Kennedy took responsibility for the Bay of Pigs failure, it is generally conceded that he took important lessons from the less than exemplary behavior of the military and intelligence bureaucracies during the episode. These lessons were later reflected in the structure of his advisory group during the missile crisis and his ultimately successful management of this most serious confrontation of the cold war.

What-might-have-been speculation concerning the uncompleted Kennedy presidency is unrewarding and unfulfilling. The success of a reformer is not measurable in policy initiatives, legislative successes, or supportive editorials alone. The final and most compelling judgment involves the lives that are changed and the degree to which those lives continue to embody the cause of reform. With the possible exception of Franklin Roosevelt, no president or political leader in this century left behind a greater cadre of young people dedicated to social change through public service than John Kennedy. Nearly thirty years after his death, the Democratic party is selecting leaders who though teenagers at that time, were motivated by Kennedy's advocacy of public service as a noble profession. There is simply no method to gauge the sweeping impact of two generations of Americans who still serve their country because they came to believe, as Kennedy told them, that "political action is the highest responsibility of a citizen."

The political importance of John Kennedy as a national leader will never be understood until viewed through this prism. In less than thirty-six short months, he motivated tens of thousands of people in their teens and twenties to become engaged in the public life of their community, their nation, and the world and to struggle for progressive change. They did so and continue to do so, and they have changed the face of American politics. The death of the leader who inspired—and, more important, who empowered and legitimized them—left a scar that would never heal. But the torch burned on, and they could not lay it down.

Even as the Great Society gave way to the Vietnam War, many who had turned away from Washington after the assassination began to stir and, ironically, returned to activism by acting against Washington's policies. Kennedy's lesson was that the reform of government policies, the exercise of a citizen's duties required active participation in government when possible and active opposition to government when necessary. Increasingly, those motivated to public service in the early sixties returned to activism in opposition to the Johnson administration's expansion of the American military presence in Southeast Asia. To oppose a misguided policy is to serve the ideal of reform; it is an attempt to substitute a preferable approach or a more worthy goal for the accepted goal.

Too much has already been written both idealizing and condemning the sixties. As a certified veteran of the decade, this reformer would come to conclude that the real sixties of his experience were never as good or as bad, as exhilarating or as threatening, as the sixties of dream and nightmare. Rather, the real decade combined a kaleidoscopic mix of movement politics, antiwar protest, cultural revolution, and random radicalism for its own sake.

Supporters of the notion of a rapidly maturing, if not transformed, Kennedy usually cite his American University speech of 1963, which was measurably at odds with the bellicose rhetoric of his inaugural speech. It was chiefly remarkable in its sober appreciation for the escalating dangers of the nuclear-arms race and for its dramatically clear-eyed understanding of the need to manage the U.S.-Soviet relationship more sanely and to avoid the mounting confrontations that the more hawkish elements seemed to savor. The historical importance of John Kennedy lies in his evolving understanding of a rapidly changing modern world and the final end of America's insular isolation. He was the first of two generations of post–World War II "new thinkers." Kennedy understood, better even than Eisenhower, how much that war had, in Richard Hofstadter's words, thrust Americans "into a situation in which their domestic life is largely determined by the demands of foreign policy and national defense. With this change," Hofstadter continued, "came the final involvement of the nation in all the realities it had sought to avoid, for now it was not only mechanized, and urbanized and bureaucratized but internationalized as well."

Containment of communism became the policy, and it was played out principally in the Caribbean (Cuba) and in Southeast Asia (Vietnam). The toll—especially in Vietnam—in lives, misplaced national treasure, and opportunities forgone would be incalculable. This militarization of U.S. foreign policy would make isolationists out of internationalists and internationalists out of isolationists. It would be a great irony, in the latter case, to see twentieth-century conservative heirs of George Washington (who admonished his successors to avoid "entangling alliances") abandon their traditional dream of America as island fortress in favor of military interventionism and covert adventurism in highly unlikely and usually strategically inconsequential outposts around the globe. Kennedy contributed to the fiction that American actions, both covert and overt, are undertaken in defense of democracy, even when America's local clients are only marginally more savory than their insurgent counterparts and are perhaps not at all democratic.

America's internationalization at Pearl Harbor would be defined for much of the twentieth century in military and intelligence terms. These two categories eventually so merged and blurred as to become virtually indistinguishable, as they were in Cuba in the sixties and Vietnam in the seventies. In both cases, even the participants were not sure where Pentagon operations left off and CIA operations took up. Stepping into this turbulent stream in the mid-1970s, this reformer was immediately required to see America's role in the world through the eyes of both the Armed Services and the Intelligence committees of the United States Senate. He would come to be surprised by very little thereafter, not even that military officers based in the Reagan White House were using intelligence services to sell arms secretly to Islamic fundamentalists in order to raise the money that would then be used to provide yet more arms illegally to anti-Communist insurgents in Central America, by way of a drug-dealing political leader. It was at once both hopelessly comic and tragically pathetic but considered completely sane and even predictable by a nation accustomed to seeing its leaders almost routinely gunned down by killers without apparent motives. In a world that made little sense, except possibly within the framework of communism's and democracy's ideological struggle, assassinations and increasingly bizarre scandals simply represented a cost of doing business.

It seemed no accident that a leader such as John Kennedy, one with a higher-than-average degree of international sophistication, would be selected to lead the nation at a time when the country was settling into a more permanent role as global citizen. If the world insisted on drawing America into its affairs, Americans would insist on leaders who knew something about, and could manage, these affairs. But managing relations among a complex matrix of former world powers and emerging former colonies was a tricky process in the best of times, and when overlaid on a contest of superpower ideologies involving paramilitary and quasi-military intelligence forces guiding proxy armies, it was nothing less than treacherous. As long as conflict and casualties were sustained by armies that were indeed proxy, this was a matter the American people could support. Vietnam proved to be another thing. Being internationalized did not mean the American people were prepared to follow their allies, the British and the French, into political sinkholes like the Raj and Indochina.

There is reason to think that Kennedy might have become a leader who could envision an international role for America above, if not beyond, the cold war. Much of both the rhetoric and the motivation accompanying the Alliance for Progress, the Peace Corps, and other international initiatives had about them ideological competitiveness, but much genuinely had to do with removing the causes of insurgency by addressing basic human needs. Kennedy, more than his immediate predecessors and successors, was willing to criticize oligarchic allies on issues of land and tax reforms.

It is too much to assume that John Kennedy, had he lived, would have become the first post–cold war president. Circumstances in the form of Soviet-sponsored and self-generated insurgencies in the third world, right-wing American political demands for confrontation, and increasing economic demands from the military-industrial complex all limited a leader's inclination to see a world richer, more complex, and more subtle than the convenient simplicity of superpower polarity would allow.

Looking back over three decades, it does a reformer no harm to wonder about the accidents of history and what might have been. On the spectrum of political light there is a hue between stoicism and fatalism that increasingly infuses all. It breaks down the bright colors of certainty and the sharp contrasts of one's early years and displays actions of the past through softer, impressionistic lenses. To know now that Kennedy could have broken out of the cold war vise is clearly not possible. But there is enormous certainty that his death led to its escalation in Southeast Asia and elsewhere. And this escalation would divide both the Democratic party and the nation.

Irony would manifest itself yet again when one of the leaders to arise in opposition to the Democratic administration's policies in Southeast Asia was Robert Kennedy. His decision to challenge Lyndon Johnson on the issue of Vietnam unleashed a tide of political energy above and beyond the antiwar movement already in existence. Combined with the protracted civil rights struggle of Martin Luther King, Jr., Robert Kennedy's presidential campaign broadened the call for social justice to the white community. Between the two men, links were formed in the spring of 1968, uniting opposition to the war, the civil rights crusade, and a campaign for social equity and justice. Increasingly as the weeks of March, April, and May went by, this King-Kennedy symbiosis intensified until it seemed that each needed the other. King helped make the Vietnam war an issue in the black community, and Kennedy helped make civil rights an issue in the white community. Together they came to represent Jefferson's appeal for generational revolution.

They also represented a vast bow wave of reform in the Democratic party, for the party's urban elements were controlled by the last generation of bosses, its southern elements were still dominated by segregationist whites, and its western reaches were still dominated by crypto-Republican conservatives. While King would draw his support from black churches and established civil rights groups, Kennedy would look to insurgent and disaffected elements in his own political party: the young, dissenters, reformers, and political outsiders. By and large, the established Democratic party structure at the national and state levels would support Johnson and the White House and oppose, often bitterly, Kennedy and the insurgents.

Unlike his older brother, Robert Kennedy would be seen as a threat to an existing power structure, the forces and interests that controlled the Democratic party, the White House, and much of the government structure. Few would doubt that, were he elected, elaborately negotiated power arrangements would be in jeopardy. Indeed, in spite of the great advantages of his birth and station, after his brother's assassination Robert Kennedy more and more took on the role and demeanor of the outsider and the rebel. Passionate and intense one moment, rueful and distant the next, he exhibited a great tragic appeal to the alienated, the despairing, and the forgotten. His brief, meteoric campaign compelled the participation of a multitude— among which was this reformer—that had walked away from public service in deep despair after John Kennedy was killed.

During an early April 1968 campaign stop in Denver, this reformer was invited to join other local organizers on the platform of the city auditorium. Four thousand people waited more than two long hours beyond the candidate's scheduled time of arrival, and when his chaotic campaign circus did appear, he seemed slight, tentative, and almost disoriented. In a brief earlier meeting in 1963, when the reformer was a summer clerk in the Justice Department that Kennedy then headed, this younger Kennedy was ruffled, shy, and quiet rather than the "ruthless," hard-boiled tough guy he was portrayed as being. Five years later in Denver, his voice rose in indignation at the dual and related injustices of war in Southeast Asia and poverty at home. It was by now a familiar theme, one that he was recounting many times each day all across the nation. But surprisingly to a young reformer, Robert Kennedy used a prepared speech, apparently as a small added measure of assurance in carrying out a role for which he felt himself ill-equipped. And as he turned each page, his hands trembled slightly.

Within days of this event, Dr. King would be dead. Within weeks, Robert Kennedy would join him and his brother in martyrdom. The cause? Call it, vaguely, progress or change or reform. But whatever it could be called, three national leaders in their forties had died in its pursuit in the space of five years. They were to varying degrees champions of civil rights, social justice, economic equity, a less bellicose foreign policy, new domestic policies, new leadership, and new institutions. They sensed, beneath a traditionalist conservative veneer, a deep cultural and political restlessness. By the time King and Robert Kennedy were killed, a cultural revolution was well under way. It would flare in all its flamboyance from the mid-sixties to the mid-seventies, with rock music, widespread experimentation with drugs, more casual sexual behavior, long hair, tie-dyed clothes and bell-bottomed jeans, protests, marches, sit-ins, and "easy rider" pilgrimages in search of America. But even after its most vivid and extreme manifestations were tempered, its deeper political impact would be felt for decades to come, mostly in the form of greater equality and access for women and minorities, "the greening of America" (the title of Charles Reich's prophetic book of the time), a heightened consciousness of the inhumanity of war, of nuclear danger, and of the birth of the arms-control movement, and a widespread demand for the reform of the rules and structures of at least one of the major political parties.

None of these efforts was successful immediately or easily. Indeed, in each case, the struggle will continue into the twenty-first century. Both Robert Kennedy and Martin Luther King, Jr., understood that reform is simply the means to the ends of justice and equality and that the victory is never total or complete. For the reformers who followed them and had earlier followed John Kennedy, their individual and collective deaths seemed but the triumph of injustice and the status quo. Thereafter, there would always be the temptation to believe in a cabal called *they*, a force that existed to prevent change or progress, to frustrate new leadership and ideas, a secret brotherhood that protected the established interests of the status quo. For decades to come (perhaps throughout history), some would seek to find the true identity of the *they*, the presumed conspirators who insisted on altering history according to their own designs. The search for a conspiracy in the wake of a plague of assassinations was a form of the search for meaning in the late twentieth century. Without conspiracy, life was whimsical, arbitrary, and coincidental. Such a conclusion made human existence considerably more problematic than did the belief that nothing of consequence happens by accident.

Whether meaningful conspiracy or meaningless accident, assassination defined the age. With Robert Kennedy's death, the Democratic party slouched toward its most divisive convention in decades. Those who had supported him—and, in most cases, his brother before him—and many who had seen a reformed Democratic party as the best hope for further strides toward the civil rights agenda of Martin Luther King now saw that party as a bastion of entrenched interests more committed to war in Vietnam than to true democracy at home. Cities were torched in the spring of 1968, as they would be again in the spring of 1992. For many, the dual assassinations of 1968 would mark the end of activism, a return to private concerns or simply dropping out of the system. Others would turn to specific causes, efforts that did not require a charismatic leader vulnerable to violent elimination. A few, like the reformer, expecting now that every progressive enterprise was doomed, would try to drop out and once more abandon public service and reform. The disastrously divisive Chicago Democratic Convention offered no encouragement to the hope that political life would ever change.

But in his brief existence as a national leader, Robert Kennedy left a powerful legacy. He repeated all his brother's admonitions concerning civic duty and the citizen's responsibility, but with a greater intensity born of immediate personal tragedies. He gave emotional content to issues of poverty, hunger, and injustice. For anyone whose sense of a just society transcended personal charity, Robert Kennedy removed the option of abandoning the quest. Opposing what seemed to be the inevitability of the death of heroes was the compulsion to continue to try, to do all that one could to make a political system more responsive and a nation more just.

Out of the chaotic 1968 Democratic Convention would come the next challenge of reform. For the grass-roots army of volunteers for Robert Kennedy and Eugene McCarthy, that convention made manifest how patently undemocratic the Democratic party actually was, how resistant it was to inclusion of the young and the disfranchised, how little its rules had to do with fairness. Even more than the riotous behavior outside the convention hall, the outrage of those who had earned their way into the hall but whose voice would not be heard represented a demand for procedural reform. The lesson for this reformer and for tens of thousands like him was this: if you want to change the policies of the country, you must first change the policies of one of its parties; if you want to change the policies of a major political party, you must first reform its rules for participation and then, within those more open rules, organize the people to take control of their lives.

Thus out of the apocalyptic series of assassinations would come yet another lesson in the lifelong education in reform: do not abandon a system until you have tried to change it from within. Only if that system will not be changed is hope forever lost. And only if reformers abandon their efforts does assassination become a metaphor.

7

LIBERALISM
VERSUS REFORM

"A thousand reforms have left the world as corrupt as ever, for each successful reform has founded a new institution, and this institution has bred its new and congenial abuses." This was the philosopher George Santayana's skeptical, if not cynical, judgment on the prospects for the permanence of reform. Whether right or wrong on the merits, he did appreciate the relationship of reform to institution. Reform of policy, purpose, or values first requires reform of institution, whether party, parliament, or presidency.

For better or worse the arena of political action in the United States has been defined by the two principal political parties. They control and dominate the election process for the selection of leaders, the initiation of policies, the legislative process, and the administration of government programs and laws. One way or another, the two parties condition the judicial process as well, through the selection of judges. American history is replete with instances of initiative by interest groups, concerned citizens, upstart organizations, or renegade dreamers. But sooner or later, all these initiatives, to become law or policy, had to be filtered through a process dominated by the two parties.

To change the direction of the country in any measurable way, two choices have been available: grassroots organization so sweeping that the political institutions are required to respond, or reform of the parties and political institutions themselves. Arguably, the Democratic party has been—with limited exceptions—the reform party of America. From 1968 to 1972, there was an insurgent effort to reform the Democratic party itself so that it could once again become a true reform party, and those efforts had a measurable effect on the 1972 election and those beyond. But the caveat concerning limited exceptions is important because it sheds light on those efforts.

The Populist movement of the 1880s and '90s attempted to recapture an agrarian ideal from the ages of Jefferson and Jackson, but it was also, in the words of the historian Richard Hofstadter, "the first modern political movement of practical importance in the United States to insist that the federal government has some responsibility for the common weal; indeed, it was the first such movement to attack seriously the problems created by industrialism." Populism arose in large part because a generation after the Civil War, the Democratic party continued to suffer from its southern elements' strong identification with the secessionist cause, and the Republican party was being taken over by the new industrial class concerned only with protectionism and the perpetuation of inhumane working conditions reminiscent of slavery. Thus, the two-party system was unresponsive to a world undergoing spectacular economic and social change.

But populism, seeking a utopia of the past, opposed

progressive change and erected a class struggle that radically threatened the status of the cultural elites. Resistance came first from the mugwumps, who, oriented toward New England's political and cultural heritage, resented the Populists' provincialism on the one hand and the "money power" of the new corporate barbarians on the other. Sensing the aristocratic elitism of their fathers, the mugwumps' successor generation exhibited much greater enthusiasm for popular democratic government and formed its own movement, which subsumed the mugwumps as well as the Populists. This movement would be called progressivism, and it so preempted the spirit of Populist issues that the Kansas journalist William Allen White was moved to conclude that the Progressives, ideologically at least, had "caught the Populists in swimming and stole all of their clothes." Whereas the Populists' critics might consider them rustic anarchists, the Progressives, according to Hofstadter, were "almost pathetically respectable" and were leaders "characterized by a fresh, more intimate and sympathetic concern with urban problems—labor and social welfare, municipal reform, the interest of the consumer." Progressivism, drawing from both, but adhering to neither, of the political parties, was the moderate, sober reform movement of the early twentieth century.

It is as convenient as it is oversimplified to say that Theodore and Franklin Roosevelt are the two great political reformers of the twentieth century, that a direct continuity exists between Theodore's early-century progressivism and Franklin's mid-century New Deal. Hofstadter quoted White's characterization of the Progressives as the " 'hundreds of thousands of young men in their twenties, thirties, and early forties' whose 'quickening sense of the inequities, injustices, and fundamental wrongs' of American society provided the motive power of reform. The ascension of Theodore Roosevelt to the presidency," Hofstadter continued, "the youngest man ever to occupy the White House, was no more than symbolic of the coming-of-age of a generation whose perspectives were sharply demarcated from those of their fathers and who felt the need of a new philosophy and a new politics." No better description could be given of the generation motivated to public service by Franklin Roosevelt (as well as a later generation brought to public life by John and Robert Kennedy). But compared with the relatively mild reforms of the first Roosevelt, the second, a young veteran of the Progressive movement, had to work a revolution to save capitalism: "It was," according to Hofstadter, "his gift to be the first major leader in the history of American reform to surmount the old dualism, so troublesome to the Progressives, between the political ethos of the urban machine and that of nativist Protestant America."

The Democratic party of Franklin Roosevelt, so dominant through the middle period of the twentieth century, was characterized by the famous political coalition of urban-rural, North-South, worker-farmer, and native-immigrant. The folly of Roosevelt's successors was to believe that the coalition would and should last forever. Even as late as the 1970s and '80s, large elements of the Democratic party establishment represented a nostalgic longing for the age of Roosevelt. It was a tribute to the Rooseveltian coalition and reforms that these elements continued to dominate Democratic party leadership and thinking forty years after the leader's passing. As comforting as this nostalgia was, however, it neglected serious changes in America and the world. The America of Truman, Eisenhower, Kennedy, and Johnson had become more suburban than urban, more technological than industrial, more middle-class than working-class, more international than agrarian, and more informed, educated, and sophisticated. In short, traditional New Deal Democrats clung to the Roosevelt model long after it had ceased to relate to reality.

To make matters even more complex, by the late sixties and early seventies, three other trends had driven deep wedges into Democratic ranks. First, New Deal initiatives had made middle-class conservatives out of hitherto marginally radical or populist workers and farmers. Second, new social elements—women, students, minorities, environmentalists—demanded more than token participation in the old political coalition. Third, Vietnam and the question of the militarization of the containment doctrine had come to divide Democrats deeply. The 1968 Democratic Convention represented a party seeking to cling to a revered past in the teeth of a social and political gale. In spite of the chaos inside and outside the convention hall, and after a springtime dominated by assassinations, the Democratic nominee, Hubert Humphrey, almost won the 1968 election.

Part of the price of a fragile unity within the party, however, was the designation of the Commission on Party Structure and Delegate Selection. The party was to act, favorably or unfavorably, in time for its 1972 convention. Two liberal, antiwar, reform members of Congress, Senator George McGovern and Congressman Don Frazer, were named as commission chairmen. The commission contained a majority of reformers or pragmatists, but it also had a strong traditionalist minority. Except within insider political circles, the commission went about its work between 1969 and 1971 with little public notice. The Commission on Party Structure and Delegate Selection recommended a series of reforms designed to open the party to greater public participation, protect minority rights by means of principles of proportional representation, and require pluralism within state delegations to the national convention. Party traditionalists saw these reforms as nuisances at best and threats to established power structures—for example, urban machines—at worst.

This reformer had retreated far beyond the sidelines following John Kennedy's death and even farther behind the sidelines following the death of the president's brother. Nothing more than the word *despair* could characterize the feelings caused by the dual assassinations. Following June 1968, there seemed no cause worth a moment's dedication, no campaign deserving of the slightest contribution. All public service, every idea of political activism, seemed hollow and pointless. The country seemed hell-bent on killing its leaders, especially those who offered the hope of progressive change. The reformer, then a young Denver lawyer, was stirred to propose radical reforms in party procedures, especially in the institution of a national primary for the selection of the party's nominee, but not until he became acquainted with Senator McGovern and thus discovered a like-minded reformer did the possibility of involvement in yet another presidential campaign arise. This occurred during a McGovern visit to Denver in the spring of 1971 and led surprisingly quickly to full-time commitment to the campaign, as a vehicle for party and national reform, by the fall of that year. But throughout 1971, there was much more interest among Democrats in the struggle for party reform than in the multitude of candidates then emerging.

Where party reforms were concerned, ironies abounded according to the laws of unintended consequences. For example, as a demonstration that not all commission recommendations were progressive, traditionalists and establishmentarians succeeded in approving winner-take-all provisions for state primary contests. Thus, a state could choose to allocate its delegates proportionately to the votes of the various primary candidates, or it could adopt a provision that the winner of its primary would receive all delegate slots.

The party establishment, secure that it controlled the party machinery in many important states, saw this as a way of shutting out reformers, dissidents, and antiwarriors from proportional participation in delegations to the national convention. California, for example, chose to become a winner-take-all state.

Even though the reforms were controversial, most were adopted by substantial majorities of the party's national committee. The party superstructure, secure after many years in power, was convinced that it could control the process and nominate its candidate when the chips were down and at the same time keep the party from fragmenting by making symbolic reform gestures to insurgent elements. Besides, the overwhelming favorite among the presidential candidates was Edward Kennedy, who seemed uniquely acceptable to both reform and traditional elements of the party. So the whole party reform effort seemed a symbolic exercise designed to appease restless fringe forces.

Lightning had already struck in the form of Chappaquiddick, and Ted Kennedy seemed to be out of the running. The new delegate-selection system became more relevant but still not determinative, given the emergence of Senator Edmund Muskie of Maine, Hubert Humphrey's 1968 running mate, as the nominal front-runner for the 1972 nomination. Muskie was seen as moderate on the war issue and generally acceptable to both new and old elements of the party. This circumstance was to prevail until the primary season, when against all odds and pundits' predictions, George McGovern overwhelmed the more moderate Ed Muskie, only to face in the later nomination stages his old friend and mentor, Hubert Humphrey. There seemed to be two lessons for reform and politics in this experience, one having to do with moderation in a period of controversy and the other having to do with static ideology versus creative change.

As for the former, it seems that the worst place for leadership during a period of polarization is in the center. The more an issue such as the Vietnam War divides an institution, whether a political party or the broader institution of the nation, the more isolated is the centrist. The only possible avenue for leadership is through mediation, bringing representatives of the extremes together to seek accommodation and reconciliation. But the passive centrist, the moderate, waits for activists in both polarized camps to seek the middle way, to discover their own moderate accommodation, and to discover the moderate leader. This rarely, if ever, happens. For the moderate is suspect to all. The moderate bears the heaviest burden a putative leader can bear: weakness, lack of conviction, and indecision. Warring factions rarely find accommodation on their own, and moderate leaders rarely have the initiative or the courage to bring them together.

But America, like most other parliamentary democracies, is a centrist nation. Its direction is determined by consensus. This is well and good as long as the process is open to all. But when the center is dominated and controlled by an establishment, then dissident, insurgent, or reform forces are rarely engaged, unless by their own determination and will. An establishment center engages the comfortable, the conformist, the acceptable elites. It is self-perpetuating. It seeks out and involves those with whom it feels itself comfortable and at ease. Its values are establishmentarian, those of the status quo. It encourages such change as is nonthreatening and marginal. It acts as a cultural filter for leaders and ideas. It rewards cleverness, courtiers, and conformity. Vietnam is a classic example of a policy of the establishment center. Containment of communism grew out of postwar Democratic administrations and was quickly embraced by anti-Communist Republicans. It became the establishment policy—well and good until its implementation required increasingly massive use of American military force in defense of a decidedly nondemocratic regime.

Thus, the establishment center tested the outer reaches of its own policy, and from substantial segments of America not part of the establishment consensus, it encountered mounting resistance. To feel that one's own democratically elected government does not listen or particularly care is a radicalizing experience. The centerpiece of radicalization is the questioning of authority. Thus, years after blue-collar workers attacked long-haired, young antiwar protesters, those same workers would wear the ponytails of the people they thought they hated. Both came to distrust an establishment center that did not engage or involve them.

The other lesson for reform to grow out of the 1972 Democratic primary race has to do with ideological rigidity and orthodoxy in a changing world. The late Hubert Humphrey was, if anything, a liberal. He boldly challenged a segregationist establishment, including that which existed in the Democratic party. He championed the rights of the poor and the elderly. He sought progressive change through government action at every step and through every avenue. He loved the fight. He was the happy warrior. He was a reformer. Yet by 1972, circumstances had reversed his role. Humphrey had become the representative of and spokesman for forces in the party that sought to contain power in back rooms and behind closed doors. The stop-McGovern and the anyone-but-McGovern forces were desperate to preserve their fiefdoms in the party and prevent the party's doors from being opened to women, young people, larger numbers of minorities, and those representing a variety of social causes. These movements and cultural forces were frightening to many not only because they were new but also because they demanded participation and a share of power. These were the direct by-products of the cultural upheavals of the 1960s and '70s. Traditional party leaders resented, misunderstood, and feared them and turned to Humphrey, one whom only a few years before they had seen as a radical threat to the status quo power structures of the 1950s and '60s. How could such a transformation have happened? How could the liberal Humphrey have become the representative of antiliberal forces almost overnight?

The answer is complex but instructive. In part, Humphrey changed. In this, his last possible chance for national leadership, he surveyed the field and saw a gaping vacuum in the center. The demise of Muskie and other more establishmentarian candidates left that most devastating of circumstances: a political vacuum. Anti-McGovern, antireform elements of the party were desperate for a rallying figure. Humphrey was the last, best hope to stop McGovern. Never mind that the two men's outlook on domestic human-resource priorities was virtually identical—Humphrey had been McGovern's mentor in national politics. Nevertheless, under these circumstances, Humphrey was comfortable leading the old liberal wing of the party. Humphrey also came to identify himself with a growing wing of the Democratic party whose adherents would finally emerge as neo-conservatives or even Nixon Democrats (amazingly not an oxymoron). These were traditional New Dealers who professed to hold socially progressive viewpoints but for whom the confrontation of communism became more important than domestic human needs. For them, the war in Southeast Asia so vastly expanded by an erstwhile New Dealer, Lyndon Johnson, was equated with Franklin Roosevelt's war on fascism. Here things become complex for the ideologically correct. Liberalism split on Vietnam. The prowar faction, which now joined Humphrey, opposed (and occasionally hated) the antiwar liberals led by McGovern.

Finally, Humphrey came to represent those stuck in

the New Deal era. The New Deal, originally such a challenge to the entrenched forces of the status quo, had by the 1970s become the status quo of the Democratic party. Government action in the form of higher taxes, expanded regulations, new programs, and administering bureaucracies were still the test of liberal orthodoxy when this reformer came to the Senate. Both the country and the new leadership in the Democratic party would come to question this previously innovative but now traditional formula. McGovern himself was seen, rightly or wrongly, as a traditional New Deal Democrat on domestic issues. But many of those whom he introduced to politics were to take a different view and pursue reform through different means.

In fact, the principal lesson of the period was this: what is reform in one era may become the antithesis of reform in another. The fallacy is in the worship of methods. All human institutions, whether political, economic, or religious, convert innovation to orthodoxy and demand obedience. But the very essence of innovation or reform is unorthodoxy. It is a process by which to question and challenge orthodoxies that have been made irrelevant or ineffective by changing times and new circumstances. The quarrel the Democratic party was having with itself in the late sixties and early seventies was over this question. Traditional Democrats, then in power, had come to worship the monuments of the New Deal and to defend the foreign policy of containment even in its gravest excesses. Reformers came to challenge the excesses of the containment policy and question the methodology of the New Deal. Not unexpectedly, the dividing line was largely generational.

The period between 1968 and 1972 is now seen by the conventionally wise as one of fratricidal Democratic feuding and destructive political behavior. As with most conventional wisdom, this too is wrong.

The procedural reforms adopted by the Democratic party during this period saved an institution that had been at the edge of a cliff since the catastrophic Chicago convention. By opening itself to pluralistic participation, the party saved both its structure and its soul. By adopting reforms so inimical to the interests of traditional power structures, the party redeemed its promise of access to the democratic process for those outside the establishment center. It regenerated itself with new leadership and new ideas, the definitive test of any institution's will and ability to survive. In part, elections were lost in this struggle, but the party remains to fight on as an instrument of reform and change when it so chooses to. It is, after all, the long term that counts.

This era revealed another significant feature of reform. It is not a zero-sum or winner-take-all game. Reform need not succeed to triumph. The principal purpose of the McGovern campaign was to stop the Vietnam war. In part—and it is impossible to measure what part—the institutionalization and legitimation of the antiwar effort in that campaign brought pressure on the Nixon administration and Congress to change the nation's policy in Southeast Asia. Indeed, President Nixon finally came to campaign on a policy of stopping the war, thus making the only real issue the question of who had the best credentials to stop the war and according to what timetable. Few would believe, absent the pressure from McGovern, Nixon's commitment to that cause.

More important, the party reforms championed by McGovern have done more to pluralize and open access to the political process than has any other factor in many decades. The Democratic party, as well as the country, is better and stronger for that effort. Old establishment factions, centrist and otherwise, have evolved, adapted, or disappeared; new ones have formed and will continue to form—that is the nature of human institutions. Sooner or later, new party reform measures will undoubtedly be required if the party wishes to avoid stagnation and irrelevance. Old orders, leaders, and methods must give way to new ones. This is the process of life itself. An institution such as the Republican party, representing concentrated wealth, conservatism, and the status quo, has less need to change and adapt. Those interests are permanent and will always be there, in need of representation and protection, come what may. But a political party of inclusion, change, and reform must itself be always in the process of reform and transition. Otherwise, it violates and offends its own nature.

Today's Democratic party is led by many who were insurgents and challengers in the great ferment of the early seventies. Some, even before settling into their middle years, are well on their way to becoming figures of the establishment. As this metamorphosis occurs, they will spend more and more energy protecting and perpetuating their position and defending the status quo against challengers and newcomers rather than struggling for change and reform. It is a tribute to the seductiveness of power that it so often overwhelms even the best of motives. It is rare, indeed, to find reform leaders who seek to perpetuate reform by engaging new and younger people in the enterprise, knowing that such people will have their own ideas about, and methods for, change and will themselves demand and deserve their own leadership within a short period of time.

This is but Jefferson's argument for generational revolution in practice. The McGovern campaign represented such a revolution. Now twenty years have gone by. There is no longer a war in Vietnam. There is no longer even the cold war that gave Vietnam its global context. The time is very near for those brought into the Democratic party leadership by the antiwar, proreform campaign of 1972 to make way for yet another generation of leaders, one that has a clear under-standing of the post–cold war future. No generation can represent reform and change for another. Each has its own life, its own experiences, and its own goals. Each generation must have the opportunity and the responsibility to achieve those goals through its own methods. The ultimate test of the reform ideal is the willingness of each generation to recognize this imper-ative and make way for its own natural succession.

8

EMPOWERMENT

For this reformer, the overwhelming defeat of George McGovern in 1972, after almost two years of backbreaking work, represented another assassination. With strong intent and all sincerity, this reformer had given up on public service after the death of John Kennedy, had briefly reentered political activism only to give up again after the death of Robert Kennedy, and now, after the defeat of McGovern, believed social and political activism was totally without effect. There seemed to be no way in which to make any meaningful contribution to one's country in the wake of such mayhem and defeat.

The values represented by the triumph of Richard Nixon seemed to be ruthlessness, power lust, meanness, and politics as usual. There was little, if anything, here with which a person of fleeting youth and tattered idealism could identify. To the degree that

Nixon represented the values and beliefs of an over-whelming majority of the American people, even the most dense of idealists could hear the message: this country doesn't want change. It was enough to dismay even a Don Quixote.

The American majority of the early seventies appar-ently wanted the Vietnam War to continue. No one seriously believed Richard Nixon intended an early se-cession of hostilities. No one seriously believed he in-tended any meaningful domestic improvements. His rhetoric about welfare reform was widely interpreted as racist and mean-spirited. In reelecting Nixon by a landslide, the American people seemed to be provid-ing their own character analysis. They wanted tough-ness—a big word for Nixon; they valued belligerency, with both the North Vietnamese and the rebellious American youth; they wanted to crack down on "wel-fare cheats," of whom they had convinced themselves there were tens of millions; and they wanted "law and order."

This last social value comes closest to capturing the American mood of the early seventies. Nixon pos-sessed that extraordinary politic attribute of being able to campaign against himself, or at least of being able to campaign against his own record. Thus, even though he had been president for four years, in 1972 he sought reelection on a platform of stamping out law-lessness, which he apparently believed had increased under his own stewardship. But law and order in this context was really a metaphor for changing social val-ues. The social and cultural revolution of the sixties and seventies featured what the rebellious young of that time summarized as sex, drugs, and rock and roll. This is really what Nixon and apparently a majority of Americans were against. This was genuine lawlessness and disorder. Layered on top of this generational up-heaval were bra-burning feminism, Black Panthers, Malcolm X, Angela Davis, Patty Hearst, urban riots,

Oh! Calcutta! and the dawning of the age of Aquarius. Traditional American society felt itself coming apart. Nixon was the man to prevent this.

Nothing is more exhilarating—or more frightening —than a society in transition. The reformer, coming from midwestern working-class stock, put his energies into political reform. Cultural revolution made him apprehensive, and hard rock music reminded him of anarchy. Only relatively late in the day would he let his hair grow, and only then to medium length. His only other concession to stylish trends was a few pairs of bell-bottomed trousers, which, typically, he would continue to wear long after they had gone out of fashion. Such symbols of rebellion always seemed somewhat silly to the reformer, but to many of his countrymen they were immediate and constant reminders that madness had overtaken the nation's youth. This madness is what Richard Nixon was hired to cure.

Predictably, the president's method was surreptitious. If the way to stop communism was to spy on it first, then the way to stop social insurrection was to do the same. Nixon seemed born to spying. It was his forte. Like that great master spy J. Edgar Hoover, he seemed to like to watch. Perhaps there was a secret thrill to be got from listening unnoticed to the conversations of others or watching unobserved their private behavior. Spying is a form of empowerment: it gives the spy a clandestine advantage. To know some secret about someone else when he does not know you know it is a form of mastery. Besides, to know is to be forewarned and to anticipate all manner of potential treachery. For some, like Nixon, spying served primarily to enhance paranoia.

In retrospect, the surprise of Watergate was not that it happened but that it did not happen sooner. For to set paranoia to achieve law and order was to invite the inevitable. The presidency possesses absolutely the best set of tools with which the former may achieve the latter. "The prevention of treachery in closed systems"—Norman Mailer's definition of plumbing (and rocketry)—has already been observed. Thus, it was no accident that the Watergate burglars were called the plumbers. They were, ostensibly at least, out to stop leaks, to prevent treachery within the closed system of government secrecy. No more should be made of the plumbing metaphor except to note that plumbing exists to deliver fresh water as well as to carry away wastes, and those mesmerized by the need for law and order seemed unnaturally preoccupied with the waste.

What troubled the reformer most about this era of law and order was how troubling social revolution was to most Americans. To prove the conservative keel of the ship of state, it is enough to note that the children of flower children had close-cropped hair, idolized the nation's oldest and one of its most conservative presidents, and attended business schools so they could make a fortune on Wall Street. So much for lawlessness and disorder. Indeed, aside from a small handful of congenital hippies, the flower children themselves turned out to be peaceful, law-abiding citizens. So what was the worry? And did it justify turning the country upside down with the threat of a presidential impeachment? Why would a strong and secure nation let itself be so frightened by so little?

To a degree, the same pattern was evident in the red scares of the McCarthy era. It was nothing but folly and madness to believe—as some of our leaders then did—that the Communists were seriously planning an invasion of American shores or that the government of a powerful democratic nation could be subverted by a handful of purported leftists in the State Department. But the folly was catching, and it swept up large elements of the public. Fear and paranoia were rampant in the fifties and, not accidentally, Richard Nixon emerged in such an atmosphere. We breed according to the climate we create. The question remains, What are we afraid of? What makes a nation created by bold revolutionaries so fearful, hesitant, and paranoid?

Even well into America's third century there are no clear answers to this question. Let us assume for the sake of argument that we are simply more conservative and more cautious than we believe ourselves to be, that we think of ourselves as bold and innovative but behave timidly, that we talk one game but play another. This duality would explain a lot. To a great extent, it would account for why we are, in the Pulitzer Prize–winning author Michael Kammen's words, "people of paradox." But to diagnose schizophrenia is not to explain, let alone cure it. Another explanation, this one economic, is the post-Depression, post–World War II rise of the middle class. To have achieved a relatively comfortable standard of living, to have a home, a secure job, reasonably good health, and the opportunity to educate one's children is, by definition, to become conservative. Why rock the boat? What else is there to struggle for? To innovate, to take risks, to experiment and explore is to jeopardize what one has. If it is not necessary to change, as it has been said, then it is necessary not to change.

Outside the peaceful domicile and community, then, change of whatever sort represents a threat. On the heels of the placid Eisenhower happy days, changes in life-style, in music, clothing, and dance, in social values, in women's and minority rights, in political behavior, in protests and demonstrations, in cultural norms (principally those sexual)—all came as a threatening shock even to a generation whose parents had stood on the picket lines, demanding union rights and fair working conditions. Relative economic success can make a whole generation conservative virtually overnight. In 1972 law and order was a simple code for suppressing the myriad changes then sweeping the country. And Richard Nixon was the law-and-order man.

Those of us deeply involved in the 1972 effort to defeat Nixon had, of course, believed all along that the Watergate affair of that year reached much further and much higher than either the official version of events ("a bunch of amateur burglars operating on their own") or the stories then accepted by the press ("overzealous campaign workers"). We lacked, however, the investigative capability of even a leading newspaper and were therefore consigned to mere allegation. But one's faith in the emergence of truth would later be summed up under similar circumstances by a Senate colleague, Gaylord Nelson of Wisconsin. When asked why he was one of only a very few senators to vote against the confirmation of Richard Kleindienst as Richard Nixon's attorney general, he said, "Something will turn up." And in both cases, it did. Mr. Kleindienst was later indicted and convicted of Watergate-related crimes, and of course, the outcome with regard to Mr. Nixon is well known.

In any case, the entire fiasco could not have been carried out without the surreptitious movement of extraordinary amounts of money. Regardless of the ultimate outcome of the question of presidential involvement and culpability, a powerful case had been made for serious reforms in the mare's nest of campaign finance. The system cried out for a wholesale cleansing, if one believed at all that the democratic process requires at least a degree of integrity in the election of public officials. To dismiss Watergate, as a surprising number advocated, was to invite the serpent into the bosom of the body politic. The same surprising number of people justified their laissez-faire attitude on the grounds that wholesale subversion of political opponents is commonplace, an attitude that says much about the degree of public cynicism toward politics in the latter half of the twentieth century.

For a still idealistic but thrice-defeated reformer, the case was a hard one. Should the scandal simply be overlooked and accepted, as many of his fellow countrymen seemed to suggest, thus legitimizing, and possibly institutionalizing, such behavior? Or should arms be taken up yet again against this sea of troubles? And if the decision was to fight, in what arena, with what weapons, to what effect? The Watergate investigation was slowly getting started in Washington. News stories began to run weekly, if not daily, concerning some new bit of evidence implicating yet another middle-, and eventually higher-, level official. Although press and public attention increasingly focused on what did they know and when did they know it, there were emerging institutional questions: What could or should be done to prevent such behavior in the future? Did the political system need fundamental reforms? More philosophically, can laws be designed to condition the behavior of human beings in a political context?

These questions took on more than academic consequence because of the surprising number of Americans who took a cynical view of their own country's politics. A reformer, albeit no longer quite young, would still be idealistic enough to find himself appalled at the willingness of numbers of people to believe that all politicians are corrupt and up for anything as long as it keeps them in power. If Watergate were a mirror held up to America's public face, then it revealed a nation so absent in idealism that it was prepared to believe the worst possible things about its leaders. This was the antithesis of empowerment; it was powerlessness. It was the political version of the cynic's adage "Very little matters, and nothing matters very much." Nixon seemed to have tapped a vein in the man on the street that contained the belief that they all do it and dog-eat-dog is the political order of the day.

Despite the 1972 drubbing by Nixon himself and the almost casual assassination of his heroes, the reformer was not yet prepared to accept this version of American democracy. Some form of protest, some symbolic gesture of outrage, was required if he was to remain true to his beliefs and raise even a small standard of his ideals. Meanwhile, the forces of democratic integrity could be seen mustering in the mists of pessimism. Honest political leaders of both parties, crusading journalists, outraged Republicans—all were beginning to be heard. The true soul of the nation might, after all, be emerging to show itself worth fighting for. In fact, this might be the real test of Watergate, a test regarding the attitudes of Americans about themselves and their country. Nineteen seventy-four seemed capable of becoming one of those watershed years, in which a redefinition of, and a recommitment to, genuine democratic values emerges from a battle between the elements of cynicism and distrust and those of integrity and idealism. This was a contest Jefferson himself would welcome.

Until this time, the thought of seeking public office had never been near the front of the reformer's mind. Contrary to popular assumption, not all candidates for political office calculate from early days how to move up the public ladder. In any case, fate and circumstance inevitably play a much larger role than cunning and calculation. Voters always find candidates motivated by service more congenial than those motivated by career. It seemed to the reformer, both intuitively and audaciously, that the platform of a contest for the United States Senate offered the greatest opportunity to make the case against Nixonian cynicism, concentrated political and economic power, and stultified institutions. Leaving aside the obvious practical considerations of a lack of campaign finances or personal wealth, a lack of any experience in public office, a lack of name recognition in his home state of Colorado, and the presence of a popular incumbent Republican senator, very little else seemed to encourage the undertaking. Such a campaign could succeed only if the reformer's faith in the ultimate goodwill, benign instincts, and anger at public corruption among average voters prevailed. But even if unsuccessful, the reformer would finally have completed his last act of public obligation and could then retire from the public arena to undertake a real—that is, nonpolitical—life. The decision and the announcement of his candidacy were made a year before the election and well before the full implications and sweep of Watergate were widely known.

The themes of this Senate campaign were all reform oriented. In every way he could, this reformer let it be known that he did not intend to pursue politics as usual in Washington, a notion that was given both resonance and credibility by his absolute lack of experience in public office and his relative youth. The reformer-as-candidate sought to present positive alternatives rather than simply negative critiques.

Against considerable odds both within the Democratic nomination process and during the election contest, the campaign proved successful. To his own surprise as much as to anyone else's, the reformer found himself elected to the United States Senate. The campaign itself had combined populist themes, attacks on incumbency and corruption, and advocacy of public-policy reforms and ideals of citizen participation. Strong statements were made against the manipulation of energy prices by monopolistic, vertically integrated oil companies. Strong commitments were made to initiate and support new efforts to improve education and health-care systems. Vigorous assaults were delivered against excessive military spending and our continued involvement in Vietnam years after Richard Nixon had promised to end the war. Most of all, pledges were delivered to do everything humanly possible to clean up campaign-finance laws and support reforms across the political process. The theme of the candidacy was reformist, anticareerist, anti-elitist, and citizen oriented. During the contest, valiant efforts were made to provide detailed proposals for changes in economic, military, energy, and foreign policies. This approach would continue throughout the next fourteen years.

There was clearly a widespread mood in the country in favor of new leadership. It went beyond merely replacing Republicans with Democrats. Watergate and the Nixon cynicism had reminded many voters of the importance of citizen involvement in government affairs and the dangers of political careerism. Democratic victories in congressional races were as much the result of the emergence of a new generation of political activists as they were simply partisan backlash against Nixon and his party. But these victories raised the question of whether these new Democratic members of the House and Senate would necessarily be traditional liberals. There was a simplistic assumption among political reporters that a host of new Democrats in Congress somehow meant a return to New Deal policies and programs. In response to a reporter's question in this regard during the 1974 campaign, this candidate was quoted as saying, somewhat audaciously (but accurately), "We are not a bunch of little Hubert Humphreys." (He later learned this had angered Humphrey and was required to apologize.) The point was not well made, but it was accurate and important. Not all Democrats, especially not all younger Democrats, equated the 1970s with the 1930s. The times were different, and the problems were different; therefore, the solutions had to be different. The reformers of the 1970s, this one especially, had many occasions on which to repeat the famous Franklin Roosevelt philosophy of experimentalism: "We will try something, and if it works we will keep it; if it doesn't, we will try something else."

It was the pragmatic experimentalism, not the orthodoxy of the New Deal, that attracted the reform Democrats of the 1970s. For those in politics' inner circle, including especially political journalists, this resistance to orthodox ideology would be the source of continuing conflict and controversy well into the next decade. Not only rhetoric but votes as well failed to follow predictable ideological lines. So new categories were invented. Neo-liberal got to be the most famous. But even that was inadequate when some new Democrats forcefully emphasized America's transition from an industrial economy to an information economy. Atari Democrats was then the cute description. For the thoughtful observer in 1974, it should have been clear that the emergence of a new Democratic majority in the Congress meant more than a more liberal Congress. It meant a Congress that was younger, more experimental, more pragmatic, less ideological, less inclined to politics as a career, and more reformist than the Congress it was replacing. Nineteen seventy-four represented a return to the ideals of the early sixties. Many Democrats, and even a few Republicans, elected in that year traced their motives to the Kennedy challenge of public service.

The real question for this class of neophyte politicians was whether the political and legislative processes were reformable. Did the people control the system, or did the system control the people? A close corollary of the native American suspicion that all politicians are corrupt is the belief that honest politicians sooner or later are co-opted by a corrupting system. Two great pillars of the traditional system militated in this direction. One was the so-called seniority system, and the other was the process of campaign finance. According to the first, longevity was rewarded by power in the form of committee chairmanships, and those committee chairmen controlled the flow of all legislation. According to the other, all politicians require funds for reelection, and those funds came in the greatest quantities from special interests, which have narrowly defined political agendas. The inevitable conclusion was that new members of Congress would learn to logroll and vote-trade if they wished to be effective and that they would have to pay considerably more attention to the wishes of the interest groups than to the national or common interest if they wished to be able to seek reelection.

Both these hypotheses were truisms, but they did not encompass the entire truth. Public outrage at Watergate and related scandals were heard in the Congress as early as 1973 and 1974, even before the Nixon resignation. In response to the outcry, Congress enacted new campaign-finance and disclosure laws designed to correct the abuses permitted under the old, looser system. Individual contributions were limited. Corporations, unions, and other groups were permitted to make contributions through devices called political action committees (the now-infamous PACs), and all contributions had to be reported to a new watchdog agency called the Federal Elections Commission. Commission membership was to be bipartisan and commission staffing was to be nonpartisan and professional.

Reform also overtook the congressional seniority system in 1974 and '75. Committee chairs did not automatically go to the most senior member; in each case, a chairman was to be elected by the prevailing majority of committee members in both houses. This made chairmen much more responsive to the will and interests of even the most junior members. Greater control of the flow of legislation was placed in the hands of diversely populated policy committees. And committee memberships were decided by steering committees, which represented diverse geographic and ideological points of view. Majority and minority leaderships were selected by the political caucus in each house, often after vigorous, open campaigning. Pure democracy had yet to be achieved in the American Congress, but it was a considerable improvement over the more authoritarian regimes of Lyndon Johnson's and Richard Nixon's days.

The sweeping victories of the new Democrats (the so-called Watergate class), the post-Watergate campaign reforms, and the impending reforms in congressional procedures—all set the stage for what might have been an era of considerable change. Many new members of Congress were returning to a Washington they had left as young staff members more than a decade before, after the assassination of John Kennedy. Many were eager to recreate at least a modified version of Camelot, in which the conflict in Southeast Asia would finally be closed down, in which new laws might be enacted to address the unfinished domestic agenda of America, and in which public service would once again be a noble profession, not a demeaned and cynical one. The atmosphere for a new reform senator was bright with promise and expectation. Opportunities for progress seemed limited only by the imagination. Previous tragedies and defeats, though never erased from memory, seemed less to overwhelm the human prospect. In one of those great ironies of politics, within twenty-four months of having helped engineer a catastrophically unsuccessful national campaign effort, the reformer found himself sitting as an equal, at least in constitutional terms, with his much-respected candidate and many other famous senators and party leaders. He would have an equal vote on all matters, many of consequence and a surprising number that were not. In committees and on the floor of the Senate itself, there were countless opportunities to introduce legislation and amendments to legislation affecting major public policies. The junior senator could vote against giant new weapons systems for which there seemed no good purpose. He could work with others to try to devise sensible energy policies and curb the growing power of a small handful of giant international energy conglomerates. He would help raise the banner of the environment, hitherto given less than the national attention it required. As much as anything else, he could participate with other new leaders in the effort to move his own party out of the rut of complacency to which its almost religious devotion to New Deal formulas seemed to consign it.

On that day of oath-of-office taking in January 1975, the awe he felt in the face of the contributions he might make was exceeded only by the reformer's surprise at finding himself in the Senate. It seemed to him then, as it does now, that this was democracy's very definition of empowerment.

9

THE ERA
OF MANSFIELD

Mr. Hart of Colorado. A reformer would have no
more satisfying experience in public life than to hear
his name called by the clerk of the Senate for a recorded vote. And he and his namesake, Philip Hart of
Michigan, would have their states named as well, in
order to distinguish them. This would last until December 1976, when Philip Hart died, too young, from
cancer.

Philip Hart needed little else to distinguish him, for
he characterized the best of a very good Senate when
the reformer took up his post there. Serving his third
term when taken ill, he was highly respected, and then
beloved, by constituents and colleagues alike. He was
everything a politician was not expected to be and
nothing resembling the stereotype. He was quiet and
gentle, thoughtful and soft-spoken. He had grown a
beard during the Vietnam War, reportedly promising

some of his several children that it would not be removed until the war was over. He outlived the war, but the beard remained.

He came to be the conscience of the Senate in many things. His coped with his disease in a way that elevated an already wise and caring man to a level between statesmanship and political sainthood. He possessed both grace and wit, but he grew increasingly impatient with the blather, blarney, and bunkum that occasionally would erupt, almost always from an expected source. Sensing, no doubt, a distillation of time, he could bluntly suggest a colleague get to the point or, in an aside, sink a fatal harpoon into the whale's carcass of a tedious filibuster. He hated the Vietnam War, the waste of public money on heaps of military weapons, human want, and all forms of political idiocy.

Yet he was kind and tolerant, endlessly helpful to a novice senator, courtly and considerate. Many of Philip Hart's qualities characterized other senators of that time as well. For the Senate then was populated by and large by serious people, who, unlike the reformer, had earned the right to be there. Many were veterans of the world war and knew its costs. A number knew history and had studied it throughout their lives. The best had their special areas of concern and expertise: Muskie and Nelson on the environment; Mansfield, Javits, and Case on foreign policy; McGovern, Church, Mathias, and Hatfield on Vietnam; Kennedy on health; Symington and Jackson on defense; Long on taxes. A number—like Ribicoff, Humphrey, Pastore, Magnuson—contributed on many issues.

The Senate of the time was remarkable for its breadth and its depth, its mentality and its attitude. A new senator then would quickly learn to respect the range of experience and knowledge, the institutional memory represented by so many veterans with so many years of service. Even discounting the awe that

the institution inspires in all but the most crass over-
achievers, the same powerful and positive impressions
hold up almost two decades later. There were, it need
be said, more than a share of ordinary mortals there
also, sent by their constituents with the explicit understanding that they were to do nothing by way of active
leadership, creative thought, or explicit initiative.
Some simply voted against everything and seemed to
prosper for it politically. But one should not attempt
to account for taste. In politics, it is largely an irrelevant commodity.

The reformer would have years both in the Senate
and thereafter to contemplate the peculiar quality of
the institution then, and the answer that always would
percolate to the surface was commitment to the national interest. These were days on the cusp, before
really big money and extraordinarily sophisticated
campaign financing, media advisers, and negative advertising arose to strangle American politics. The
process still allowed for some distinction and even
greatness.

The Senate majority leader in those days, Mike
Mansfield of Montana, qualified for that description.
In his own laconic way, he was, and is, an extraordinary man and leader. He shares many of Philip Hart's
best human qualities. His demeanor is reserved. But
when amused, there is a devilish Irish twinkle in his
eyes, as he puffs on a pipe. I heard him laugh aloud a
few times, but I heard him raise his voice only once.
He didn't need to. Few of his peers crossed him know-
ingly, and none in memory did it more than once.
Mansfield served in three branches of the military
while still in his teens; he has been a hard-rock miner
and a university professor. Most of his life has been
spent in public service. He would complete his career
by serving as United States ambassador to Japan for
almost ten years. The people of Japan came to revere

and respect him as much as his former Senate colleagues did.

Mansfield represented the Senate at its best. The young reformer could think of no more ideal senator. He followed Mansfield through troubling procedural minefields, trusting explicitly his dedication to the protection of the Senate as a sacred political institution. Early in the reformer's first year in the Senate, a great debate occurred over the issue of the Senate's unique filibuster rule. The filibuster, the popular name for unlimited debate, sprang from the Senate's original and continuing respect for each senator as the voice of a sovereign state. It was believed throughout the history of the Senate that a senator, speaking for his state, should be heard as long as that individual felt strongly enough about his position to hold the floor. Great deference is traditionally accorded Senate colleagues in this regard unless the right is so abused as to deny the Senate the ability to carry out the business of the nation. The filibuster was practiced during early civil rights debates by Strom Thurmond of South Carolina, among others, but had come to be used increasingly by southerners like Jim Allen of Alabama and Jesse Helms of North Carolina simply to obstruct action on a whole range of issues.

Normally, the rules of the Senate provided that debate could be limited only by a two-thirds vote of the full Senate. But things had come to such a pass by the mid-1970s that progressive and liberal forces in both parties had launched a full-scale effort to reduce to three fifths of the Senate the vote necessary to cut off debate. For traditionalists such as Mansfield, this was a complex question. Should one respect the historic traditions of the Senate or the nation's need to address a myriad of problems? In a classic way, it was the two-century debate between the rights of the states and the rights of the national government. To complicate matters further, there was a complex series of rulings by the Chair and, through him, by the parliamentarian of the Senate (the principal authority on matters of procedure) concerning the number of votes required on preliminary procedural matters before the principal vote to change the filibuster rule could take place. The forces for change—the progressive, reform forces—took the position that legal and traditional niceties ought to be set aside temporarily to allow for the urgent business of changing this rule, and they were, in effect, prepared to run roughshod over the Senate procedures to achieve this result.

Mansfield, as was his custom, did not try to exert influence on the senators, including those of his own party, but left all free to vote their conscience. He made it clear in caucus discussions, though, that he was personally troubled by the skirting of strict Senate rules and traditions to reach the principal vote and, in the interest of upholding proper Senate rules, could probably not support the majority position on that question. The Senate parliamentarian, who tended not to intervene in matters of such delicacy, would only privately confirm the strict correctness of Mansfield's position. The young reformer's great respect for Mansfield and Mansfield's great respect for the Senate, plus the obvious correctness of Mansfield's position on the matter, led the reformer to vote with Mansfield and against the reform forces on this close procedural question. In his first few months in the Senate, he earned the distrust of a number of liberal interests and senators, few of whom, in their rush to achieve the benign objective, were inclined to care about creating a highly unwise precedent, one that might later be used against them.

A principle, it seemed to the reformer, was involved here. And principle in this case came face to face with expediency, albeit expediency in a worthy cause. It was the kind of internal struggle so often romanticized in political fiction but which seldom occurs in real political life. The reformer thought at the time, and so discussed with his wife, that if the life of the Senate meant an ongoing series of such tormenting struggles of conscience, he would be a broken man before he completed his term. Few would understand the dramatic nature of this issue because it was so clouded in arcane rulings and procedures. But it was one of the most difficult issues a reformer would face in his twelve-year legislative life. Should the traditions central to the Senate's uniqueness be waived in the interest of legislative progress? Which comes first, integrity of the democratic institution or achieving pragmatic results? What is most important, the system that makes progress possible or progress itself?

Mansfield was a great mentor. He may not have provided easy answers to these and other thorny questions, but like the teacher Johnson before him, he was a great teacher, a teacher by example, by putting his trust in new senators, and by always showing character and acting on principle. As with so many in the Senate at that time, the reformer would come to treasure the experience of having known, and served with, such a great figure.

Despite the presence of imposing and serious legislators, reform of any kind was not easy in the mid-seventies. Nineteen seventy-four marked the effective emergence of the Organization of Petroleum Exporting Countries. World oil supplies were restricted by the principal producing nations, largely in the Middle East, and prices consequently rose sharply and continued to rise until 1980. Unwisely, the United States had systematically increased its imports of foreign oil rather than develop its own reserves, reduce unnecessary consumption, or increase its reliance on alternative, renewable resources. Gradually, throughout the 1960s and early '70s, our economy had become a hostage of foreign oil producers. Caught off guard by the lack of any national energy policy and having become the most energy-intensive nation in history, America found its economy in a downward spiral, caught between inflation driven by dramatically higher energy prices and recession and unemployment brought on largely by the same factors.

Economists, accustomed to believing that inflation and recession are not supposed to coexist, could contribute only a new name, stagflation (stagnation-inflation), to describe the phenomenon. Otherwise, they were not especially helpful. At roughly the same time, cracks and decay in America's urban structures became so obvious as to be no longer avoidable. Following the assassination-induced riots and urban unrest of 1968, a special commission appointed by Lyndon Johnson (the Kerner Commission) had recommended major new national initiatives in employment, investment, transportation, and housing in older urban areas. Only some of these initiatives had been pursued, and matters had gotten considerably worse. Cities like New York were increasing their demands for federal money, money that was not available in the quantities demanded in large part because of the stagnant national economy. The Ford administration's rejection of these demands led to the classic New York newspaper headline: FORD TO NY: DROP DEAD! Anyone who knows even the vaguest thing about New York knows that dropping dead is the last thing that city is about to do. But going bankrupt was a distinct possibility, and only through a heroic rescue effort, involving the federal government substantially in loan guarantees, was this disaster avoided.

So despite a higher-quality Senate than might be seen in later years and all the good intentions in the world, the problems faced by the country seemed especially intractable. Senate Democrats were not loath to lay the blame for the economy and the energy crisis at the doorstep of the Republican White House. President Ford was considered particularly vulnerable as the nation prepared for the 1976 national election, due to his notorious pardon of his predecessor, Richard Nixon, gone but not forgotten in his involuntary retirement to San Clemente. Much of the fiscal straitjacket in which the country and its Congress felt themselves was created by conservative Republicans desperately concerned about budget deficits. When the reformer arrived in Washington in the mid-seventies, the national debt hovered at just over $950 billion, and annual deficits, thought by many to be so outrageously excessive that no new spending measure, however worthy, ought to be considered, averaged $25 billion to $30 billion annually. In retrospect, obsession with fiscal integrity at such relatively paltry levels seems quaint and almost touchingly naïve.

Nevertheless, major new initiatives in human needs and resources were severely restricted by budgetary concerns and uncertainty about the economic future. The energy crisis put everything under a strain and made major reform problematic. Furthermore, there was disagreement within the majority Democratic ranks in the Senate over economic policy. Traditional Democrats, represented by Hubert Humphrey, favored classic Keynesian pump-priming devices, such as tax cuts, to jump-start economic activities. Newer Democrats, this reformer among them, felt strongly that such measures would simply exacerbate the deficits, which were already of great concern to markets and the public, and would do little to address a new set of economic realities that were only just becoming apparent. Though the Vietnam War was finally grinding to a halt, over its ten-year life it had generated a war-production machine that demanded attention and feeding. The bill for our lackadaisical dependence on foreign oil was just coming due. Foreign competition in steel, autos, appliances, food, and a host of other products was making itself felt in plant closings and unemployment. Nonmilitary research into new technologies and new products was practically nonexistent. There were, all in all, a host of new, unprecedented challenges to American competitiveness that traditional economic measures, such as tax cuts, would not cure and might even exacerbate by covering over structural and institutional problems.

These debates in the mid-seventies demonstrated the emergence of a new wing in the Democratic party, one that would gradually make itself dominant over the next two decades. In philosophical terms, its members were as progressive and as dedicated to the reform and improvement of human conditions as more traditional liberals. But the new Democrats, less worshipful of the battles and achievements of the past, were more skeptical of the applicability of traditional New Deal methods to the problems and challenges of the day. New government programs, requiring large, new administering agencies and bureaucracies, Keynesian tax cuts and government-spending measures, additional volumes regulating economic activities, and looser control of the money supply, all were questioned by the new Democrats of the class of 1974.

Sadly, traditional liberals had enshrined these and other methods and made them the test of one's liberality and even of one's compassion. In their respect-bordering-on-worship for the achievements of the New Deal, they had forgotten that, at heart, it was experimental, not dogmatic, in attitude and approach. The socially progressive elements of the Roosevelt coalition—the labor unions, minority groups, human-service organizations, and a host of others—continued to produce ideas for new programs and annual legislative agendas and demanded that all those who considered themselves progressive Democrats support these measures virtually without question. Often the details of particular new initiatives would be negotiated with prominent congressional liberals, such as Kennedy, Bayh, Jackson, or any one of a number of others, with the thought that all other liberals would automatically fall in line. Of course, it was immediately and universally assumed that "the former campaign manager for George McGovern" (an automatic key on every political reporter's typewriter following the reformer's name) was a sure thing on whatever new social legislation came along.

But the neo-liberals and the Atari Democrats often saw things differently. Study and discussion groups were formed to explore root causes for structural problems in the economy, in the use of energy, in urban areas, in the military, and in technologies and to examine new methods of dealing with them. The bolder of the new Democrats refused to be swallowed up by the surviving New Deal legislative machine, which had controlled the party since the forties. Some interest groups in the party, not understanding the sincerity and seriousness of the new Democrats, came to distrust them and even to consider them traitors for their lack of predictability and dependability. For those that had contributed campaign funds, as some unions had, there was an assumption of virtually automatic votes on all items on that organization's legislative agenda. Deviation or the exercise of individual judgment was considered heretical and suspicious.

The reformer considered that he was elected to represent a sovereign state—in his case, Colorado—and to seek in all cases the nation's interest. Where his philosophy, convictions, and beliefs coincided with those of the coalition groups in his party, he would seek their support, and they could seek his, and so much the better. But even after the bruising experience of managing a presidential campaign and the internecine bitternesses it produced, he was nevertheless amazed at the degree to which those party interests assumed they owned him and casually expected his unquestioned loyalty regardless of the issue. It was as if he should not exercise—and perhaps not even have—judgments of his own in matters affecting those special interests. An innate stubbornness and vein of independence, evident from his early years, began to show themselves more often under the pressure of the Senate experience. These are not admirable traits for anyone contemplating a career in elective politics, the reformer came to understand, and this insight strengthened his early instinct not to pursue politics as a career.

But if ever an institution was devised by the clever artistry of politicians to permit independence in its inhabitants, it was the United States Senate. It is also not a bad place to hide for those with little to do. Early on, one of the reformer's favorite colleagues, a quiet third-term senator from a quiet midwestern state, took the reformer aside to offer some rather languid advice. "Do you want to stay here a long time?" he asked, assuming the answer to be affirmative. The young reformer said he wasn't quite sure but that he did not think it was forever. "Well, I can tell you how to do it, how I do it, if you want to know," he continued. Looking sideways and speaking very quietly behind the closed fist covering his mouth, he said slowly and with great gravity, "Don't do anything." What? "Don't do anything," he repeated. "The people back home sent me here because they knew I wouldn't do anything, and so I don't." Fair enough if that is the understanding. But somehow the reformer had neither sought nor received that signal from his constituents in his long, recent contest to replace a very nice man who summarized his legislative achievements after twelve years in the Senate as having sponsored one measure permitting American citizens to own gold (something most Coloradans might aspire to but never quite achieve) and another requiring that homing beacons be placed on private aircraft (a fair number of which did, it must be said, go down every winter in Colorado's snowy mountains).

On many occasions, the American people did make

it possible to reward those politicians who saw their job as opposition to everything. If a politician saw his destiny in this light, then why not vote against everything in one of the more prestigious environments, the United States Senate? The salary is better than that of the common state legislatures (from which many senators had made their escapes); it is, as one of the reformer's colleagues used to remind him, "indoors and there is no heavy lifting"; and the title enables one to get into most of the better restaurants. There are, in fact, some senators who have spent most of their lives there, and very few in America, including the citizens of their home state, have ever heard of them.

The Senate could boast of having both America's most illustrious leaders and its least well known citizens, all in a body of one hundred. This alone would make it unique. It also permits, if not encourages, independence of thought and judgment, however. Its six-year term was designed for this purpose. As Jefferson saw it, it was created to be the saucer in which hot liquid, in the form of expedient legislation, can be cooled before being consumed. Senators, as has already been observed, are meant to speak for the will of their sovereign states in the federal assembly and thus are presumed to have some authority, subject to forfeiture for willful or persistent ignorance or lack of preparation.

The Senate day was becoming impossible to manage, with myriad committee hearings, visiting constituent delegations, evening receptions, official dinners, votes, and—by the way—debates on the floor of the Senate. By contrast, a very senior senator, John Stennis of Mississippi, told the reformer that in his early years in the 1940s, he would personally write answers to all his correspondence, refer all constituent issues and complaints to members of the House (these were not the job of a senator, he said), and travel back to Mississippi four times a year on the train. This reformer, in

1975, found stacks of mail awaiting his arrival, mostly containing requests for help and complaints, days that began with early working breakfasts, and countless meetings and votes throughout the day; for almost twelve years he spent an average of one day a week traveling throughout Colorado, fifteen hundred miles away.

All this having been said, however, the great issues of the day, domestic and international, were framed in the Senate, and unless one chose, out of ideology, lassitude, or cowardice, to vote no on everything, the opportunity was there to participate in it all. The 1970s were a time of transition—in the nation's economy, in its energy situation, in its use and structuring of its military and intelligence operations, in its industries, and in its position in the world. Transitions are history's way of inviting reform. Many historians—including the Schlesingers, *père et fils*—believe that American history does in fact arrange itself in cycles of conservatism and reform, conservatism and reform. True or not, what had promised to become a reform era in the sixties with John Kennedy was frustrated by assassination and war. Even so, the Johnson Great Society was arguably at least a type of social reform. But now economic and social institutions required fresh and imaginative restructuring, not simply marginal prescriptions and therapies. If reform was to take place, in both the Democratic party and the nation, there seemed no better point of origin than the new Congress and, particularly, its chamber designed for independent thought and action, the Senate.

The very sweep and scope of the modern Senate's activities, however, represent an almost hypnotizing invitation to inaction. Where should reform begin? A professional lifetime could be given to fundamental changes in economic structures, let alone to military institutions, education systems, national energy policies—and the list continues. Virtually every modern issue requires at least vague and elementary knowledge of technology and science. There was often more data than could ever be absorbed, let alone reduced to usable, simple information from which judgments could be reached. So-called experts, whether scientists, economists, militarists, or others, rarely agreed even on fundamental principles. It was difficult to impossible to create consensus on technical questions. How could a policy maker, not to say a reformer, know the proper course? It was maddening for one not expert in complex fields to sort out conflicting advice and opinion. Often hearings, staff meetings, and policy sessions would dissolve into bitter exchanges between conflicting experts while senators scratched their heads or headed for the calm of the cloakroom, where they had only to consult their equally puzzled colleagues, their own common sense, and the smoke of their cigars.

The confusion of senators on matters of great technical or theoretical complexity led too many so-called experts to adopt an attitude of benign contempt for them. On more than one occasion Henry Kissinger felt obliged to lecture congressional committees on the intricacies of foreign policy. Caspar Weinberger, the Reagan administration's secretary of defense, would adopt an imperious tone on matters of national security, especially with senators who might not share his views. Military "experts," in particular, seemed inclined to use their knowledge of intricate weapons systems as the principal means of cowing recalcitrant committee members. Economists, whether from the administration, the academy, or Wall Street, were adept at M-1, M-2 mumbo jumbo when they did not have a serious clue as to why things were going down when they should have been going up. In his two Senate terms, this reformer could not recall one fundamental principle of economics that was not, at one time or another, proved demonstrably false by actual facts and occurrences. It was enough to throw all expert opinion into doubt and tempt the legislator and policy maker to trust his own instincts and common sense.

All these forces and factors weighed heavily on the reformer and the institution in which he was elected to serve. Colleagues were great statesmen, or they were ordinary people hiding out from their constituents. Parliamentary rules, designed to protect the Senate's integrity and institutional genius, were often barriers to change. The party ideology's self-worship and self-perpetuation created an orthodoxy resistant to new approaches and new ideas. Constituent interest groups demanded obedience in exchange for campaign support, whereas the Senate insisted on the independence of its members. Theoretical experts quarreled among themselves over complex technical questions and employed their professional credentials like bludgeons to cow bewildered senators. The nation's structures and institutions begged for fundamental reorganization to address a world engaged in rapid and dramatic change, and the entire political system dawdled and dithered. All in all, it was a glorious time to serve in a grand assembly, the United States Senate.

THE OCTOPUS
OF INTELLIGENCE

At no time in human history has the sport of espionage
been so rampant as in the second half of the twentieth
century. It was the weapon of choice in the cold war; it
excited men's fantasies, and it spawned fictional careers, careers in fiction, and vast agencies and bureaucracies. As with all other human endeavors that result
in organizations, sooner or later America's huge and
powerful intelligence community would exceed even
the very large and lax boundaries established by its
most ardent supporters, and it would become an octo-
pus that had escaped its aquarium and made its way
into the family swimming pool. And so it was in 1975.
Sensing, no doubt, the reformer within the man, Senate Majority Leader Mike Mansfield appointed this
reformer to the newly established Senate Select Committee on Intelligence Activities three weeks after he
arrived in the Senate.

It was both a fantastic blessing and a terrible curse. The CIA and its sister agencies—the National Security Agency, the FBI, the Defense Intelligence Agency, and others—lift the veils and remove the cloaks of secrecy no more than once in a lifetime, if that, and a new reform senator from Colorado was given one of eleven exclusive ringside seats. Over the course of the year-and-a-half investigation and report, the intelligence agencies made the performance more of a striptease than it might have been, and it is widely suspected that they presented, in the manner of Gypsy Rose Lee, only the illusion of baring all. Nonetheless, many of its more lurid memories would last a lifetime.

To set the stage, Watergate and subsequent misadventures suggested less than total professionalism and, in some cases, downright ineptitude and possible illegality on the part of some or all of the intelligence agencies; demands were made for exposure and elimination of abuses of authority; the Rockefeller Commission (so-called after its chairman, who was then vice-president), appointed by President Ford, was thought to have been less than eager to carry out a full-scale, let-the-chips-fall-where-they-may investigation; and so the Senate passed Resolution 21 on January 27 of its Eighty-ninth Congress, establishing a select committee "in order to clear the air, in order to cleanse whatever abuses there have been in the past, so that we can recite, once and for all, the proper parameters within which [the intelligence organizations] can function," according to its sponsor, John Pastore of Rhode Island. The resolution had been the idea of Mansfield, who had sought intelligence reforms for almost two decades.

Democratic members of the committee included Philip Hart, Walter Mondale of Minnesota, Dee Huddleston of Kentucky, Robert Morgan of North Carolina, and Gary Hart of Colorado. Republican members included Howard Baker of Tennessee, Barry Goldwater of Arizona, Charles Mathias of Maryland, and Richard Schweiker of Pennsylvania. The committee vice-chairman was John Tower of Texas, and its chairman was Frank Church of Idaho. It would quickly come to be known as the Church committee, after its chairman and not because it served a confessional function. Highly professional staff members drawn from both parties quickly began to plan and organize hearings and investigations, establish timetables, negotiate with intelligence agencies and the White House, and hunker down for a long, bitter struggle for documents and records. The overall relationship of the committee to its subject agencies, especially the CIA, was one of wary antagonism, never one of cordial cooperation.

During this period, the CIA and the other agencies saw their ultimate mission as survival. They claimed constant concern for, and therefore the ultimate right to deny to the committee, "sources and methods." Their more hard-core officers saw the undertaking as nothing less than a covert effort to destroy the CIA. The committee saw its ultimate task as not simply the exposure of abuses of authority for sensational purposes but, rather, the achievement of a clearer understanding of how the massive intelligence operations of the United States had operated in the past, how they had managed to wander into un- or extraconstitutional areas, and what form of congressional oversight might make the system work better while avoiding illegalities and abuses of citizens' rights. Simply put, the committee was engaged not in the destruction of a wayward system but in its reform.

One of the earliest starting places for inquiry was a report commissioned in 1973 by a previous CIA director, James Schlesinger, who had ordered the agency to draw up a list of all incidents of actual or potential abuses of authority. To his surprise, the list included close to seven hundred such incidents. This closely held, highly secret report—even inside the CIA—was known as the family jewels. Among the jewels were at least five plots to assassinate foreign leaders, beginning in the late 1950s and continuing into the mid-1960s. By May 1975, CIA Director William Colby, responding to intense pressure, detailed these plots before a committee whose most senior, hard-bitten members were bug-eyed. No other word but *stunned* could summarize the reformer's response.

In three of the cases—Ngo Dinh Diem of South Vietnam, Rafael Trujillo of the Dominican Republic, and René Schneider, a general in the Chilean army—the leaders were killed by dissident factions, but in each case the CIA had supplied weapons and supported the dissidents. Each was killed in a coup attempt that the American government, through the CIA, had supported. But the committee ultimately failed to discover direct evidence or obtain concrete testimony connecting the agency directly to the deaths. Questions were raised regarding alleged CIA efforts to assassinate François Duvalier of Haiti and President Sukarno of Indonesia, but with even less effect.

Most troubling were the cases of Patrice Lumumba of the Congo (now Zaire) and Fidel Castro of Cuba. Lumumba was a firebrand revolutionary widely believed by the United States government of the late fifties to be interested in directing the former colonial nation into the Communist camp. The CIA provided both deadly toxins and a rifle, by diplomatic pouch in both cases, to agents dedicated to Lumumba's death. The Army Chemical Corps provided the deadly biological agent, which was sent with rubber gloves, a surgical mask, and a hypodermic syringe. For backup purposes, the Congo CIA station officer cabled headquarters, "Recommend HQS pouch soonest high powered foreign make rifle with telescopic scope and silencer," and concluded, "Would keep rifle in office pending opening of hunting season." The agent obtained by the CIA to carry out the assignment was a professional European assassin given the code name QJWIN. Before the agent could take action either with needle or bullet, Lumumba was killed by counterrevolutionary forces inside the Congo.

Castro was another matter. Over a period of several years, the American government, through the CIA, demonstrated an almost demented insistence on his elimination, one way or the other. And the ways selected were not without imagination. He might be killed by Cuban agents with sterile (untraceable) rifles, .30-caliber M-1 carbines, .38-caliber pistols, fragmentation grenades, or 64-millimeter antitank rockets—all supplied by the CIA. His beard would be made to fall off as the result of someone's putting thallium salts (a depilatory) in his combat boots, and so his charisma would dissipate. He was to be blown up by a seashell packed with high explosives that would be planted to attract his attention on one of his periodic recreational scuba dives. He was to be injected with a highly toxic substance secreted in a fountain pen, which was passed to the agent designated to carry out the unlikely task in a hotel in Paris on November 22, 1963. The longer the mission continued, the more ingenious— and problematic—the methods became.

Obviously, none of it worked. And a reformer or anyone else might pass it off as paranoid folly, except for several aspects. The project engaged two administrations composed of otherwise sober men and women. It became an almost endless obsession to those occupied by it. It characterized to an extreme the American preoccupation with communism in small states. Most of all, it was under way at the time John Kennedy was killed by a man who had tenuous but real connections in two equally murky worlds, one pro-Castro and one anti-Castro, in two cities, New Orleans and Dallas, where anti-Castro sentiment ran high. Finally—and perhaps most important—the CIA had engaged the services of three leading figures of the North American Mafia in its efforts to kill Castro.

Even the densest of senators would find it important to pursue the Castro matter as far as the trail might lead. How could a plot to assassinate a foreign leader continue for so long? How many people knew about it? Who actually ordered the job done? Was it the president? If so, which president? Was there ever a thought of retaliation? Did the Warren Commission know about the Mafia's involvement in the Castro plots? Why was the Mafia being used in the first place? Who, might we know, was Judith Campbell Exner, and why did she have more than a friendship with the president of the United States and at least two of the three Mafia figures trying to kill Castro? The further it went, the more totally bizarre it became.

The full Church committee designated Richard Schweiker and this reformer to pursue these and other questions. The two senators did so under the auspices of a Subcommittee to Investigate the Performance of the Intelligence Community During the Warren Commission Investigation. They found—if that is the correct word—the following answers. There was no direct evidence linking either Eisenhower or Kennedy to the Castro plots or indeed any evidence that they knew these efforts were under way. On the other hand, the efforts continued because those in authority at the CIA and elsewhere thought both presidents wanted Castro got rid of. No thought of retaliation arose, even after Castro insinuated that removal of foreign leaders was a two-way street. The Mafia figures were used because they had long experience in Havana, controlling gambling casinos, prostitution, rackets, and virtually everything else under the former dictator Batista. They, in turn, were eager to cooperate with the CIA not because of the thrill of it but because they wanted Castro out and Havana back in the hands of a dictator more congenial to the United States and to them. The Warren Commission apparently had no knowledge of their involvement in the Castro plots or even of the Castro plots themselves (even though a commission member was the former CIA director Allen Dulles). Judith Exner held herself out to be merely a "friend" of the president and a "friend" of the Mafia figures by virtue of introductions in each case by Frank Sinatra. So.

Sometimes the cause of reform requires overturning rocks under which even a reformer might not wish to look. The Schweiker-Hart subcommittee found exile Cubans who swore under oath that in meetings where the overthrow of Castro was the topic, they had seen Lee Harvey Oswald in the company of a man described without doubt as an intelligence case officer. The agent, who used the name Morris Bishop, bore an uncanny resemblance to one George de Mohrenschildt, the nominal White Russian who had helped welcome Lee and Marina Oswald to Dallas. De Mohrenschildt, who was interviewed without effect by the Warren Commission, was a European with a complex and murky background in the "oil business" throughout the Caribbean. The names of the Mafia figures involved in the Castro plots were John Rosselli, Sam Giancana, and Santos Trafficante. The reformer also discovered, almost by accident, that the CIA had engaged a professional in the Castro plots as an experienced "adviser." His code name was QJWIN.

What could possibly be made of all this? This reformer was up for finding out. Shortly after learning of the assassination plots from Director Colby, the reformer and his wife participated in a Senate delegation visit to the Soviet Union. Colby had been asked to try to find QJWIN, if he still existed, so that the reformer might speak to him as the group returned from the Soviet Union. Colby promised to put his best man on the problem and said he would communicate with the reformer after his group had departed Soviet soil. On the last day in Moscow, an anonymous man "from the U.S. embassy" quietly slipped the reformer an unsigned note, which simply said that contact had been made and the senator would receive further instructions on the first return stop, which happened to be Amsterdam.

While in a restaurant in Amsterdam shortly thereafter, the senator-reformer received a call from Colby's man, giving instructions for reaching him very late that night. Following the instructions, the senator made his way to the bar rendezvous without attracting the attention of anyone but his wife ("committee business"). Having convinced himself that the senator had not been followed, Colby's man took the senator aside to deliver the following message: he had found QJWIN after all these years "in a nearby country" and had persuaded him to come to that place earlier in the evening "to meet one of our friends." QJWIN, he said, had asked whether the "friend" had anything to do with the ongoing CIA investigations in the States. Colby's man chose to answer truthfully, whereupon QJWIN had fled. Possible explanations abounded. QJWIN had never been contacted or no longer existed. The CIA was performing a charade to humor the reformer and the committee. The CIA man made an honest mistake by telling the truth (unlikely). Or the CIA agent did not want the committee talking with QJWIN for whatever reason—perhaps because of information QJWIN might have concerning the connection between the Castro plots and Kennedy's death—and he knew the assassin would flee if the truth were told. How would a reformer ever know the truth of the matter? There is one footnote only: Colby did send his top man; his name was John Stein, and later he became deputy director of operations, the top covert job, before being dismissed under unclear circumstances having nothing—one hopes—to do with reform of the CIA or anything else.

Some weeks later the committee secretly summoned one of the Mafia figures, John Rosselli, to give testimony on the Castro plots. After negotiations, he appeared without press notice and was later asked to return to try to shed even a small beacon of light on the curious circumstances surrounding Judith Exner. This time his appearance before the committee was leaked to the Miami press. Some time thereafter, Rosselli disappeared, only to be discovered within weeks horribly mutilated and disfigured in a fifty-five-gallon drum afloat off the Miami shores. Since Rosselli had not been active in Mafia affairs for some time, one had to be extraordinarily simpleminded not to believe a connection existed between his committee testimony and his cold-blooded demise.

Another Mafia figure, Sam Giancana, semiretired boss of the Chicago-area mob, was then notified of a request to appear before congressional committees looking into CIA operations. Now a man in his seventies, as Rosselli had been, and under round-the-clock surveillance, Giancana was nevertheless promptly assassinated in the basement of his home before even responding to the requests. Neither murder has ever been solved.

By now the mysterious George de Mohrenschildt had also aroused sufficient new interest to prompt a House committee also pursuing CIA abuses to request his presence and testimony concerning anything he might know regarding connections among Castro plots, the Mafia, the CIA, and Kennedy's death. Very soon after receiving this notice, de Mohrenschildt was found dead in his home of "self-inflicted wounds" from a very large shotgun.

This reformer, who only months before had been a struggling self-employed legal practitioner in the city of Denver, would not know what to make of these events even years after his own campaign for the presidency and his departure from public life. To say they were, and are, puzzling is to understate the case grossly. While struggling to cope with these strange circumstances, he incorporated parts of this complex story, particularly the effort to find the mysterious QJWIN, in a novel he wrote in collaboration with a Senate colleague, William Cohen of Maine. And in his national campaign effort in 1984 and afterward, he made it abundantly clear that were he ever elected president, he would turn the CIA upside down in search of further information on President Kennedy's death. But nothing, in the cause of reform or otherwise, came of either venture.

Despite tense controversy and conflict, the Church committee continued its hearings, investigations, and disclosures, all with an eye to reform of the intelligence community. For some, the immense concentration on assassination plots represented a frolic and a detour from the original purpose of the committee: to investigate and further prevent covert operations carried out by intelligence agencies against American citizens. But the committee counsel, Fritz Schwarz, saw a policy benefit in the early, sensational focus on assassination: "It was vital to make the politicians and the American people really *believe* that reform was necessary. You couldn't speak in abstractions; you had to have something real and concrete. This the assassination report provided, in memorable, horrifying detail."

But additional abuses, the direct result of congressional oversight of intelligence operations, were equally shocking in their implications for constitutional liberties. Using the code name COINTELPRO, for domestic counterintelligence activities, the FBI and virtually all other government intelligence agencies conducted massive invasions of citizens' rights for years. One account of the committee's work summarized its findings on domestic political abuses as follows:

> The results were shocking. The CIA program to open mail from or to selected American citizens produced a secret computer bank of 1.5 million names; the FBI intelligence unit developed files on well over a million Americans, and carried out 500,000 investigations of "subversives" from 1960 to 1974 without a single court conviction; the NSA computers were fed every single cable sent overseas by Americans from 1947 until 1975; Army intelligence units conducted investigations against 100,000 American citizens during the Vietnam War.

The same source accurately characterized the record of this sorry period in American history:

> The tactics sometimes used were alien to the principles embraced by the Bill of Rights and the body of statutes that have evolved to protect civil liberties in the United States. They were, in fact, more reminiscent of the means resorted to by Hitler's SS and Beria's secret police under the Stalin regime: drug experiments conducted by the CIA on unsuspecting subjects; assassination plots attempted against foreign leaders in peacetime; murder and other violence incited among blacks by anonymous FBI letters; the families and friendships of dissidents disrupted by concealed bureau harassment; burglaries carried out in the homes and offices of suspected subversives; elections manipulated in democratic countries; tax information misused for political purposes; academic and religious groups infiltrated.

The Church committee represented the first and only full-scale congressional inquiry into United States intelligence operations since the formation of the CIA and related intelligence bureaucracies in 1947. For almost three decades, the growth of this awesome community's power had proceeded virtually unchecked or unquestioned even by presidents whose oath of office required such control. The Church committee's mandate was not to destroy intelligence capabilities through exposure of misdeeds but, rather, to strengthen those capabilities by requiring that they be focused on their true purpose: the collection and analysis of information for the use of duly elected and appointed policy makers. The committee's final report, containing ninety-seven specific recommendations for change, represented reform at its best.

Of these, the most far-reaching was the proposal for the creation of a permanent Senate Committee on Intelligence, with authority to oversee and approve the budgets and operations of the CIA, the NSA, and other intelligence agencies not under the jurisdiction of an existing Senate committee. The FBI, for example, was in theory, at least, an arm of the Department of Justice, which comes under the jurisdiction of the Senate Judiciary Committee. After considerable heated debate in 1976, the oversight recommendation, contained in a resolution that itself incorporated a number of other key Church-committee recommendations, was adopted by the Senate. Since then, the CIA has operated under more or less thorough Senate oversight and has proved the stronger for it. Dire warnings from intelligence officials and political conservatives that such oversight would destroy American intelligence capabilities, that massive and continuous leaks of classified information would emanate from Congress, and that foreign sources of information would cease doing business with United States agencies for fear of exposure have all proved false. Except for concerted efforts by the Reagan White House and the late CIA director William Casey to return to the bad old "cowboy" days, the intelligence community has worked effectively under the new regime and has, apparently, stayed clear of the kind of misadventures that led to the investigations and reforms in the first place.

There are undoubtedly many lessons for reform to be drawn from all this. Some are obvious. Secret agencies do not like to share their secrets. Zealous people, even those zealous in the cause of defending democracy, will violate the democratic freedoms of others in order to further the cause of democracy. Many legislators whose job it is to see to the proper functioning of agencies of government do not believe that their job applies to the security forces. Liberals are more willing, if not more eager, to find fault with intelligence agencies than conservatives. Sunlight is a prerequisite to genuine reform. The more secret the institution, the more likely it is to require reform over a period of time. Power corrupts.

The cold war was used to justify illicit and undemocratic behavior by United States government agencies. The ends were believed to justify almost any means. It was a very short distance from a doctrine of preventing the other side from winning to a doctrine of winning. We came to believe that we had no choice but to play by rules defined by the other side, even if those rules defied our own best principles. Politicians, elected government officials, found it too easy to let someone else do the dirty work. They did not want to know what was being done in the name of democracy and in the name of their own country because it was clearly distasteful and unprincipled. What you don't know can't hurt you or cause you sleeplessness. Real justice would have called to account the many politicians, presidents, and members of Congress too cowardly to do their job during those three decades.

Though often said, it must be said again: it is right and proper that a nation have the ability to collect and analyze information that may prove vital or even helpful to its security. That was never the issue, except perhaps for a fringe handful who wished to destroy the CIA. The issue was whether such a capability could exist in a free, democratic society without exceeding its authority or violating the rights of the citizens it was pledged to protect. The motto of the CIA is telling, and biblical: "You shall know the truth and the truth shall make you free." It is impossible to imagine that the desired death of Fidel Castro had anything to do with knowing the truth. It is possible to imagine that the death of Rosselli, Giancana, and even John Kennedy had something to do with knowing the truth.

The barriers to reforming the CIA and the intelligence community were these: the Ford White House; the CIA itself; many conservative senators; the ambitions of committee members; former intelligence officers and retired government officials who did not wish to defend past practices or policies or change traditional procedures and methods; elements of the press eager for sensation; senators who had not done their job under the old regime; national security hard-liners; the FBI, the NSA, the IRS, the Defense Intelligence Agency, and all elements of military intelligence; virtually everyone who knew anything about the dark past; QJWIN.

All those considerable barriers were overcome, however, by a public aroused by the press's legitimate and serious exposure of abuses of intelligence authority and political power; the public finally empowered reform-minded Senate leaders like Mansfield, Pastore, Ribicoff, and Church to undertake a task they could not have undertaken with any real effect before the intelligence scandals. In short, the democratic system finally worked—which leads to yet another important lesson for reform: timing is everything. All the good intentions in the world cannot make up for the wrong circumstances. The people of America possess much more power than they think. They just do not use it often enough. Lethargy, lack of concern, personal preoccupation, defeatism, and cynicism sap the power of protest. There are often leaders, like Mike Mansfield in the case of CIA reform, who urge change and issue warnings of danger. But if the public is inattentive or unconcerned, those prophetic leaders are isolated and forgotten. The Senate, like most political—that is to say, human—institutions, is composed of one third who want change, one third opposed to change, and one third who don't know and are waiting to be told which way the wind is blowing. When the public wind begins to blow, most of the "pragmatic" one third will go with the wind.

But it must continue to blow. It blew sufficiently hard in late 1974 and early 1975 to enable one of the most sweeping and important congressional investigations in American history to take place. It must be said, however, that by the time the committee concluded its deliberations, issued its report and recommendations, and sought legislative reforms in oversight and control, public interest had dissipated greatly. Consequently, antireform, traditionalist forces were able to qualify and weaken the reform package and prevent the passage of the strongest measures necessary to prevent future abuses.

Thus, the last and most basic lesson for reform in a democracy: reform does not take place when the public is apathetic. Or, put the other way round, public interest and insistence is necessary for reform. The corollary of this principle is that reform will continue, deepen, and take root in direct proportion to continued public demand. The middle third carry the day, and the middle third always hold up a dampened finger to test the breeze of public opinion.

ENERGY FOLLIES

No other aspect of American life and its economy so characterized the nation in recent years as the country's complex attitudes toward energy. Energy has been seen as plentiful to the point of inexhaustibility; it has been readily available; it is believed to come automatically from the nozzle of a pump, from a thermostat, or from a light switch; its price should always be reasonably low; no effort to alter its source, supply, patterns of consumption, or cost will be tolerated. Energy is part of America itself. It is a definition of America.

With regard to the suppliers of energy, Americans have had a curious relationship. They resent but have come to accept that the giant vertically integrated oil companies (the majors) represent a carefully constructed, well-managed cartel. They widely believe that the members of this cartel manipulate the price of their product virtually at will. They have come to accept, also, the argument that the majors must control the flow of the product from the well to the gas pump (cross-subsidization through vertical integration). They believe this handful of companies has too much power in the marketplace and too much power over government. In short, they accept that the energy industry in America operates on the margin of democracy and outside the normal market forces of capitalism.

They will continue to accept this situation, however, under one condition: that the price of gasoline, home heating oil, and other widespread supplies of energy remain at roughly one third the price paid in most of the rest of the world. The most readily available historical analogy is the Romans who continued to permit a series of unpalatable emperors to preside over the decline of their empire as long as there were bread and circuses. However questionable the structure and practices of the oil industry might be, they will be permitted as long as supply and price remain secure.

A similar attitude toward the government prevails where energy is concerned. The mandate of the people of the United States to their government is clear and simple: the price of energy is not to increase by taxation, even to encourage conservation, and the government is to do whatever it must to maintain a continued supply of energy. The sum total of this popularly acculturated attitude—for it does not merit being called a policy—is just this: we will continue to consume energy even if we do so below its replacement costs and even if we do so wastefully, and we will fight anyone who interferes with this practice.

The latter is important, for it is an unspoken but integral part of a de facto American energy policy and has been so for decades. The American military force incorporated this reality into its sizing, planning, and deployment long before the OPEC price rises of 1974. Our foreign policy has followed our military policy, which has followed our attitude toward energy. In the Middle East, we have overthrown governments, supported dictators and a variety of undemocratic governments, provided more sophisticated arms than we can count, conducted covert operations, subverted democratic oppositions, intervened in regional conflicts (in some cases, on both sides), violated our own laws, and perpetuated political scandals (such as Irangate) all for one purpose—to keep the oil flowing.

It was all somehow easier during the cold war. Then we had to keep the rich oil fields out of the hands of the Soviets—never mind that the Soviets were already the world's largest oil producers. But now our reasoning is less clear. Now we go to war in the Middle East to preserve "democracy" in places like Kuwait. Since everyone knows there is about as much democracy in Kuwait as there is in Mongolia, that fiction never held up. Well then, we went to war in the Middle East to punish a dictator. Our leaders never got around to explaining their earlier friendship with this dictator, as well as with a variety of others in the region who happened to be helpful to us. The secretary of state at the time felt uncomfortable enough to come closer to the truth. He said we were going to war to protect American jobs.

This is simply an oblique way of saying the American economy is dependent on continued supplies of relatively cheap oil imported from the Middle East— which is the truth. The question is, Does it need to be? The answer is no. America is an energy-rich nation, rich in petroleum, rich in coal, rich in uranium, rich in natural gas, rich in oil shale, rich in geothermal steam, rich in wind, and rich in sun. It also consumes much more than is necessary for a growing economy. Why, then, spend billions of dollars creating a Rapid Deployment Force and risking the lives of thousands, if not tens of thousands, of young Americans to secure supplies of oil from the Middle East, oil that does not belong to us?

The only plausible answer lies in this: many years ago the same major oil companies that dominate the American oil industry entered into enormously valuable concession agreements with the Middle East and invested very large sums of money in developing petroleum fields there. The resources were so vast and the costs of production so cheap in terms of the United States economy that it made certain economic sense at the time. It makes even more economic sense now that the original costs of exploration have largely been amortized and the oil being produced is almost dirt cheap; it would be far more costly to develop new wells in the United States and certainly more costly to develop alternative supplies of energy.

Yet this equation does not take into account the enormous military costs involved in securing those Middle Eastern oil supplies. Added to the cost equation, however, is the fact that environmental-quality controls in the middle of the Saudi desert are certainly less stringent than they would be in most parts of the United States. And local labor is less costly. Almost all the economic inputs, to use an economist's term, favor Middle East production over domestic production. Isn't it true, one might and should ask, that the American oil industry has fallen on hard times recently? That is true, primarily because we are importing roughly half of all the petroleum we consume and because most domestic exploration is carried out not by the majors presently making profits in the Middle East but by the so-called independents, the relatively small mom-and-pop companies, the heirs to the classic wildcatters. Almost all the independents produce under some form of agreement or contract with a major company. The independents are not vertically integrated; they do not have pipelines, refineries, and distribution networks. The major finances the deal; the independent drills the well, and if he finds oil, he sells it back to the major and keeps a little profit for himself.

That doesn't sound very independent, a novice might say. The novice would be correct. There are thousands of independents and only a few majors. But one had only to be an energy reformer in the hothouse days of the late seventies to know that the majors control the industry, including its political and lobbying positions on energy issues. The bravest of the brave independents would say it aloud, but those merely brave would tell the reformer privately, "We can't go against the big boys; they finance our deals." So much for an industry of thousands of independent producers free to speak their mind on matters affecting the future of their industry and their country.

The Senate of the mid-seventies was indeed a hothouse on energy issues. Prices were rising, to the frustration of consumers, who were demanding that they be kept down simply because supplies were being rationed and controlled by the producing nations. There were—perish the thought—lines at gas stations. Frustrated, angry people shouted, and occasionally shot, at each other. How could this happen? Cartoons featuring greedy, grinning Arab sheikhs holding guns to the backs or heads of American consumers were everywhere. Few thought to question the profits the Arabs' partners, the majors, were making as prices rose. But they were enormous. Few thought to remind themselves that this was in fact Arab oil—not our oil—and the owners could demand for it what the market would bear. It was classic capitalism. Except that the consumers had little choice. Because the majors had made their lucrative deals in the Middle East, because we were importing then (as we are even now) half our oil, because we were not developing our own supplies, because we were consuming much and conserving little, because we did not have a national energy policy, the mighty United States of America was over a barrel, an oil barrel that was not ours.

So a hue and cry went up in the Congress of the day: "We need a national energy policy." Suddenly, every American in every coffee shop across the land—and, needless to say, his or her congressman—was an expert on energy. The problem was that all these experts disagreed. Some wanted to bludgeon the Arabs into submission. No one was exactly clear on how to do this, nor did anyone want to be reminded yet again that the oil belongs to the Arabs. Some wanted a massive increase in domestic production overnight. But they had to be reminded by head-scratching oilmen that, dang it, you just don't set a rig overnight, let alone ten thousand of 'em. Some wanted a hundred new nuclear power plants. Some wanted solar heaters on every roof. Some wanted to develop a massive oil shale industry, also overnight. Some thought if you just drilled a hole deep enough, you would have enough steam to heat America forever. How to run the cars was unclear. Some wanted railroad trains and streetcars, now, in 1975, all rusting in junkyards. Some discovered fission, others windmills, and yet others gasohol, made from corn. It was all a grand show, full of fun and folly, except the United States economy was sinking through the floor, factories were closing, people were losing their jobs, and the elderly feared the winter.

Americans, natively dubious about government power, have always resisted national policies, anything that smells of government planning, except in extremis. Since the oil crisis of 1974–75 qualified as in extremis, it became permissible for politicians to discuss a national energy policy. In fact, little else was being discussed. Energy was topic A. The structures and names of congressional committees are often good barometers of the mood. The Senate quickly reorganized its old, sleepy Interior Committee into a brand-new Energy Committee, and it was the place to be.

Otherwise dignified senators elbowed and jostled each other fiercely for membership.

Herein lies another central lesson for reform: if major changes are desired, create a crisis. If an issue dominates the news for a period of time and the people are aroused, the political process will be close behind. *National energy policy* was the crucial phrase on every word processor in Washington. Editorial writers, columnists, pundits, journeymen reporters, staff members, and senators—all became instant experts. A policy, a national plan, was what was needed. Predictably, much finger pointing occurred to fix blame for the mess, except few wished to point a finger at the American consumer, addicted as he was to wasteful uses and low prices.

The national atmosphere for the reform of energy policies and practices could not have been better. The lonely prophets of solar, geothermal, and wind energy —the renewables—suddenly were the toast of dinner parties in fashionable Georgetown dining rooms. Scruffy wildcatters who believed they could drill holes two or three miles into the crust of the earth and produce virtually unlimited amounts of clean, natural gas to fuel the nation's boilers were hailed as saviors. Endless hours of testimony from people who but a few days before would have been frogmarched out of Senate offices were heard in great earnestness by senators who could not seem to learn enough about intricate laws of thermodynamics, levitating trains, Israeli solar heaters, Canadian tar sand technology, the oil equivalent of a ton of rich oil shale, the laws of fission, and wind-driven generators. A new reform senator could not seek the solace and quiet of the Senate reading room to absorb the energy wisdom of the nation's great newspapers without being interrupted by a colleague fresh from yet another hearing, thoughtfully puffing a cigar and wishing to repeat some startling revelation from a crackbrain who had spent an isolated lifetime preparing a paper on the conversion of moon-beams to megawatts and whose hour had now come.

The nation being this desperately preoccupied with a solution, some serious thought eventually did filter upward through the system. The Congress and the people were prepared to get at least some energy religion, if not a full-blown conversion. Listening to the cacophony of opinion, the reformer came to believe in four basic principles of energy reform: the introduction of genuine marketplace competition; a systematic but sharp reduction in reliance on foreign oil imports; the development of all practical alternative domestic supplies; and the reduction of wasteful consumption through increased taxation. To say that each element of this proposed new national policy was controversial would represent wild understatement.

The first—stimulation of real competition—simply required restructuring and reorganization of the domestic oil industry. The simple, stunning term for this is *divestiture*, a term of science in the body of antitrust law requiring the breakup of monopolies. From the earliest Standard Oil days of the original John D. Rockefeller, those who controlled the supply of oil in America—and to some degree, in the world—have seemed almost genetically attracted to monopoly. As the Teapot Dome scandal and other such incidents demonstrated, the oil monopolists often tried to monopolize the United States government as well. The basic idea was to control the supply of petroleum from the well that brought it from the ground, through the pipeline to the refinery, from the refinery to the service station, and thence into the car. If one owned the well, the pipeline, the refinery, and the gas pump, one was then considered vertically integrated, a nice term for a monopolist. But if the government would not let one company control all the oil, the capital costs of constructing such a giant empire would guarantee that very few companies would control the oil. Even the most novice antitrust student knows that the fewer the companies, the easier the formation of a cartel, a cartel being a de facto monopoly of a few companies that controls the distribution of a commodity or product and regulates the price at which it is sold to the consumer.

Under the Sherman and Clayton Antitrust acts, monopolies and cartels are of course illegal, and sporadically antitrust-minded administrations, like tired referees in a desultory boxing match, have found it necessary to push the waltzing companies apart and make them punch. When a price-rise hiccup occurs, the curious man-on-the-street consumer pushes his cap back, scratches his head, and wonders why the prices all seem to jump just exactly the same amount at almost exactly the same hour. Then prices go back down, the consumer forgets, and gas pumps all across America still register exactly the same price in this "highly competitive industry."

Within a few months of taking the Senate oath of office, the reformer would join a small band of like-minded antitrust, procompetition senators—Abourezk of South Dakota, Nelson of Wisconsin, and Philip Hart of Michigan—in sponsoring a bill requiring the divestiture of all vertically integrated domestic oil companies. This bill affected roughly six or eight companies at the most. The independents would not have been affected, except to be given a more favorable climate in which to work. The majors would be required to decide, within a reasonable period of time, whether they wished to produce oil, transport oil, refine oil, or distribute oil. They would no longer be able to do all four. The idea was to create genuine competition at all levels of the petroleum stream, from well to gas pump, thus, according to classic Adam Smith economics, producing the greatest supply at the lowest price.

A new reform senator would learn many important

lessons about economics from this enterprise, not least of which was that those who talk the loudest about free enterprise usually practice it the least. Monopoly loves power. Power loves money, monopoly loves money. Monopoly loves power loves money. All love a government that will leave them alone or give them what they want. As the White House and Congress continued to flounder on energy throughout 1975, the mood of the people darkened. The divestiture bill had no chance of being heard, let alone acted on, by the new Senate Energy Committee, due to intense, powerful lobbying by the majors. So the divestiture quartet, now supported by consumer groups, genuine antitrusters, and a small, brave band of independent producers, took the bill to the floor of the Senate as an amendment to a pending energy measure. To the shock of all, it almost passed—it received forty-seven votes.

The majors went berserk. Full-page adds sprouted in newspapers across America. Mass mailings went out to widowed shareholders. Inflammatory industry orators fanned out into every service club in the land. Lobbyists crowded every Senate office, demanding an audience. Checkbooks came out. Service station operators were terrorized. Industry employees were threatened with job losses if the measure passed. Consumers were given dire warnings of giant price rises. Everyone who had anything whatsoever to do with oil was mobilized against the idea of real competition in the oil industry. The battle continued throughout the year, but the heat generated by the majors, far exceeding that of their total domestic oil production, prevented the divestiture measure from ever again coming close to passing.

There were not to be the "destructive gales of capitalism" and competition, to use the economist Joseph Schumpeter's phrase, in the American oil industry. The titans of capitalism would not tolerate it. Most disturbing for energy—and perhaps for any other reform in America—was the manipulation of the independent oil producers by the majors. Aside from the consumers themselves, no group in our economy would have benefited more from the competition introduced by oil-industry divestiture than the several thousand independent producers. The majors would have had to negotiate much more favorable farm-out agreements to obtain new supplies. Independents could have formed cooperatives to refine their own products, or they could have negotiated more favorable refining agreements among a variety of newly independent refineries. The shake-up of the industry would have revitalized domestic production and saved many hundreds of failing independents, most of whom were benefiting not at all from the OPEC price run-up. Yet almost to a man, they opposed the divestiture measure. Puzzled by this opposition to self-interest, a reformer would want to know why. Always the same the answer came back: the majors control this industry, and they demand that we support their position. So much for an industry made up of thousands of independent oil companies and so much for capitalist, free market competition and free enterprise.

The struggle then shifted to a second policy arena: the reduction of dependence on foreign imports. Here the reformer thought the simplest measure would be a direct, straightforward tax of about ten dollars per barrel on all such imports. He proposed it several times in the 1980s. But this notion came to be received with even less enthusiasm and at least as much opposition as divestiture. Alas, the oil-import fee sank due to the weight of its own merits. It had so many attributes of energy reform as to frighten away all but the most ardent reformers, of whom there are always too few. It was simple and easily administered: imports would have been assessed a flat fee on every barrel at the point of entry. It would have encouraged conservation across the board: unlike a gasoline tax, a tax on imported oil would have been distributed on all petroleum uses throughout the economy and would have reduced unnecessary consumption in all uses. It would have encouraged domestic production: the value of oil would have risen to meet the increased import level, thus encouraging domestic petroleum production as well as the development of new, economically marginal, environmentally clean alternative sources, such as solar power. It would have reduced the risk of our going to war for oil: reliance on foreign supplies would have declined, as would the probability of our need to fight for them. It would have returned substantial revenues: more than twenty billion dollars per year would have gone into the federal treasury, an amount that represented a healthy contribution to a reduction of the deficit. It would have helped liberate our foreign policy: the temptation to turn away from a democratic ally, Israel, in favor of the oil-producing Arab states or to support undemocratic regimes in the region would have been reduced. There was simply no other energy-reform idea that achieved so many desired objectives simultaneously or as simply.

It just would not fly, however. The Reagan White House was opposed. Some lame and thoroughly laughable excuse about interfering with the free market was given. The oil-industry majors were opposed for the same reasons and, of course, out of deep concern for the plight of the consumer. There would be no admission from them that the tax would simply be a transfer of their profits and those of their Middle East partners to the American treasury. Consumers were opposed because prices of energy would increase. Never mind that energy prices were increasing at a furious pace and that the lives of their children might be the final price of continued reliance on foreign imports. Even the so-called independent oil producers could not be mustered in support, even though the tax would have meant a huge boost to their languishing prospects. They were still taking orders from the majors.

Like the divestiture measure, there was never a prospect that the Senate Energy Committee would act on an oil-import fee. Therefore, this reformer would offer the proposal as an amendment to a variety of other germane energy-related bills, with almost no effect. A rough dozen or so senators might be stirred to lend a vote here and there. One might have some sympathy for the opposition of senators from oil-consuming states—there would be some rise in the price of home heating oil, after all, and constituents might be displeased with that. But the opposition of senators from oil-producing states would be confounding. No single measure would have stimulated the economies of Louisiana, Oklahoma, and Texas more than the import fee, and yet the senators of those states stood in opposition. One could only surmise that they got a call or two from major company executives concerned with their reelection prospects and their need for campaign funds.

In 1979, President Carter supported a proposal for an extraordinarily modest gasoline tax of ten cents per gallon. Predictable cries of outrage from so-called consumer groups managed to frighten away many senators who knew quite well that the proposal was in fact modest and necessary. The reformer joined only ten other stalwarts in the losing cause. The president of the United States was quite powerless to deliver votes even from his own party on a measure this unpopular. Coming at the height of the energy uproar, there would be no better measure of the lack of real seriousness about the energy issue.

By contrast, the later Reagan White House was totally hypocritical on the issue. By the mid-1980s, international terrorism had distracted attention from the ongoing energy dilemma, and the laissez-faire attitude

of the Reaganites in every respect precluded any serious attempt to achieve the national energy policy so
devoutly sought in the late seventies. In fact, most of
the real progress finally achieved in the Carter years—
in price restructuring, stimulation of alternative
sources, research in new technologies, increased conservation, and energy security—was simply thrown
overboard by the Reagan administration in the final
capitulation to the so-called free market. Again predictably, the chart representing reliance on foreign imports, which had slowly been driven down by these
initiatives in the late seventies, began to climb back up
quickly, and Reagan sought and received vast new
sums for military forces in the Middle East, equipped
to fight and die for foreign oil.

Hypocrisy was the theme throughout. While Reagan was literally targeting Muammar Qaddafi of Libya,
sending a squadron of B-111s from bases almost three
thousand miles away, in England, to try to assassinate
the Libyan leader by aerial bombing (surely a first in
the annals of assassination), the United States was importing, and paying the Libyan government for, sizable
amounts of its oil. While decrying Qaddafi's terrorism,
we were providing funds through oil purchases to help
him finance those operations. A reformer, now in his
second Senate term and therefore no longer supposed
to be surprised by anything, could still not fathom it.
So he would take the Senate floor to offer yet another
amendment, in this case to ban all oil purchases from
Libya. He should have known what everyone else in
the world had figured out—his amendment was
doomed to overwhelming defeat for the same reason
the oil-import fee was defeated: one or two major
American oil companies had lucrative Libyan contracts and were making a good deal of money from the
Libyan trade. Regardless of Qaddafi's bad behavior and
our efforts to remove him surgically by aerial bom-
bardment, they were not ready to close up shop and

kiss those profits good-bye. They so instructed a compliant but embarrassed White House, which in turn trotted out the chairman of the Senate Foreign Relations Committee, Charles Percy of Illinois, to oppose the reformer's amendment on the grounds that these were delicate diplomatic matters that should not be confused by prohibitions on a few billion dollars in oil trade.

Throughout the period of the late seventies, Carter's years, energy prices soared, and supplies remained short. By the early eighties, in large part because of the policies of conservation and domestic production and because of the worldwide recession brought on by oil-price shocks, demand had fallen, OPEC was thereby fractured, and prices of energy in the United States dropped. The high oil prices that produced inflation and stagnation had made Carter unpopular, and the lower oil prices that produced growth and prosperity made Reagan popular. In neither case did the leaders involved have anything to do with the situation. Ironically, in fact, unpopular Carter energy measures had brought about the conditions contributing to Reagan's consequent popularity. There were lessons for reform here: credit for hard choices arrives later; timing is everything; it is better to be lucky than smart.

As quickly as the energy issue burst forth with the price shocks of 1974 and 1977, it quickly disappeared with the falling prices of 1980 and 1981. *Supply-side economics* was the new phrase on Washington's word processors. The old one, *national energy policy*, was used only by hopelessly out-of-date commentators. Being inevitably a long and difficult process, reform requires an attention span of some duration. Modern American culture does not lend itself to long attention spans. Currency is the currency. And the currency of the day was not energy. President Reagan went for years without once even mentioning the issue that had dominated the national debate of the previous decade. No one thought a thing of it. The once-fashionable Senate Energy Committee gave way to the Senate Finance Committee and slowly slipped back into the anonymity of its former Interior days. Once again it became a place to hide, not a place to be seen. The energy gurus packed up their technical fixes and gave way to a new army of economic theorists with puzzling curves on cocktail napkins, fast-talking theories about the supply side, and promises of economic growth so swift it would boggle even the most skeptical mind. If anyone talked about fixing the roof while the sun was shining, or even mentioned the word *energy*, official Washington would consider him quaint and hopelessly out of touch with the political fashions of the day.

Alas, divestiture, oil-import fees, and conservation taxes had all failed, even during the heyday of the energy debate, and would be given no attention or credibility thereafter. But efforts to continue to focus on new supplies and sources of energy would survive in the back corridors of the Senate. To be a reformer implies doggedness, if nothing else. Like a terrier with its teeth sunk firmly into the backside of a Brahma bull, a reformer could not let go so easily. There would be continued encouragement of at least an experimental oil shale industry, even though falling world prices had taken much air out of the prospects for commercial development. A national Solar Energy Research Institute, created in Colorado by President Carter, would need financial and political support long after its glamour days in the public spotlight had passed. Encouragement would be sought for enhanced and tertiary recovery of existing petroleum deposits. There were a variety of conservation measures to be supported and encouraged. The battle to reduce foreign imports would continue, without effect, well into the 1980s. And the reformer would doggedly continue his controversial support of reduced taxation for new supplies of domestic oil and gas discovered by independent drillers.

In the turbulent years between 1983 and 1988, when this reformer would seek to enter the national stage, he insisted on repeating a theme that few then cared about and seemed to find no resonance in an era of cheap, readily available energy. The warning was that foreign oil imports were climbing back to the critical levels of the early seventies, that dependence on other people's oil was folly, that we were wasteful and inefficient, that continued reliance on oil from the chaotic Middle East was an almost sure guarantee that sometime in the future supplies would be cut off and we would be involved in a war for oil in the region.

In 1991, 146 Americans lost their lives, securing the transfer of oil supplies from Kuwait to their country and the Western world. Most Americans would celebrate this great military victory and congratulate themselves, their military commanders, and their president on the low casualty figures. That celebration would not include the families of the 146, a few of whom were killed by "friendly fire."

In *The March of Folly*, the late Barbara Tuchman analyzed a number of historical occasions on which societies and nations have exhibited folly. Tuchman defined folly as having an alternative to a dangerous course of action, knowing that alternative to be preferable and more advisable, and choosing to pursue the less preferable course regardless. Were Ms. Tuchman alive to revise and update her book, a puzzled reformer would assume she would add a chapter on American attitudes toward energy in the latter decades of the twentieth century. Unless those attitudes change, America will once again find itself at war in the Middle East over the issue of oil. And that will be nothing but the grandest folly of all.

12

REFORM AND
THE PRUSSIAN MIND

No nation in history has reformed its military without having suffered a major military defeat. Though the recent Persian Gulf War was the first pure military victory since the Inch'on landing in Korea forty years before, the United States—the mightiest military power in the history of the world—has yet to suffer a major military defeat. (Vietnam represented a defeat only if one considers the failure to achieve one's objectives a defeat. Historically, defeat has usually implied occupation or serious erosion of national security.) In fact, the cold war, which ended without shots being fired, might be defined as a major military victory. And so the United States once again has an opportunity to make history by reforming its military in the wake of political, diplomatic, and military success. The odds are heavily against this occurring.

To understand why this is true, it is necessary to

know that a small but dedicated effort at military reform has existed in America for a decade. The fact that almost no one knows of its existence is the best commentary on its effectiveness to date. Building on the pioneering work of theorists and practitioners of military reform, this reformer helped found the military-reform caucus in Congress in 1982. It was, in fact, this country's lack of success in Vietnam and a few instances where it was successful that led these innovative thinkers to question traditional military theory, doctrine, strategy, and tactics. Isolated questioners have a way of finding each other, and so the small movement was formed.

A mythology was created in the 1970s that assumed opponents of United States involvement in Southeast Asia were also opponents of the United States military. It is one thing to be antimilitarist and another to be antimilitary. In fact, this reformer's first committee request upon entering the Senate was for membership on the Armed Services Committee. This decision sprang not only from a lifelong interest in military history but also from a strong sense that the defense establishment represents a central part of American life and American history. In the 1970s and '80s, it most certainly represented an important part of the United States budget.

For decades after World War II, roughly one third of all federal spending went to the military. This figure includes not only the annual Pentagon budget but also intelligence operations applicable to the military and programs for the development of nuclear weapons, which were regularly hidden in the budgets of the old Atomic Energy Commission and the newer Department of Energy. However it was calculated, it represented a great deal of money and a substantial allocation of national priorities. It always seemed a mistake to a reformer that so many of his progressive allies and liberal colleagues chose to have so little to do with the military establishment of our country. It is difficult to understand the whole picture without taking into serious consideration the country's national security apparatus.

For the better part of a year, the reformer tried to learn the elaborate process by which the United States government structured its defenses. It was more complicated than it might seem. Almost everyone in the Senate focused on the astonishingly complex weapons —so complex they were now routinely called weapons systems. But that was to focus on the teeth of the animal rather than the animal itself. The more sophisticated analysts would put it this way: first there are political commitments; then there are force structures to meet those commitments; then there are threats to one or more parties involved in those commitments; then there are military doctrines that govern the use of the forces to counter those threats; then there are strategies to implement the doctrines; then there are deployments to carry out those strategies; then there are tactics to be used by the deployed forces in carrying out their strategies; and only then are there weapons to be used in fulfilling the strategies and the tactics. A plebe at West Point would find such a summary horribly unsophisticated, but it nevertheless serves to make the point that there is more to defense than guns, planes, tanks, and ships.

Most of the debate in the Armed Services Committee and virtually all the debate on military matters before the full Senate related to weapons procurement, yet the procurement of weapons represented only 30 to 40 percent of the annual defense budget. The cost of maintaining a standing military force of more than a million persons was enormous. Those costs included not only the payroll but also housing, a huge military-education infrastructure, health care, transportation, facilities for families, military construction, and a host of other human-resource-related items. Yet personnel issues received relatively little attention from Congress. Politicians, including presidents, were clearly more interested in missiles than people. Almost no attention was given by the committee or the Senate to issues of doctrine, strategy, and tactics. The unspoken rationale was that these were matters for military experts; they were arcana beyond the reach of mere amateurs. Yet only a moment's reflection and even an elementary knowledge of military history would reveal that if we were pursuing the wrong doctrines and strategies, having the most and best weapons would not avail. It became commonplace for reformers, in making this point, to remind anyone who would listen that in 1939 France had more tanks and more men under arms than the Germans, and France fell in forty days.

Three things, then, were important to a strong defense: people, ideas, and weapons. Throughout the seventies and eighties, every senator found it regularly necessary to declare himself in favor of a strong defense. In twelve years, this reformer would never hear a senator announce his support for a weak defense. It had become such a litany that any and all votes having to do with military spending were couched in terms of being for or against a strong defense. Anyone voting against a proposal, however idiotic, narrow, or self-serving, was voting for a weak defense. Likewise, those opposing a military-spending measure would always have to begin their argument, "Mr. President, I am for a strong defense, but . . ."

Nothing attracted extremes more than defense matters. The Pentagon annually offered a budget it knew to be loaded with items it would not get and, truth be known, probably did not even want. These were bones to liberals and those who wished to build a record of "cutting military spending." This artificial waste (as opposed to real waste) would be hacked off in committees and on the Senate floor to the crocodile tears of the services, all of whom had let their congressional friends know ahead of time the list of expendable items. There was the other side of the coin also. Superhawks would add items the military did not request and sometimes did not want. Thus, to please a contractor and/or a union at home, a flying tank or an amphibious whirligig would be added on. This was sometimes done in collusion with the military and sometimes in spite of their adamant opposition. Much of it was an elaborate, scripted ballet, a pas de deux designed to make a record of "being for a strong defense." Aside from wasting time and money, the principal detriment of this folly was that it distracted attention from the first two components of the defense equation—people and ideas.

The Pentagon welcomes attention to personnel matters, both because they are serious and because so few in Congress seem to care about the care, feeding, housing, and general welfare of the service personnel and their families. These matters were not sexy political issues—like MX missiles, stealth bombers, or Trident submarines—that could be used for profit on the campaign stump. To a degree, this cruel truth is a reflection on the American voters. We want "a strong defense," but we do not want it to cost so much, and we certainly do not want to be bothered with the plight of career military people. Citizens, under the guidance of their political leaders, have also come to define strength almost exclusively in terms of weapons.

So those few in Congress who took a genuine interest in the often-neglected human factor in the defense equation found a very receptive welcome from uniformed commanders especially. But the Pentagon did not welcome civilians tampering with military education, the aspect of personnel having to do with doctrine, theory, and strategy.

A military reformer would come to believe that the

critical aspect of America's—or any other country's—defenses had to do with military theory. The best people with the best weapons would be defeated if they were operating according to the wrong doctrine or strategy. The gospel of military reform was, simply put, people, ideas, and weapons, in that order; the best-trained and best-cared-for personnel, following the proper strategies, tactics, and doctrine and using weapons that work in combat. Our motto was "People win wars; weapons don't."

The middle and late seventies represented a winding down of, and final withdrawal from, the war in Vietnam. The Republican Ford administration began to make reductions in military forces and expenditures during 1975 and '76. After great debate, the draft, or compulsory service, was replaced by the all-volunteer force. The ten-year military bulge represented by Vietnam was on the downside of the curve. During the second and third years of the Carter administration, however, military spending began to climb again. This was in part because a voluntary force is more costly, and the maintenance and operation of technically sophisticated weapons, as well as the training of skilled personnel in their use, are all more expensive. In a rush to do away with the hated draft, many neglected the reality that a volunteer force competes in the job market. Higher wages are necessary to attract the increasingly higher-caliber people the system requires. Then came the Soviet invasion of Afghanistan, and the cold war got hotter.

Ronald Reagan built his case in large part on the Soviet threat, accusing the Democrat Carter, who had already begun a military buildup after the Ford years, of being soft on defense. To no one's surprise, Reagan was for "a strong defense." After his 1980 election, we found out what real military spending was. The Pentagon blew the dust off every weapons system ever conceived, and every one of them all came to Congress in the burgeoning military budgets. Democrats, panicked by the pundits into believing Reagan had a carte blanche mandate to get whatever he wanted, gave it to him for several years with regularity.

Woe unto the senator who questioned a Reagan defense budget. He would be suspected of harboring suicidal tendencies. Those were the years when military spending was not government spending. Reagan and the Reaganites recited their little catechisms deploring "wasteful government spending"—except in no case did that awful spending include the largest agency, the largest bureaucracy, and the largest element of the government's budget: the Pentagon. Out of fear or religious fervor, senators and members of Congress refused to point this out. Reagan managed to define a government that did not include the Department of Defense, the good bureaucracy. That department deserved everything it could get. That agency never wasted a nickel, and even if it did, so what? It was all in a good cause.

History will simply stand in awe of the Reagan era. With the help of many Democrats, discretionary nonentitlement spending was cut, and quite severely in the case of some very good, very effective programs for the unemployed, the poor, children, and the elderly. All the while taxes were also massively cut in the face of the largest peacetime military buildup in human history. Federal deficits went ballistic. Reagan's annual deficits averaged four times those of the man he labeled a wasteful spender, Jimmy Carter. And the national debt more than tripled in eight short Reagan years. Throughout, Reagan played the role of Claude Rains and while pocketing his earnings could state with a straight face, "Close this place immediately. There is deficit spending going on here." The reformer watched in horror and years after would still be amazed that the real victims, the American taxpayers, would seem to love every minute of it.

Needless to say, the military-reform movement, officially formed in Congress in 1982, would not find fertile soil in the atmosphere of this giant military casino. Who would wish to think seriously about military training, ideas, and doctrines during an unprecedented shopping spree? It was much more fun to hear the president describe, with a straight face, how thousands of our missiles would shoot down every one of their thousands of missiles. We were drifting through the ultimate military Disneyland with the Great Communicator as our guide. Who cared whether the structures of our military establishment's institutions were sound or creaking? A young army colonel became a heretic and an outcast in the military profession in the 1930s for warning France that the Maginot Line was obsolete, obsolete not only in theory but, even more important, in fact. His name was Charles de Gaulle.

With limited exceptions, the opponents of reform were the senior officers of all the services; the most senior retired military commanders and the traditional institutions to which they belonged; the industry of defense contractors concerned only with next year's contracts; the national security establishment, a self-perpetuating network of so-called experts who frequented the same lecture circuits, spoke to the same audiences, said the same traditional things, dined together, and drank from the same intellectual cup; most members of Congress, liberal and conservative, including those most noted by the political press as military experts; and the political and military press.

Supporters of reform were a small number of members of Congress and senators of both parties, liberals and conservatives alike, increasingly disturbed by the lethargic, simplistic, and ritualistic rhetoric about "a strong defense" and the ineffectual quibbling over weapons systems; younger military officers who had served in Vietnam and seen the folly of old doctrines and methods; a few retired officers—like John Boyd, sometimes called the father of military reform—who saw the desperate need for new approaches; a few genuine defense experts—like Stephen Canby and William Lind—who also proposed alternatives to established practice; and a few senior commanders, mostly marines, and retirees like Admiral Stansfield Turner. This represented a solid but small nucleus.

The reformers proposed changes in military education and promotion, strategies and tactics, and weapons design and procurement. A central reform principle was training officers to think in combat. This required major changes in curricula at the military academies and advanced officer-training colleges. Instead of the heavy emphasis on engineering, physics, and science, young and mid-career officers would study more military history and theory. Promotions would go to those who learned and demonstrated battlefield leadership and could encourage esprit de corps. Changes in force structures were also proposed. Instead of heavily emphasizing the rotation of military personnel (and the rate of that of the United States military is the highest of any modern military power), the Pentagon was urged to adopt something like the British regimental system, which keeps troops and officers together for long periods of time, if not throughout their careers. The idea was to build confidence and esprit and thereby strengthen battlefield competence.

As to military concepts, one of the most central to reform thought was the notion of maneuver warfare. Like large, successful armies before them, the United States land forces were trained and arrayed to invite and prosecute head-on assaults. This doctrine had become a more advanced form of attrition warfare, in which one side traded bodies and weapons with the other until victory was achieved by the army left standing. Attrition essentially describes the military doctrine of World War I (classically) and World War II, except for the island-hopping aspects of General Mac-Arthur's campaign in the Pacific, in which he succeeded in going around dug-in Japanese installations and severing supply lines. Leaving aside the morality of this doctrine, it was deeply troubling to NATO military planners in Central Europe because of the vast size of the Soviet and Warsaw Pact armies. These armies represented a force that might be able to conduct attrition warfare and win. So we hoped that better-trained and better-motivated soldiers and marginally more sophisticated weapons might prevail in a conflict against an enemy of superior numbers. Nonetheless, our doctrine essentially remained attrition warfare—we planned to win by killing more of them than they killed of us.

By contrast, the theory of maneuver warfare is based on the principle that an adversary's will is more important than his size. If his will to fight can be destroyed, his forces will collapse of their own weight. The enemy's will is most effectively destroyed by surprise, by creating unexpected adverse circumstances. Classic examples are the destruction of communications and supply lines, appearing where not expected, the rapid and unexpected movement of forces, and the refusal to present a front that can be attacked directly. Historical examples are the battles fought by Stonewall Jackson and Robert E. Lee's cavalry forces, practically every war fought by the Israelis, and the early fights of Cassius Clay (before he became Muhammad Ali and invented rope-a-dope, which, when one thinks about it, is essentially attrition warfare in reverse). Maneuver requires speed, mobility, and imagination. By implication, this means lighter weapons transported faster, and it means rewarding and promoting battlefield commanders who can seize the moment.

Maneuver warfare is a classic example of how doctrine has an impact on both people and weapons. The style of fighting conditions the kinds of personnel and instruments used. The greatest early proponents of maneuver warfare were middle-level army and marine officers who had served in Vietnam in their early days. They experienced firsthand the mistakes of taking old theories and impractical weapons into an environment in which they did not work. Lives were lost needlessly as a result of this folly. Nothing angers a professional soldier, sailor, or marine more than the unnecessary loss of lives. Many of these career officers who were veterans of Vietnam became the strongest advocates of maneuver doctrine as they rose through the ranks, and many risked their careers to promote this and other reform theories within their service, often over the official theories and practices advocated by their senior commanders.

Their persistence finally and dramatically paid off. In early 1991, the United States deployed roughly a half-million combat and support forces to Saudi Arabia and the Persian Gulf. They were supplemented by British, Saudi, and other forces. They faced an Iraqi military force, including the vaunted Republican Guard, of roughly the same size. Familiar terrain, shorter supply lines, desert training, and defense of the homeland were all to the Iraqis' advantage. Most expert analysts anticipated heavy allied casualties because they assumed traditional attrition doctrine would be employed. Instead, under an American strategic command in large part made up of reform-minded officers who were Vietnam veterans, highly mobile armored units, imaginatively commanded and flexibly gaining agreed-upon objectives, surprised the dug-in Iraqi forces by going around them, swiftly appearing behind them, and severing communications and supply lines. Confronted by the unexpected, the Iraqi command collapsed, and thousands of casualties and tens of thousands of prisoners were taken. Allied casualties were amazingly light. Under American command, the allied forces had followed classic maneuver-warfare doctrine, and it had worked.

Whether the lesson will carry over into the future remains to be seen. Two factors augur well: military officers who planned and carried out Iraqi land operations will be rewarded with promotions and will take their beliefs, now confirmed in practice, with them, and the Gulf War will now enter military-history books, to be studied by future officers. Almost as important is the question of whether the politicians learned anything. If Congress plods methodically along, equipping the military with weapons designed to fight the Soviets in Central Europe, nothing will have been gained.

One clear signal of congressional attitudes will be the naval ship-building program. More than a decade ago military reformers strongly advocated that the Navy begin the long process of moving away from a fleet structure that requires fewer more sophisticated cruisers, destroyers, and frigates supporting huge, expensive, and vulnerable aircraft carriers. The Navy high command, then still heavily composed of officers who had been young carrier pilots in World War II, loved the giant ninety-five-thousand-ton, $3.5- to $4-billion nuclear-powered *Nimitz*-class aircraft carriers. And well they might. They are magnificent tributes to advanced American technology. They had only two problems: they were becoming increasingly vulnerable to Soviet torpedoes and antiship missiles; and they, their planes, and escort ships were so expensive we could afford only about a dozen of them. The same conditions essentially applied to attack submarines. They had become so sophisticated and so expensive we were building fewer and fewer of them.

The battle over the naval ship-building program continued through much of the eighties, as long as this reformer was on the Senate Armed Services Committee, for it was his greatest concern. America is, in practical terms, an island nation. Almost a century before, the American captain Alfred Thayer Mahan, in his classic work on sea power, had demonstrated that the modern world would belong to the nations that built effective, modern oceangoing navies. The British had proved the point in the century and a half after Trafalgar, and the Germans used Mahan's theories in building up their navy before World War I. The United States Navy in the 1970s and '80s was rivaled only by the Soviet navy of Admiral Gorchkov. We were superior in technology but inferior in numbers.

The battle over the naval ship-building program could not have been described as either large scale or particularly effective. It was largely waged by this reformer, who, in this case, was operating well beyond his supply lines. Essentially, for a number of years he advocated a program that would include more but smaller ships, forty-thousand- to forty-five-thousand-ton and twenty-thousand- to twenty-five-thousand-ton conventionally powered carriers, more and less expensive escort ships, battery-powered submarines in greater numbers, new technology roll-on, roll-off transports, hydrofoils, Hovercraft, and so on. Over a decade or two this program would have increased the overall size, capability, and flexibility of the United States Navy and given it a much wider capability. The only problem was that senior naval commanders did not want it, the White House did not begin to comprehend it, and the Congress could not be bothered.

Happily, as in other such military matters, the end of the cold war has removed some of the urgency. The potential for all-out global conflict on a superpower scale has been sharply reduced and, for the time being, quite possibly eliminated. But, as with energy reform, the roof should be repaired while the sun is shining. Tanks and planes have a useful life span of ten or fifteen years. Ships last forty or more years. Well into the 1980s, we were still operating ships whose keels were laid during, or which even saw service in, World War II. The giant nuclear aircraft carriers we are presently building will be in the service of the United States until the decade of the 2030s. We have no idea what the world will look like then. But we do know what Nelson's smaller, more agile ships did to the outdated Spanish behemoths, what German naval guns did to giant British dreadnoughts, what the Japanese navy did to the Russian fleet in 1905, and what our planes did to the Japanese carriers at Midway.

Naval ships, like modern combat aircraft, are increasingly simply carriers of weapons systems. They are increasingly, to use a popular military word, simply platforms. In our defense, we will need platforms at sea as far into the future as one can imagine. Weapons systems are made redundant and obsolete by technology much faster than the platforms are. It is not uncommon for military laboratories to turn out better versions of or replacements for a weapon, guidance system, or radar even as it is beginning to enter production, thus making it obsolete before it is deployed. Even more ominous is the notion that antiweapon weapons—that is, countermeasures to a new weapon —often outpace the weapons themselves. We have no idea what the naval weapons of the twenty-first century will look like. But they will need platforms on the surface and beneath the sea. Even the most novice reformer could understand and appreciate the notion that we should now build more and simpler platforms for our nation's future defenses and equip them to accept whatever modern weapons unborn inventors may devise.

The great mystery of the cold war is how it ended so swiftly and so peacefully. Few intimately involved in the arcane military debates of the 1970s and '80s thought it would happen, and no one envisioned it happening in the way that it did. The urgency of defense and military issues has receded. Yet the great juggernaut rolls on. We created the vast military-industrial complex that President (and former general) Eisenhower had warned us against. Democrats in Congress accede to the continuation of giant defense appropriations not because of threats to our national security but because of threats to their political security if defense plants are closed wholesale. America continues to build staggeringly expensive weapons that it does not need, will never use, and that will eventually rust in some military graveyard, and we do so for one simple reason: jobs. We had no plan to convert our defense factories to domestic production, and we still do not. It was not even a topic of debate in the first post–cold war national elections of 1992. Of necessity, our leaders will be tempted to create threats and enemies to demonstrate the awesomeness of America's military power even as our economy, burdened by these unnecessary defense expenditures, continues to grind downward into obsolescence. We have trapped ourselves in an economy that is now obsolete, and we have no plan or leadership that would convert it to the kind of economy that is required for participation in a new century of economic, not military, competition. The history of the world is littered with the carcasses of dinosaur nations caught in the tar pits of time.

A reformer always prays that someday soon the lion will lie down with the lamb. But until then, America will require a Navy, an Army, an Air Force, and a Marine Corps. We will always require some defenses. That it the nature of our world. But no politician on the scene has a clear picture or a sound plan for the kind of forces we will need and can afford in the next century and the next millennium. The reformer, scarred and fatigued from more than a decade of friendly combat over the reform of our military establishment, still believes that the principles of military reform offer the framework for such a plan. People, ideas, then weapons; maneuver doctrine, less costly and more flexible platforms, weapons that work in the combat zones of the third world, combat leadership, imagination and esprit de corps—these and other basically commonsense notions offer a key to an uncertain future.

The traditional defense establishment—which includes not just the senior serving officers but also the civilian "experts" from the serious institutes and prestigious academies, the defense contractors who produce the weapons, their labor unions and local chambers of commerce, the congressional committees and their staffs, armchair admirals and clean-desk generals—now has a unique opportunity, an opportunity given few nations in their entire history. It is the opportunity to restructure, rethink, and revitalize—to reform—the entire defense complex of the United States to meet a new, uncertain future. This is a very great blessing, and history will condemn us if we waste it. Even more important, our sons and daughters—those who will bear the financial costs of the defenses we bequeath them and those who make the ultimate sacrifice—will condemn us if we waste it.

Reformers, by nature from the so-called liberal ranks, have found military matters awkward and unappetizing. Too many have adopted the posture of watching the battle from above and then, after it was safely over, going onto the field to shoot the wounded. Liberals have found it easy to condemn and occasionally demean the military career, those who have made national defense a career and a profession. The reformer would repeatedly have occasion to recall one of his favorite scenes in modern fiction, from Herman Wouk's *Caine Mutiny*. After having been essentially exonerated, the mutineers gather to celebrate and are given a drunken toast by their military defense counsel, Lieutenant Greenwald. After listening to their prideful boasts and peals of self-congratulation at their clear intellectual and moral superiority over the hapless, destroyed Captain Queeg, Greenwald says, "Gentlemen, while I was studying law . . . those birds we call regulars—those stuffy, stupid Prussians, in the Navy and the Army were manning guns. Course they weren't doing it to save my mom from Hitler, they were doing it for dough, like everybody else does. . . . Question is in the last analysis, what do you do for dough? [Captain Queeg] for dough, was standing guard on this fat dumb and happy country of ours. . . . So when all hell broke loose and the Germans started running out of soap and figured, well it's time to come over and melt down old Mrs. Greenwald— who's gonna stop them? . . . Who was keeping momma out of the soap dish? Captain Queeg."

The reformer's creed is that we will serve our nation, our children, and the cause of democracy better by having a reformed and effective national defense than by having an outdated, outsized national defense or none at all.

13

REFORM AND
THE DISMAL SCIENCE

The most daunting task facing political leaders and private citizens alike is reaching an understanding of the constantly changing new global economy and then embracing the structural reforms necessary to assure America's place in it. This is not made easier by the very real fact that the science of economic theory and practice is decidedly dismal. Dismal or not, however, this newly elected Senate reformer would be forced by bitter reality to appreciate that only through the dreadful gateway of economics could one hope to achieve enfranchisement for the disadvantaged, an improved quality of human existence, and stability for emerging democracies around the world.

Bitter reality began to make itself felt in 1974, when the Organization of Petroleum Exporting Countries reduced its oil exports, thus raising world oil prices by a factor of four and then, in 1977, to a total of ten times higher than the sleepy, comfortable 1974 price levels. More quietly, but equally dramatically, beneath the surface the national economies of Japan and Germany were beginning to emerge as internationally competitive, especially in the areas of technology and manufacturing, which had long been assumed to be subject to United States supremacy in perpetuity. Totally unnoticed at the time were the ominous downward trends in real income in America and in gross domestic product growth and the institutionalization of public deficits. There were also suggestions that public school test scores might not be all they should, that the economies of great cities such as New York were startlingly fragile, that giant corporations might not be as solid as their advertising suggested, and that we might be poisoning ourselves with, among other things, chemical and nuclear wastes.

It was not as if the United States had not had difficulties before, having faced at one time or another, for example, national bankruptcy. But a student of the nation's history would be hard pressed to recall a time when such a great number of massive structural problems began to emerge out of the mist of the New World like so many monstrous icebergs swirling around the U.S.S. *America*. In almost every case, the political and financial systems of the nation responded with traditional, marginal solutions—bailouts; quick fixes; makeshift, jury-rigged ad hoc schemes—and little else. The discovery of flaws and fractures in the national economic infrastructure occurred so gradually and incidentally that few thought to cry danger and most were concerned that the public not panic. Many political leaders of both parties refused to admit the seriousness of the challenge for fear of being thought alarmist and, more important, because they had no solutions.

Complicating matters was the network of safety nets woven during the darkest days of the Great Depression. The system of buffers against individual or systemic collapse—Social Security insurance, Medicare and Medicaid, federal insurance for banks and financial institutions, regulations of the stock and commodities markets, and a host of other programs—effectively pledged the good faith and credit of the government of the United States against disaster. Once burned, twice taught. We would never again let things get so far out of hand that whole structures collapsed. Yet this philosophy neglected forces beyond our control: international economic competition, the internationalization of financial markets, the nation's subtle dependence on foreigners to finance our public deficits, the massive flow of American capital offshore for Middle Eastern oil and Far Eastern television sets.

So while economic structures rusted and cracked, they were propped up by federal guarantees that themselves never contemplated an age of internationalization. Predictably, the political response to the rusting and cracking was paint and patches; the response to international competition was threats and warnings. For fear of what they might discover, few would think to explore the subterranean caverns of the national infrastructure or consider that foreigners must simply be turning out better products at lower prices. In part under pressure from constituency interests, the Democrats—long the free trade party of America—succumbed to protectionist measures. Quotas, duties, and tariffs were the answer for American industries operating outdated plants and equipment with workers unskilled in modern manufacturing techniques. Beyond that, the best that most Democrats could devise were half-baked Keynesian tax cuts or spending increases to jump-start an economy perilously close to falling off its tracks.

For their part, the Republicans of the seventies were satisfied to recite ritualistic incantations of nineteenth-century laissez-faire. Equally predictably, this merely became a Pavlovian conditioning exercise for supply-side economics, the great economic fraud of the century. In the 1980s, taxes were massively cut for individuals and corporations in the hope that taxpayers would save and invest income and profit in new productive ventures. This was surely the most naïve or calculated mistake in recent history—naïve in the belief that a consuming culture would not simply increase its consumption (which it did) and calculated if the real intent (as this reformer believed all along) was to destroy the government's social functions through starvation and bankruptcy. In whichever case, the national budget was brought near the edge of ruin, and most important, traditional macroeconomic levers were jammed or broken.

In the 1990s, further tax cuts or spending increases, to stimulate economic growth in traditional Keynesian ways, were proscribed because it was assumed they would contribute to already mountainous deficits. Throughout 1992, the reduction of lending rates by the Federal Reserve Board ("printing more money") was effectively urged by an increasingly desperate Bush administration, but with the result of lowering interest rates to the point where foreign lenders were no longer interested in purchasing public United States debt instruments. Massive cuts in defense spending were unacceptable because of the negative effects such cuts would have on local economies, unemployment rates, and the giant defense industries' corporate profits. Indeed, the 1992 presidential campaign witnessed the sorry but predictable exercise of incumbent and challenger promising more contracts for unneeded weapons systems as a bizarre kind of public works jobs program.

Ronald Reagan left many strange monuments, but none stranger than something called the Strategic Defense Initiative (Star Wars), a colossal exercise in learning to shoot bullets with bullets. Leaving aside the endless list of demerits for such a phantasm, it gave this reformer the springboard for his own economic reform plan in the late 1980s. It would be called a Strategic Investment Initiative and would focus on the following principles: rewarding savings and productive investment after the fact; taxing consumption, especially energy consumption; reforming the defense establishment to make it more effective and less costly; empowering workers through investment in education and job training; massively rebuilding infrastructures; establishing federal incentives for new product and technology research; planning for a balanced reduction of the deficit; and promoting universal education and literacy.

Admittedly, this set of policy reforms ran contrary to the laissez-faire mood of the day. They required the federal government to become a catalyst that would induce private-sector initiatives. This was so because markets are politically neutral: they have no sense of the national interest and commonweal. Markets do not invest in the minds of children, in the roads of the nation or its communities, or in innovations of the future. Markets do not provide milk for babies living in poverty, nor do they preserve the homes and communities of steelworkers when mills are shut down. *Markets* was the watchword for those who extolled the virtues of the engine of free enterprise while refusing to maintain and modernize that engine.

Economic reform, whether in the form of strategic investment initiatives or national investment policy, should be built on the notion of economic empowerment. Present and future workers deserve the assistance of their government in achieving and maintaining the skills necessary to equip them for the jobs of the future. Students, for example, including those who cannot presently afford the degree of higher education they desire, could receive loans guaranteed by the national government in the form of equity investments. Through private lending organizations or a new specialized bank, the government could establish a line of credit for all who wish to be students. The amount of the loan would be equivalent to the cost of tuition and other expenses associated with a postsecondary education and would be paid back over a worker's productive lifetime by a surtax on the income that was enhanced by that educational opportunity.

For existing workers, a similar system of individual-training accounts would maintain skills. This system would also have to be enhanced by a reformed system of trade-adjustment assistance and expanded job-training partnerships with the private sector. This new social compact with workers would require job-relocation insurance, advance notice of plant closing, and guarantees of pension portability and retirement security. Worker empowerment should also include a sense of owning a job through employee stock-option plans, quality-of-life programs, gain sharing and profit sharing, and rewards for incentive and productivity.

As needs for defense production decrease substantially at the end of the cold war, defense industries and their organized workers should be given new national tasks to perform rather than encouraged to build totally unnecessary weapons (for resale abroad, contributing to the international arms-proliferation race). This work should be in rebuilding the national infrastructure of roads, bridges, dams, highways, ports, and inner-city transportation systems. To finance this project, a national-infrastructure fund should be created and funded at a rate of three billion or so dollars per year for ten or more years. This fund would make twenty-year loans at no interest to the states and would be repayable over the life of the loan out of state revenues. The states, in turn, would set up infrastructure banks or revolving funds that would allow them to enter into contracts with private corporations, including former defense contractors, to carry out construction and repair projects. The original thirty-billion-dollar fund could leverage up to seventy-five billion dollars or more in new infrastructure spending over the thirty-year life of the program.

Taxes on energy, especially a ten-dollar-per-barrel fee on imported oil and a fifty-cent increase on gasoline taxes graduated in ten-cent increments over five years, would raise tens of billions of dollars in new revenue for deficit reduction, scholarships and school loans, and projects for rebuilding the infrastructure while also reducing unnecessary use of energy and stimulating the development of alternative sources of renewable energy. Such measures would do more than any others to turn a wasteful consuming nation into an effective producing nation.

Further savings can occur through wholesale military reforms. America's security needs are now drastically different from what they were before 1991, but we have yet to acknowledge this historic fact in any concrete way. No better argument for this proposition can be made than that which the historian Paul Kennedy put forward in a magazine article as early as 1987:

Although defense expenditures amounted to ten percent of GNP under President Eisenhower and nine percent under President Kennedy, America's share of global production and wealth were at that time around twice what they are today. . . . The United States now devotes about seven percent of GNP to defense spending, while its major economic rivals, especially Japan, allocate a far smaller proportion. If this situation continues . . . then it seems inevitable that the American share of world manufacturing will decline steadily, and likely that American economic growth rates will be slower than those of countries dedicated to the marketplace and less eager to channel resources into defense.

When the full force of the tidal waves of internationalization began to strike America's shores in the
second half of the 1970s and in the 1980s, nothing
would stun the still-naïve reformer more than the intricate avoidance mechanisms that grown political and
corporate leaders could invent. While innovations
from American laboratories were being developed,
commercialized, and marketed by overseas firms,
while America was running the risk of becoming simply the world's library and not its most advanced fac-
tory, leadership was sadly lacking. One captain of
industry, famous for his televised fulminations aimed
at his foreign competitors, whose enterprise "out-
sourced" the manufacture of automobiles abroad,
endorsed harsh protectionist measures one week
after depositing his twenty-three-million-dollar bonus
check.

Such protectionism comes at a very high price.
Though acknowledged as such by few protectionist
politicians, America is one of the world's greatest protectionist nations, with quotas on foreign cars and tariffs, duties, and quotas on textiles, food products,
steel, and many other items. Because of existing protectionist measures, American consumers spend tens
of billions of dollars in higher prices, but the protected
industries have not become any more competitive or
any more productive. Investment in new plants and
equipment does not increase. Workers' jobs are not
saved—or they are saved at incredible costs. Only corporate profits are really protected. In the late eighties,
the cost per job saved by protectionism was regularly
more than $100,000 per year per worker. It was
$290,000 per year for orange-juice processors,
$500,000 for steelworkers, and only $30,000 for rubber workers. Perhaps the workers so protected might
simply prefer a one-time direct payment.

The great albatross and the Reagan legacy to America—quadrupled annual deficits and national debts—

weighed down all thoughts of economic reform. It represented the greatest test and greatest failure of American democracy in the last two decades of the twentieth century. By effectively eliminating one of the central ingredients of a healthy federal budget—revenues—the Great Communicator laid the groundwork for a generation of political cowardice. The best Congress could produce in the form of deficit control —not reduction—was the so-called Gramm-Rudman law. Seen by some as well intentioned, by others as a sinister plot, and by too many as nothing but a convenient political escape hatch, it became simply a weapon that allows Congress, like Bill Sykes in *Oliver Twist*, to use "the knife not I killed the lady" defense for cuts in favorite programs.

Until all the items listed in the federal-spending, defense, and entitlement programs and the panoply of sacred cows are on the table to be considered for reduction and reform, and until the occupant of the White House and Congress can agree on a range of new revenues from consumption, not income, there is no chance the albatross of public debt and national deficit can be shed by the American economy. And until that anchor can be shed, it will be difficult or impossible to work the kind of economic reforms the nation so desperately needs in order to help shape the new global economy.

When America faced collapse in the 1930s, we rebuilt the very foundations of the national economy. We marshaled our strength behind national investments, experimental policies, and institutional reforms: a renewed infrastructure and manufacturing base, a reformed financial structure, and a new national commitment to a better standard of living throughout society. Enlightened leadership made national recovery possible, but it had to overcome forces of inertia and traditionalism and the old voices calling for only marginal change.

With our democratic allies a decade later, we created out of the ruins of war a remarkable engine of world economic growth, which offered hope and opportunity to the Western world. Visionary leaders created the International Monetary Fund, the World Bank, and the General Agreement on Tariffs and Trade, the Magna Charta of international trade. These new institutions of reform permitted us and our allies to enjoy more than three decades of prosperity, helped to secure a durable peace, and insulated Western Europe against Communist threats.

Now, almost a half century later, we need leaders of the same caliber, vision, and action—Roosevelts, Churchills, Marshalls, and Monnets—leaders who recognize the truth of Lord Keynes's observation that "the difficulty lies not in the new ideas, but in escaping from the old ones." At a time when America must look inward and outward at the same time, the reformer would wonder why a broader-gauge, bigger-picture coterie of leaders did not emerge. Political careerism, media leveling, and political cowardice would account for some of the dilemma, but not all of it. Perhaps the crisis has not deepened enough. Perhaps people have to become gravely frightened before they will find a Roosevelt and give him or her the authority to do bold things, to experiment and reorganize, to undertake the sweeping institutional reforms necessary to remake America for the new millennium.

But the social, economic, and political protections adopted during the last great national crisis help buffer against similar shocks today. Therefore, we are insulated against the new, harsh realities that are less visible but no less threatening than those of the 1930s. By comparison with a wholesale remodeling of the American economy, the reforms of the intelligence community, of our energy policies and practices, and even of our military and defense establishments would seem relatively simple.

As a science, economics might be seen as dismal. But nothing could so consume every practical aspect of America's life. Having passed through an era of simplicity (if not of simplemindedness) with many unpaid debts to mark the experience, Americans perhaps were ready to listen to voices of reason, seriousness, and honesty. Citizen Ross Perot, had he had a firmer grasp of the political realities of his own country, might have performed a historic service, the service he really wanted to perform as the late-twentieth-century Paul Revere. When he finally found both voice and sea legs, one pillar of a reformed economy—fiscal sanity—was there. Alas, the messenger let other considerations obscure the message.

The opportunity would remain, whether for President Clinton or someone else, to enter the pantheon of great reformers by educating the American people to the new economic realities of the late twentieth century and the great chances of the twenty-first century, by proposing the sweeping new policies of productivity, learning, inventing, and trading, and by forming the new national consensus to create the economy of the future.

14

THE ERA
OF QUAYLE

The United States Senate changed its character in 1980, or more precisely, its character was fundamentally changed by the national elections of that year. It became younger, more media-alert, better looking, more focused, more orderly, better controlled, more businesslike, smoother, more suburban, more efficient, more bland, more presentable, and more certain of almost everything. It also became meaner, more glib, more superficial, more intolerant, more menacing, more regimented, much more right wing, and in many ways much, much sillier.

Gone were Mansfield, Muskie, Pastore, Ribicoff, Nelson, Philip Hart, McGovern, Church, Bayh, Magnuson, Javits, Case, Symington, Stevenson, and a pantheon of senior, serious figures. In most cases, much different men replaced them. Decades of institutional memory disappeared overnight.

The Republican party had suffered in the minority for more than a generation, and it was in the mood for control, if not also vengeance. Many felt oppressed by what they saw as the Democratic majority's heavy-handedness and arrogance over the years. There was undoubtedly some merit here. The way of politics is this: power brings control, and if you have control, use it. Over the years, the Democrats had used it, often quite heavily. Now things would change. Democrats, rudely shocked by their new minority status, would find the position more uncomfortable than they might have imagined.

When majority control of a house of Congress changes, the leadership also changes, as does control of the committees, where the tedious work of preparing authorization and appropriation bills, budgets, and preliminary legislative drafts goes on. In some ways, most important of all, control of the increasingly important staffs of the committees also changed, passing to the Republicans. Howard Baker of Tennessee, a tolerant and fair man of the pre-Reagan school of Republicans, became the Senate majority leader, replacing Robert Byrd of West Virginia, and all committees were chaired by senior Republicans. Their collective mandate was first to enact the Reagan programs and second to restore traditional Republican values to government.

Alacrity characterized the pace of action on the Reagan program. A sense of mission—in some cases, even destiny—seemed to permeate the work of the more ardent Reaganites. The atmosphere was feverish. The White House, wielding a sturdy whip hour after hour and day after day, seemed to believe the real rulers might show up and throw them out or, more ominously, that the people might sober up and discover that the sentences did not parse and the equations did not add up.

First, massive cuts in spending on programs for human beings and the public infrastructure had to be made. This death of a thousand cuts was cleverly carried out en masse so that no single constituency could identify its particular sacrifice and cry for help. It took the form of something called the Gramm-Latta bill, after its congressional sponsors, and it was also cleverly rushed through the House of Representatives, where the most opposition from majority Democrats was to be expected after the bout of Reagan fever had subsided. The sponsors need not have worried. It sailed right through, with the happy support of both "leaders" and rank-and-file Democrats, in spite of the fact that the bill was more than nine hundred pages long and so crudely and sloppily drafted that telephone numbers were written on the pages of the draft submitted for enrollment. It was a legislative travesty, a joke, and everyone knew it, and everyone laughed about it, and too many people voted for it. Congressional Democrats were slaughtered in their tents, and the revolution was on.

Next, the Republican-controlled Senate Armed Services Committee pounded through a whopping defense budget for fiscal 1982, just the first of a large number to follow. It was much bigger than the nation's defenses required and contained weapons and programs the Pentagon did not even have the heart to request. Under this mandate, Congress would eventually authorize a six-hundred-ship Navy (of the wrong kinds of ships) built around several giant, new nuclear aircraft carriers; the MX missile; the B-1 bomber, whose costs doubled and then tripled; the Trident submarine and the Trident missile; full-scale production of F-15 and F-16 combat aircraft; the stealth bomber and the stealth fighter; the M-1 "Abrams" tank; the Bradley armored infantry carrier, which was a rolling tinderbox; and a list of major weapons-procurement initiatives that choked defense production lines for years to come. Like the budget cuts, the idea of the

Reaganites was to get keels laid, production lines open, programs under way, contractual commitments made, workers hired, designs drawn, orders placed—all before the total costs, and questions about paying for it, could be raised. Everyone knew that it is much more difficult to stop a new weapons program than to start one. The public stocks of defense contractors soared.

The third element of the equation was the crucial one, the centerpiece: tax rates were to be lowered substantially and tax brackets reduced in number. The grand theory, repeated throughout the late seventies and early eighties like a catechism, was that this would stimulate investment and growth and generate tranches of new revenues more than sufficient to pay for the hoard of new military purchases and eliminate the deficit. This was demonstrably false, and at least some of those who proclaimed it—including the soon-to-be-infamous budget director, David Stockman—knew it to be false. The clear history of the decade should erase any doubt. In any civilized society, the authors of the ruse—Gramm, Kemp, Stockman, and an assortment of editorial writers and columnists, mostly from *The Wall Street Journal*—would have been sent to Elba or clapped in irons. But America is too polite to its real political victimizers.

Throughout those heady days of the early eighties, the Senate was a kind of controlled madhouse. Major legislation, much of it unwise or outright bad, was routinely enacted with only the justification that "the president wants it." Endless singsong speeches, more appropriately litanies, were chanted on the Senate floor, proclaiming yet again the wonders and the glories of the Reagan revolution. Young, scrubbed new senators, sounding and looking very much alike, routinely and increasingly tiresomely announced the dawn of a new era, the birth of a new age, the coming of a new millennium. It was, God save us, "morning in America."

There was not a moment's true thought in any of it. It was nothing but the tritest pomp and circumstance, bluster and blather, bunkum and hokum. The mindlessness of it all would make a reformer weep for years thereafter, weep for his country and for its sanity. The big balloon was going up, and to watch it go while one's feet were unalterably rooted in reality brought on a lonely feeling. There is something about even the meanest parade that makes one want to march. This was the parade of a lifetime. The dark night of oil shortages and price shocks, of stagflation, of embassy hostages, of malaise, and of national doubt was over. It was all going to be all right.

The aging reformer would grasp at any straw of reality in this whirlwind of political bliss. Just to test his sanity, he would seek out a colloquy on the vacant Senate floor with his learned and thoughtful friend Daniel Patrick Moynihan of New York, who for seriousness of scholarship and appreciation of the lessons of history stood out like a tall pine in short grass, and he would ask whether the nation really might spend and tax-cut its way out of deficits, whether the Russians really were thirty feet tall and just over the horizon, whether all those on public assistance, including increasing numbers of very small children, really were bums and malingerers. Moynihan was a blessing because he would provide a periodic reality check and do so with little of the anger and frustration demonstrated by the reformer.

Much else that characterized this period in the Senate was nothing but the utmost nonsense. Many new senators seemed obliged to point out the obvious at excruciating lengths, as if those who had gone before were total ignoramuses. They felt divinely inspired, as if just sent down from heaven with the truth. They considered repetition an art form and practiced it often. Like all zealots, they felt the heathen would eventually convert or go mad if the gospel were repeated often enough. It was occasionally a little frightening to see across the committee table or the Senate floor those innocent faces earnestly preaching the gospel according to Reagan, sent up that very day by apostles in the White House for the edification of the remaining savages on the Hill. It evoked sadness in the reformer, who longed for the days of literate rhetoric and reasoned debate, of serious statesmen and reverence for history. But it had the consolation of proving once again that America was strong enough to survive anything, including this hopefully temporary invasion by the new righteous.

More disturbing than this onslaught by the Reagan pure was the overall performance of the Democrats. Too many caved in and went along, not out of conviction but out of political expediency, acting against the principles and history of their party either because they were afraid to face the voters as serious opposition figures or because their party had not discovered an alternative to Reagan policies. Here reform offered an answer, one of those rare answers that was both right politically and right in principle.

The Democrats of the Reagan years had become the minority party of the Senate and were on the run in the House because no comprehensive set of ideas transforming or superseding the New Deal had been constructed for a new era, an era of transition. By the 1970s, the New Deal, as updated by the Great Society of the sixties, had come to represent three things: Keynesian macroeconomics, according to which selected tax cuts and spending increases would be used to level out the periodic downturns in the economy; entitlement programs such as Social Security, Medicare, and Medicaid; and individual new program initiatives to address society's social problems. Increasingly in the 1970s, the Democrats had been called on to bail out failing industries, such as Chrysler, the Penn Central Railroad, and others, and even failing cities, such as New York. The federal government was fast becoming the ultimate guarantor against failure, a troubling thought to many newer Democrats.

The Reaganites adopted Keynesianism and dramatically raised the ante. In their zeal to destroy the New Deal and all its vestiges, they briefly toyed with the notion of limiting the entitlement programs, and they got their fingers badly burned. Thus, they found the permissible limits of the Reagan revolution. So the real battle was over discretionary spending—all those other ad hoc programs in health, education, job training, community assistance, and so on that the Democrats had enacted, often with the compliance of Republicans, to respond to some social or political demand. Contrary to Reagan's constant harping that the Democratic Congress would not cut spending, these programs were cut, and cut severely, with a majority of Democrats in both houses in the fore.

In the late sixties, the Democratic party had been deeply divided over the militarization of foreign policy and the nature of the Communist threat. The division was over Vietnam. But by the seventies, divisions were also occurring over economic theory and practice. National economic growth had greatly slowed because of increases in energy prices. There were fewer discretionary dollars in the treasury to finance the new spending programs that older, more traditional Democrats continued to seek. Newer Democrats, this reformer among them, sensed the country's growing resentment of deficit spending and its resistance to adding new programs. The public itself was hardly consistent. Repeatedly throughout the seventies and eighties, the reformer had in his Senate office constituent groups from Colorado bearing two messages: the federal deficit is too high—cut back spending; and, by the way, can you help us get some money for that new dam we want? Most of these same people would vote for Reagan because of their first request, and later they would be shocked to find there was no money for the second.

The new congressional Democrats of the period were more cautious about new social programs, sharing their constituents' suspicions about government effectiveness; they were more inclined to resist the commitment of military forces here and there and to question in considerable detail the need for new weapons; they were interested in stimulating the growth of the emerging service and information sectors of the economy; and they were drawn toward seeking technological solutions to the energy crisis and other new challenges. Most of all, there were hundreds of individual, largely unorganized efforts under way to redefine the role of a government that their ideological forebears had fashioned and become comfortable with. In short, there was a quiet but highly important generational revolution going on in the Democratic party.

During the period of the Republican majority in the Senate, new Democrats—Bradley of New Jersey, Rockefeller of West Virginia, Gore of Tennessee, and a number of others—began to appear. By and large, they were progressive—what conservatives would pejoratively label liberal (certainly by comparison)—as well as skeptical, pragmatic, and searching. As graduates of the sixties, they combined a social conscience with a keen awareness of the evolution in social values in areas such as race and gender relations, environmental concerns, and culture and life-style. Being closer in tune with the country's desire for change, they were more open to ideas for reform in the economy, defense, and foreign policy.

Politically, the new Democratic leadership of the eighties did not arrive soon enough to head off the Reagan dominance and the antireform mentality it represented. But history is history and cannot be changed. This emerging group of new Democrats did not fit the stereotypes used by Reagan for his partisan lampoons and therefore made it increasingly difficult for the Reagan flacks to mischaracterize the Democratic party. More important, they were head and shoulders above their new Republican counterparts. The contrast was striking. The newer Democrats were verbal, thoughtful, capable of reason and debate, well read, and intelligent. Even if the Democratic party had a liturgical grab bag of trite phrases—like supply-side economics, strong defense, and tax-cuts-investment-growth—its newer leaders were not inclined to rely on them totally.

The Senate of the early eighties, like the president, fit the public mood. There was widespread hunger for simple answers to complex problems. Regular people were tired of partisan pettiness and confusion. They felt, particularly after Vietnam and the Iran hostage crisis, that the United States was being pushed around by tinhorns and petty tyrants. They did not want leaders who tried to reason with them or who tried to engage them in the confusing dilemmas facing the nation. They wanted "strength," and it mattered less in the short run that the strong defense, or the strong economy, or the strong leader were the wrong ones, just as long as they were strong. It was a word that came to symbolize the decade.

It certainly dominated Senate debates in the early eighties. The reformer heard it endlessly, echoing up and down the Senate corridors, bouncing between ceiling and floor of committee rooms, and always punctuating every speech in the ornate cavern of the Senate chamber. *Strong*—it was the adjective of choice regardless of the circumstance. *Strength*—it was the very word to prevail in any debate. To question the wisdom of the policy or program was, ipso facto, to favor weakness. Any question raised about deficits or new weapons systems or unjust enrichment of the wealthy would draw a contemptuous smile and the suggestion that the questioner wanted to return to an era of weakness, subservience, submissiveness. The fact that such a time had never existed was beside the point.

There was a lot of the bullyboy about all this, a bluff designed to silence dissent. Vast shifting of wealth upward, stealing from the poor and the middle class to enrich the rich, plundering accounts, raiding corporate treasuries, wholesale aggrandizement of greed—all were swept up in the era of strength. The Darwinian notion that the strong were rich and the rich strong was implicit in Reaganomics. Anyone who seriously believed that unregulated markets would lead to a substantial increase in the standard of living for the middle and lower classes was a bounder or a fool—a bounder for peddling patent poppycock or a fool for believing it. It never had happened, and it never will. Unrestrained financial land rushes benefit only the large hogs. Those with wealth beyond the dreams of avarice would reap staggering benefits from Reagan tax cuts while a million more American children fell below the poverty line.

There was no trickle down. Those who preached it in the eighties should be placed in public stocks, pilloried, and publicly mocked. It was a travesty. But it was strong. The Reagan disciples in the Senate either did not know or did not care that the scheme was a fraud. Either way they deserve at least to be dismissed from public service. Reaganomics represents the greatest raid on the public treasury in American history. But it was clever. Instead of simply stealing existing public money, the Reaganites stole future public money. They just mortgaged the store and passed the mortgage money out to their wealthy and powerful friends. It was not their money, and it was not your money. It was your children's money. They stole money from your children and had a great party with it. The 1980s represent nothing less than an extravaganza carried out by and for the rich. The bill is waiting for your children when they grow up. Simply remember that, when you feel inclined to congratulate Ronald Reagan on his strength.

Abandoned in the mad rush toward strength for private wealth and weakness for the people's government was any sense of social conscience or public obligation, of the commonweal and the common good, of responsibility for future generations and the public trust. These were notions incompatible with strength. They were beliefs held only by weak Democrats and softhearted liberals. To be that most contemptible of creatures, a liberal, was to be the weakest possible form of life, a spineless amoeba that deserves nothing better than to be crushed by the strong. Liberalism was, and still is, used to characterize all those who disagree, to denigrate dissenters, to pillory and shame those who do not subscribe to the Reagan far-right values.

The American people, recovering from the binge, are beginning to discover that there were certain costs involved in abandoning the values of community, conscience, and the public interest, for these were part of the liberal values so contemptuously dismissed by the strong of the eighties. Like it or not, poverty has increased, especially among children, deficits and debts continue on a ballistic course, the tycoons of Reaganomics languish in cells, the monstrous bill for collapsed, unregulated thrift institutions has come due, the cost of health care soars, our children are no better educated, our cities are no safer, our roads and bridges are no stronger, and we have a lot of weapons we do not need. The orgy of strength was fun, at least for some, while it lasted. But it carried some bitter costs. The champagne has gone flat. It is no longer "morning in America."

The United States Senate, the fulcrum of the Reagan revolution, is back in the hands of the Democratic party. The burden of fashioning policies that work, policies based on national interests rather than special interests, is shifting back to the former opposition. It is a time ripe with possibility for reform. It is unfortunate that the early eighties were not better used by the Democrats to fashion a national reform agenda for the day when power and responsibility would return. While the Reagan senatorial royalists and loyalists were carrying on about strength and chanting their mantras about supply-side theory, newer Democrats could have been quietly shaping ideas and policies for the 1990s and beyond. A plan for national energy independence could have been discussed and shaped. An agenda for military reform after the cold war could have been anticipated. New economic structures could have been examined and tested. A post–cold war foreign policy could have taken shape.

In fact, some of this preparation had begun to take place. Ad hoc discussion groups began to spring up among new, progressive congressional Democrats in basements on Capitol Hill. New thinkers were brought in to discuss advanced industrial policy, creative military theory, innovative economic ideas, health-care systems, and the like. Names like Gephardt, Baucus, Bradley, Fazio, and many others represented regular attendees. The military-reform effort continued on its singular and lonely course, largely behind the scenes, as the Reagan military juggernaut grew and consumed all in its path. Small progressive think tanks around Washington and around the country became hothouses for new species of ideas designed eventually to replace Reagan policies when they failed or were dismissed. It would not equal the intense ferment within American conservatism throughout the sixties and seventies, but it was a start.

The start, however, would not be sufficient in scope or in time to represent a comprehensive programmatic alternative to the Reagan agenda as displayed in the Senate of the first half of the eighties. Howard Baker would play at least as fairly with the Democrats as the Democrats had played with him, but his party controlled the high ground and the big guns. Scaffolding from which to dismantle environmental, safety, transportation, and banking regulations was swiftly erected, and destruction was eagerly begun. Along with much regulatory dross, basic protections of the public interest were rather laughingly crumpled up and trashed. Programs that even the Republicans of the more bipartisan, statesmanlike era of the fifties and sixties had agreed to were summarily drawn and quartered. As Democrats scrambled to scavenge and save what few treasures they could carry from more enlightened times in their desperate retreat from the rapidly advancing Visigoths, political prisoners, especially the detested liberals, were routinely rounded up and shot.

Rather than stand and fight, many Democrats capitulated. Reasoning as others in similar circumstances have done throughout the ages, that the national heritage is better protected by collaboration with the conquerors, they stayed behind to try to seek accommodation. The strategy succeeded only rarely and then at great cost. To seek negotiations with those who reject one's basic premises is to be forced to adopt an alien frame of reference. Furthermore, in the case of the Senate from 1981 through 1986, the Republican majority did not need Democratic votes. Democrats had no strength from which to bargain. All they could hope for were political crumbs and the conquerors' promise of survival under menial conditions.

Sadly, there were Democrats who collaborated in exchange for the hope of political survival. Reagan's vaunted popularity, which the reformer never thought was as deep as did the wise pundits of Washington, frightened many insecure Democrats, including a surprising number who regularly won by landslides in their states and districts. These landslides were the result of years of piling up considerable hoards of political capital. Rather than spending some of that capital in defense of the values of the Democratic party, if not its programs and policies, these Democrats, including a number who were considered leaders, chose to negotiate peace terms with the Reaganites. In exchange for votes on tax cuts for the rich, military expenditures, and cuts in human resource programs, the names of those cooperating were removed from the list of recalcitrant Democrats regularly thrashed by the White House. There were other important rewards: invitations to state dinners (Washington's coin of the realm and most important barometer of status), a benign grin and nod of the head from the popular president himself, appearances on Sunday-television analysis programs to give the "opposition" point of view, a kindly word from leading Republicans back home for "supporting the president."

Guerrilla warfare is the alternative to collaboration, and it is never a pleasant one. The guerrilla sacrifices the comforts of polite society, takes to the political hills, and conducts unexpected raids that often distress and embarrass his accommodationist allies. Resistance is alienation, from friend and foe alike. It means challenging premises and frames of reference quietly accepted by conqueror and conquered. It often appears mean-spirited and last-ditch not to go along with the merriment of the bright new era. Resisters and guerrillas quickly earn unpleasant reputations in polite society. Those on the lam receive few dinner invitations. De Gaulle was hated by the Vichy French.

Daniel Patrick Moynihan, a real resistance fighter, as befits his race, would have none of it. He told the truth, fired at will, and devil-take-the-hindmost. Together with this reformer, he early and often promoted the theory of a sinister Reagan agenda. Using as evidence the infamous confession of an original supply-sider, David Stockman, he argued that the real purpose of the Reagan team was to dismantle as many publicly supported social structures as the times would permit. He believed, correctly, that what was really going on reached far back, before the Great Society, to the New Deal, that, amazingly, harbored deep within the conservative breast was an abiding anger with Franklin Roosevelt, the hated socialist, that had lasted a half century. Reagan represented the Restoration, the return of the economic royalists banished for five decades by progressive, reform governments to the darkest recesses of the reactionary social clubs, traditionalist boardrooms, and old-school secret societies. The tool for the destruction of the awful works of liberal government was the federal budget itself. The plot was simple. Under the guise of Keynesian tax cuts and military buildups, they would bankrupt the federal treasury. They would literally starve the government, a government they had come to hate when it ceased to serve them and became an instrument of the common people. Except for its defense functions, most of this cabal no longer considered it their government. So down with it.

If the plot succeeded, there would simply be no money for health programs, federal aid to education, assistance to the cities, public works, jobs programs, meals for the elderly, and most of all, *welfare*—the blackest symbol of government at its worst. There are only two choices: the supply-siders were fools, or they were up to something. Reagan himself and perhaps one or two others, including a future vice-president, may not have quite understood it all. *Fools* would be a reckless, uncharitable charge even for an angry reformer. But there were some there who could do and had done their math. It did not add up because it could not add up. The real agenda was to kill the domestic side of the national government by starvation. What else could George Bush have possibly meant in his moment of epiphany when he harpooned it in the heart with the most telling and supremely accurate phrase he would ever utter: *voodoo economics.*

The royalists of King Reagan had made only one minor but significant miscalculation. The American people might applaud their antigovernment, antiliberal, antispending rhetoric; they might make the rafters ring with cheers for free enterprise and freedom from government regulations; they would hoot themselves hoarse at the despised welfare cheats and unemployed bums. But do not touch my Social Security check. Do not even think about Grandma's Medicare program. And by the way, can you help us get some money for that dam we need?

A few Senate Democrats of the Reagan years took to the hills and carried out their resistance attacks on unneeded weapons systems, unjust cuts in programs for children's nutrition, and the highly suspect, screwball math of supply-side economics. The effort was largely futile but occasionally valiant, and the few, like Moynihan, who kept alive the flame of social justice, human community, and commonweal, would live to see the day of vindication and rejoice in the knowledge that they had not capitulated under pressure. But resistance was not reform. The Democratic party still had no program to recapture the field from the restored royalists. Nineteen eighty-four and beyond loomed as a time of terrible testing. Would traditional or new Democrats prevail? Could the new Democrats produce a progressive and innovative program for governance sufficient to win back the confidence of a nation only beginning to doubt whether the rosy perceptions created by the image makers of the Reagan era were all they were cooked up to be? The reformer's role in seeking answers to these questions would make the trials of previous reform struggles seem very small.

15

UP OR OUT:
THE ULTIMATE TEST
OF POLITICAL REFORM

To run for the presidency is an act of either the utmost egoism or the utmost patriotism. The true scale of justification tilts more frequently to the former than to the latter, but there is nothing particularly wrong in this. Egoism has simply been given a bad name by most politicians.

All who have undertaken one in today's climate agree that a national political campaign is also an act of extreme masochism. A new reform candidate for president would be surprised at the number of fellow citizens who ask in all seriousness, "Why in the world would you want the job?"

The only answer that was both true and made sense, that the candidate cares about his country, sounded more high-minded than it was intended to and usually masked the more selfish reason, that he also cares about his children. Politicians are also not without their competitive instincts. Early in their contests, the young reformer had occasion to ask both George Mc-Govern and Jimmy Carter the same basic question: "What made you decide to make the race?" Both gave the same appealing answer, startling in its directness: "I looked at the field, and I decided that if those people could be president, I could be president."

There is that to it. Raised in a small Kansas town at a time when national figures, particularly presidents, were considered exceptional and extraordinarily gifted individuals, simply by virtue of the fact that they were national figures, it was a form of revelation to meet people of prominence, leaders in their field, those routinely expounding this or that on television, political celebrities. They were all very human. They did not always look so handsome or sound so wise up close. They were not ordinary so much as they were mortal. They seemed to possess no secret wisdom or truth. They were where they were almost always because of the age-old combination of hard work and luck, in that order.

The basic requirements for president are elementary (and seem to become even more so as time goes on): a reasonably congenial personality, a basic understanding of government (underscore *basic*), the confidence of one's party sufficient to become its leader, at least a minimum of common sense, a sturdy ego, and the ability to live with ambiguity—there being no simple solutions or easy answers. Having survived the race for his party's nomination in 1984, the reformer would also learn of a final and perhaps most important precondition: a very sturdy physical constitution.

It is also helpful to have a reason for running. Napoleon occasionally employed a strategy that military historians term campaigns of opportunity. He would order his army out of Paris with no particular objective in mind except to look for trouble or see whether a fight were already under way that he might join. ("Is this a private fight, or can anyone join?'' the Irish have been known to ask.) In Napoleon's case, the practical framing of the strategy was this: let's start a fight and see what happens. In effect, a contested race for the nomination being a prizefight arranged for high stakes, a surprising number of candidates follow Napoleon in waging campaigns of opportunity.

The system encourages this. Often a governor, senator, or congressperson knows the chances of being nominated are slim, but there is always the consolation prize, the vice-presidency. To the reformer, it seemed neither consolation nor prize. But there is also a cabinet office or, for those tired of governing or legislating, an ambassadorship. One has only to wage a respectable race to receive national recognition and, in some cases, national acclaim. Only those exceptionally good at what they do or with superb press secretaries will receive such recognition otherwise. This is not to be cynical. Deep within the heart is a glimmer of hope and in the recess of the eye a glint of recognition in even the darkest-horse, longest-odds candidate for president that he just might make it. But of greater concern to the nation than the unlikely success of the dark horse is whether the dark horse will know what to do once in the Oval Office. Capitalizing the very name of that office suggests the regard in which it is normally held.

Upon observation and experience, the reformer formulated a belief that a direct correlation exists between sense of mission and likely success. The American people can spot an opportunist forthwith. Whatever else one might say—and in the reformer's case, that would be volumes—even to his severest critics, Ronald Reagan did not seem to be an opportunist. He was a man with a mission, and the mission was to dismantle the federal government.

Occasionally, presidential candidates have as a principal motive the revitalization or reform of their own party. This, too, is a worthy cause, in which only the avenue to the presidency offers itself. Presidents and, usually, the previously unsuccessful candidate of the opposition party are normally their parties' leaders. William Jennings Bryan, thrice unsuccessful candidate for president, had enormous impact on the Democratic party at the turn of the century. But no one runs to lose.

This reformer entered the contest for the Democratic nomination for president more than a year before it was to be decided in 1984. The Democratic party, as evidenced by the performance of its representatives in Congress, was still very much adrift. The old Democrats had not given up, and the new Democrats had not yet taken control. Sufficient cracks were appearing in the Reagan façade to encourage Democrats to oppose his policies, albeit selectively and cautiously. Much of the caution had to do with a lack of consensus within the party over what the alternative to Reaganomics and other Reagan policies should be. At this time, the careful criticisms of Reagan were merely criticisms, and they offered little by way of choice. Even those Democrats who had supported the policies were beginning to say what should not have been done, but they were saying very little about what else should be done and how to do it.

The Democratic party would not win in 1984 with traditional policies and ideas. To succeed, to regain voters lost to Reagan, reform leadership would be required, new leadership that had developed sound proposals for basic changes in the structure of America's public systems. But the party rank and file who participated in the selection of the eventual nominee would have to know and understand a new reform platform for the party. The party, like the country, was large, diverse, and complex. A campaign of ideas was more complicated than a campaign of personality. It was not simply a matter of convincing people to like and accept a candidate personally. It was a very long process of information and education. The reformer's only gamble was that people would be ready to listen. They were.

They were ready, and they were eager. Official Washington is pleased to delude itself into believing it is in the vanguard: Washington speaks, the nation listens. The vast majority of citizens are far beyond that childish fantasy. They have ideas of their own and very strong opinions. They increasingly resent politicians who talk down to them. Most politicians seek to amuse them, entertain them, lecture them, or occasionally berate them, but few listen to them. The reactions the reformer would receive in response to his own ideas for change were routinely superior in quality and thoughtfulness than anything he would hear in Washington. The country was becoming increasingly uneasy about the Reagan reign and was searching for a plausible alternative. That alternative, the reformer was totally convinced after only a few trips around the country, would not be a traditional Democrat with a traditional message.

Eight years later the hunger for ideas would be even more profound. Businessman Ross Perot would briefly become the sensation of Washington in the spring of 1992, not only for helping to fill the vacuum of boredom in political circles in the capital, but also because he was thought to have ideas. Public response was both great enough and spontaneous enough to justify the belief that many Americans were desperate both for truth and new policies. Leaving aside Perot's bungling of his candidacy as largely irrelevant to history, he did become the focus for many Americans deeply displeased with the entire political superstructure and clearly resentful at being treated like children by politicians and press alike. As the initial response to Perot proved, millions of Americans—certainly enough to constitute a formidable base for a new, progressive reform political party—will respond virtually to anyone willing to challenge political orthodoxy, speak clearly and directly, and offer new solutions for restructuring political and economic institutions.

But in 1984, the reformer was seeking a platform for national reform through national party leadership, and this presented a much more complex challenge. For better or worse, the Democratic party is a coalition party. That is, it is made up of organizations and interest groups, most of which agree on some points but all of which have their own agenda. By the mid-eighties, these groups had come to dominate the party. Indeed, they were the party. There was very little party independent of them. And because there was no strong party structure, the political vacuum was filled by the increasingly dominant and demanding interest groups.

In the latter part of 1983 and in the first half of '84, the interest groups increasingly maneuvered to dominate the nomination process. Instead of allowing the party leaders to select the candidate, the interest groups were determined to select the candidate or at least exercise a veto over candidates they did not favor. The methods for exercising control included lengthy questionnaires requiring the candidate's explicit commitment to particular agenda items and appearances before screening groups and audiences of interest group representatives for the same purpose. This system was neither enlightening nor helpful in establishing the fortitude of the potential leader. It gave the American people the impression of a group of grown men groveling and capitulating before a series of bosses with their own agendas. Various elements of the party have always disliked lengthy debate and so in 1984 sought to shorten the process by giving endorsements to candidates before primary voters at large were ever heard from. The process was unprecedented and looked to the outside world like the worst kind of machine control.

As a senator from a nonlabor state, on labor issues the reformer had one of the strongest voting records of any westerner and one as strong as that of most national Democrats, yet in 1984 he would be opposed by organized labor for two reasons: he refused to support the protectionist-of-the-year measure, called domestic content (requiring that certain percentages of cars sold in America be made in America), and he had upset the group's hand-picked candidate, Walter Mondale, in the early primaries. Thus, he managed to anger and embarrass labor leadership sufficiently that its most visible representatives would travel the country, making extravagant (and false) proclamations that "Gary Hart is as dangerous to labor as Ronald Reagan." (Months after the nominating convention and the national election, the Mondale campaign would be required to pay fines in excess of three quarters of a million dollars for accepting $1.5 million in illegal labor donations in critical primaries.)

In any case, the contest was to go to the convention in San Francisco in July of 1984 and would ultimately be decided by so-called superdelegates, elected officials and party leaders given automatic delegate votes. They would officially confirm the nomination of former vice-president Walter Mondale.

Fritz Mondale and the reformer disagreed on many things, especially the need for reform and renewal within the Democratic party itself, but the two men shared deep loyalties to the principles and values of social justice, equality of race and gender, and economic equity. Their differences were in outlook and methodology, and their roots were in somewhat different wings of the party. Fritz was the protégé of Hubert Humphrey, the greatest heir of the 1970s to the classic New Deal traditions. The reformer would trace his influences more to the pragmatic reformism of John and Robert Kennedy. Essentially the same contest had been fought between these two wings of the party in 1960.

Throughout his life and despite considerable thought, the reformer would be unable to decide whether those who represent the ideas and ideology of former reformers resist further change and reform out of reverence for the legacy or more simply because of a desire to shepherd power. By the mid-eighties, many liberals were conservative when it came to their brand of liberalism. The conundrum can be explained only by the human tendency to reduce a liberalism that is progressive, innovative, experimental, pragmatic, and reformist to an orthodoxy. Orthodoxy simply means the narrow way. Adherence to the New Deal orthodoxy became the test of true liberalism. But reform by definition is experimental and pragmatic. It cannot be bottled or caged. Within the frame of reference of traditional values, it seeks new solutions and new structures to address new challenges. Reform simply means adapting to the times. This can be done while preserving old values, but it must be done.

The reformer, frustrated with conservative liberals, would conclude that the party hierarchy had lost its reform nerve, its instinct to innovate. It was cautious, and it essentially wanted to return to the glorious days of its victorious past. Thus, America was faced with a choice between a Republican party that wanted to return to the pre–New Deal era and a Democratic party that seemed to want to return to the New Deal era itself. Both looked to the past rather than to an uncertain future. Given the choice of varieties of conservatism, the majority turned its back on the party that was supposed to be the agent of change but was not. The three presidential contests of the 1980s prove this point as clearly as anything else.

It is all history now and probably not particularly important history for all that. The reformer did about as well as a candidate could do in 1984 without receiving the nomination. He would win all the New England states; he would carry seven of the nine super-Tuesday states; he would win all the western states, including the largest, California; and he would win eleven of the last twelve primaries. More often than they should have, critics and media analysts would dismiss his candidacy with the suggestion that it had briefly surged with the surprise New Hampshire victory and then quickly disappeared. The true history is otherwise. His twelve hundred delegates to the national convention would be proof of that. But history, as it has been said, is written by the winners, and he was not the winner. The reformer and thousands of his supporters would thereafter go on to do all they could publicly and privately for the Democratic ticket. But it was not enough. The outcome at least in part justified the reformer's belief that only a new voice and a new message could have had even the glimmer of a chance.

With the exception of the bitter contest of 1968, one of the hardest fought within the party in many decades, the 1984 Democratic contest revealed more startlingly than any other the serious fault lines running through the party. The reformer won states in regions that were doing well economically, where there was hope for and optimism about the future, where the benefits of international trade were evident, and where independents and non-Democrats could participate in primaries and caucuses. Former vice-president Mondale won in states that were economically depressed, where older constituent groups of the party were dominant, where international trade had hit industries hard, and where voters were older. There were clear generational and income divisions. But the reformer won the votes of half the members of labor unions in many states, despite the desperate warnings of national labor leaders. And he received many more votes from the elderly and traditional Democrats than pundit analysts gave him credit for.

For him, the dominant lesson was that the Democratic party and the country were already looking for a generation of leadership that was newer, younger, more progressive, and more experimental than that of Ronald Reagan and George Bush or that of the traditional leadership of the Democratic party.

Throughout 1985 and '86, the reformer attended to his Senate duties while seeking to continue to solidify a reform platform for the remainder of the decade and beyond. This platform included *America Can Win*, a book on military reform, written with the close cooperation of his adviser William Lind. A series of foreign policy lectures at Georgetown University, incorporated under the title *Enlightened Engagement*, was presented as the framework of a new foreign policy in anticipation of the post–cold war era. The lectures were based on visits with the Soviet leaders Gromyko and Gorbachev and Prime Minister Peres, King Hussein, and President Mubarak of the Middle East as well as consultations with dozens of the nation's most creative international experts. With the help of many, the reformer also compiled a plan for economic reform, *A Strategic Investment Initiative*. This included many ideas for education, health-care, and energy reform, environmental leadership, worker-training initiatives, new directions for research, and an overhaul of the nation's economic engine for the twenty-first century's race for economic leadership.

The Reagan program had lost steam and stalled. The economic and fiscal costs of the great supply-side experiment were beginning to be seen. Congress and the nation were awakening to a queasy dawn after the fiscal binge, and the people were restless and looking for leadership. It was a disturbing time and an exciting time. The reformer felt that the chance for national renewal was as great as it had been at any time since the death of John Kennedy a quarter century before.

From 1983 to 1988, the reformer-as-presidential-candidate was both seeking and seeking to offer the holy grail of late-twentieth-century American politics: the "new paradigm." This grand phrase refers to nothing more nor less than a new way of institutionally, structurally, and conceptually looking at and addressing a new set of challenges: a new economic model, a new defense approach, and a new set of policies for a massively changing global environment. This effort requires a fundamentally different national campaign than is conventional not only in terms of candidate and ideas but also in the use of metaphors, symbols, and language.

Most people are looking for new and better leadership. But the political establishment—by definition, protective of old, negotiated arrangements—resists new leadership. Those who intermediate between candidate and voters, those more rooted in the political establishment than they would ever admit, more often than not succumb to the temptation to make newness threatening and fearful, mostly by obsessively magnifying anything different about the bearer of the new message.

Among the many mysteries involving the media and the politics of the era, the reformer would find none more curious than the almost-demented insistence that national campaigns be "political" events requiring "political" reporters. In many months of presidential campaigning, the reformer could recall no instance where, outside Washington, an economics reporter covered an economics speech, a military reporter covered a defense speech, or a foreign policy reporter covered a speech on international relations. A national campaign would be seen by the intermediaries only on the one-dimensional plane of politics. There would be more experiences than the candidate-reformer could possibly document in which he would appear before a crowd of concerned citizens who were insistent on discussing ideas and policies, an event quickly followed by a formal or an informal press conference where every question would involve campaign politics or political controversy. There were constantly two strikingly different campaigns: that of the people and that of the press.

Efforts to devise new symbols, metaphors, and language included rejecting all PAC contributions; organizing new-leaders conferences, which demonstrated contact with a new generation of leaders worldwide; conducting seminars around the country on military reform; visiting locations where "new ideas" were demonstrably in practice; and encouraging supporters to undertake practical social reforms, in advance of obtaining political power. In 1984, the reformer did not locate the symbolic holy grail, but he believed that had things gone differently, he would have done so in 1988, and in the process he would have created a new political vocabulary. In any case, he would continue to believe that between 1983 and 1987 his campaign went about as far as it could in staking out new political categories, structures, and paradigms without totally alienating the political establishment.

Major reforms are, by definition, structural in nature. Macroeconomic, military, and foreign policy institutions are the focus. No single individual, including a reform president, can work out to the decimal point the implications and microimpacts of structural reform. Franklin Roosevelt could not have begun to know the detailed ramifications of the New Deal as that massive set of reforms was implemented over an uneven decade. America is a great, vast social enterprise composed of countless facets and factions. No president, however reform-minded, can manipulate all the levers. But some levers are more connected to national systems than others. Tax and fiscal systems, monetary systems, defense-contracting authorization, financial institutions, regulatory structures, intelligence networks, virtually all foreign policy including the war-making power, and a number of others represent the arena for major reforms. Move and change these levers, and much happens below. This was this reformer's notion of reform.

Had he achieved the position of national leadership in 1988, his plan would have been both simple and complex. He would have reversed the normal course of events by focusing first on two major foreign policy initiatives and then devoting the bulk of his term to major domestic economic reforms. He had in mind to negotiate a quick but massive arms-reduction treaty with President Gorbachev and to seek to set up a series of bilateral U.S.–Soviet treaties designed to encourage and support Soviet political and economic reforms. Simultaneously, he would have begun behind-the-scenes negotiations for a sweeping new Middle East peace agreement, using every ounce of United States authority to bring all interested parties face-to-face at a neutral bargaining table. Based on a lengthy visit to the Middle East in the summer of 1986 and meetings with Gorbachev and Shevardnadze in Moscow in December of that year, he strongly believed both initiatives to be possible and necessary.

Having then addressed, immediately and dramatically, the two most important foreign policy problems America had faced for forty years, he would have had a freer hand to take on the structural changes necessary at home. By the fall of 1989, he would have put before the American people and their elected representatives in Congress, in a series of television talks, a set of reforms of education and health-care systems, a proposed shift of the tax system from income to consumption, proposed taxes on imported oil, the major military reforms documented in his 1985 book, and plans for large-scale infrastructure-renewal programs designed to modernize the country while providing hundreds of thousands of jobs. These and other initiatives would have represented the focus of the national debate and, it is hoped, congressional action for the remainder of one term, if not two. The goal would have been a rebuilt and renewed nation for the twenty-first century.

But another presidential campaign was not to be. Of the abrupt conclusion to that campaign much has been written, often false and mean-spirited, sometimes stretched beyond recognition, and, very rarely, close enough to the mark to be singularly painful. Two aspects cause the greatest regret: hurt to family and supporters, and setback to an agenda of reform ideas, trivialized or totally lost in the media focus on messenger rather than message. Further discussion of this incident contributes neither to a good nor a productive fight. Nevertheless, a brief comment on the mentality that allowed such an incident to combust beyond reason's control does seem relevant, in the hope that unnecessary damage to others may be prevented and a responsible press may consider reforming its own behavior.

Public officials must be accorded basic rights of privacy which should not be violated by the news media any more than by the government. The press should not have greater right to invade one's privacy than the FBI. In the case of clandestine surveillance, the media has wrongly claimed an even greater right of intrusion than that accorded to law enforcement agencies.

No constitutional amendment grants the press a special privilege to assume final judgment regarding the character of others. The First Amendment, as American courts have held, provides the press a shield, not a sword. Nor does the Constitution or laws of the United States have anything at all to say about "the public's right to know." This is a fictional "right" used to justify printing anything that comes along or, increasingly, that can be generated, whether disguised as "opposition research" or "investigative journalism."

Very personal details of a private life are relevant to the public only as they affect the conduct of the public's business. As to the search for clues to "character," they are revealed throughout a lifetime and principally in the very visible conduct of public service.

The reformer continues to bear a sense of great responsibility to his family and supporters for his mistake in permitting a chain of events to be set up that would make continuation of a serious national campaign of ideas, issues, and reforms impossible. But the real loss was not a campaign or a candidacy. The years thereafter were constantly punctuated with trivial scandals, all of which had the effect of demeaning the nation's leadership in both parties. The real loss was the erosion of the nation's dignity, the impression American politics was giving to the world during this nightmare period of silliness, triviality, and adolescence. It was demeaning to a great nation, its leadership, and its people.

While the quality of journalism spiraled downward, while desperate efforts were being made to separate the responsible press from the irresponsible press, while the world watched in confusion and bemusement, America continued to avoid any serious discussion of its future. National campaigns, following the trend, became more bitter and more negative. The presidency was won by the campaign whose negative television advertising was the most misleading and whose candidate had the least to say. What should have been, what the American people wanted the age to be—an era of reform—became instead an era of diversion, distraction, and petty scandal. Editorial writers in newspapers whose pages were filled with exposé and silly gossip would thoughtfully ponder and lament low voter turnouts. The Russians, blinking in the bright new light of democracy, would follow American politics and the American press and wonder whether this is what they had risked their lives for.

New ways had been found to stimulate newspaper-circulation drives and boost television ratings, to attract advertising revenues and compete in an increasingly cutthroat media environment. But America was without direction in the strange post–cold war world and no closer to her destiny.

As time went on, there were glimmers of hope. Paul Tsongas of Massachusetts, a former Senate colleague, would attract attention and be rewarded with early political success in 1992 by issuing a booklet of policies and proposals very similar to one prepared by the reformer five years before. The Democratic nominee, Bill Clinton, a friend and fellow campaign worker from two decades before, would enter the national campaign far ahead in the polls (despite a bout with scandalmongers), largely because he had formulated concrete plans for future change. By 1992, the generation of new, reform-minded Democrats had finally taken control of the party. The political pundits would attribute President Clinton's success to his moderation from traditional liberalism. A reformer would believe his success was a tribute to his age and to his understanding that the American people were hungry for new ideas, for a new road map of the country's future.

Even as press coverage of the campaigns became more trivial, the candidacies and the campaigns of the newer Democrats became more idea- and issue-oriented. From the 1970s onward, the reformer would believe and argue that voting citizens want to know in advance of elections what to expect in the way of policies and governance once a candidate is in office. Traditional politics and the conventional wisdom were that people cared only that they feel good about the candidate, that the candidate seem generally well organized and able to give a rousing speech, that the candidate could lash out articulately at the perfidious opposition and declaim in the most general terms that things have to change. The conventional wisdom was that voters were bored and confused by ideas and policies. That wisdom was too often shaped by political reporters who themselves were bored by policies and preferred to cover only the horse-race aspects of campaigns and the inside gossip of their workings—who had raised how much money, what the latest polls said, which shrewd strategist had joined which campaign, who would win the endorsement of what other politician.

In fact, the American people in the last quarter century have become much more sophisticated about their own government and the policies that affect their lives than the traditional political press ever gives them credit for. They are much less willing to trust a vague politician to do the right thing. They understand a good deal about fundamental economics, the environment, health-care and education issues, and the trends and tides in the world. Unlike Washington political insiders, they have been bored by campaigns and politics. They want to know before a candidate is elected what positions he or she will take on crucial issues and whether he will lead or follow. From 1974 onward, the reformer would build campaigns, including national campaigns, around ideas. The generation to follow would increasingly do so as well.

There could be no American reform without a blueprint or guideposts. Admittedly, Franklin Roosevelt made up much of the New Deal as he went along. But he was operating under conditions of immediate desperation. The reformer hoped a new reform era would anticipate and prevent such conditions. By waging a campaign of ideas, he would have forced his opponents to respond; a debate over change would have been joined in considerable specifics; and the voters would have been required to accept or reject the plan for basic reform. If they had accepted it and the reform candidate had been elected, he would have a mandate to take to Congress, and Congress would feel much more obliged to follow the will of the voters. His theory, then, was that a reform president, having run on a platform of fundamental structural, institutional, and programmatic change, would have a mandate from the people to carry out those changes.

In a certain way that was the 1980 campaign of Ronald Reagan. His message was simple: I will cut taxes, strengthen the military, get tough with the Russians, reduce the size and power of government, and balance the budget. It was clear, neat, and fit the sound-bite requirements of the evening television news. As events later proved, it was also wrong. It all came true except the wild deficits. But Reagan's impressive victory in that campaign whipped Congress into shape; he did what he had promised, and the American people got what they thought they wanted. It was only the most simplistic blueprint, and it was not reform, but it was direct and straightforward. Real post–cold war American reform requires much more thought, more complex blueprints, and more elaborate preparation. It does not need to begin from scratch; much of the work has been done, and some of the ideas have already been debated. But a way must be found for a reform platform to be communicated to the vast electorate through a media filter whose frequencies are jammed with trivia and amusement and demands tabletlike condensation.

Even this plague, so confounding in the 1970s and '80s, might possibly be abating. Ross Perot's brief foray into 1992 presidential politics contributed one important innovation: bypassing the political press in favor of talk show campaigning, Perot communicated directly with the voting public. He outflanked the media's political establishment, something the reformer tried briefly and unsuccessfully to do in 1988. In the spring of 1992, when he became briefly very popular and controversial, raising the potential of a third-party candidacy, he performed political jujitsu on the traditional media establishment, forcing it to go to him instead of him begging it for attention. Morning chat shows, increasingly devoted to promoting their network's latest sitcom rather than news events, found time to preempt whole hours of invaluable broadcast time for Mr. Perot. They permitted him to talk at length and even permitted voters to call in with questions and discuss issues and ideas directly with this upstart, unconventional candidate.

This having been done with Perot, broadcast fairness rules required that equal and similar time be given to Governor Clinton and President Bush. For a month or two, something totally unprecedented took place. Privately owned and operated television networks (broadcasting under license on publicly owned frequencies and channels) became the medium for the American people to listen at length to presidential candidates and ask them questions directly on the air. It was a staggering phenomenon, one the reformer thought would never happen. And it was the greatest thing to happen to American politics since the Kennedy-Nixon debates. The candidates were forced to state their positions on crucial issues in more than clever sound bites, very large audiences listened attentively, and ordinary people asked much more serious questions about serious issues than political journalists ever did. It was a great day for the republic. It was political television at its best, the way it should have worked in the past and hopefully will work again in the future. If institutionalized, this format will totally reform national political campaigns and thus national politics and government.

Part of the reason for Mr. Perot's brief popularity and his ultimate withdrawal was revealed by this extraordinary experiment. Perot cleverly articulated vast public discontent with both political parties and their policies. He discovered (not created) a ground swell of citizen desire for different leadership, a ground swell sufficient to form a new party if the other candidates refuse to respond. But, having done that, he ran into a policy stone wall. Voters wanted to know, after a while, not just that he shared their anger but also what he would do about it. When he retreated in the late spring to ponder this, he discovered two important realities (both of which a reformer could have told him for the cost of a phone call): the answers are not that simple, and the answers will not be popular.

After Mr. Perot discovered these truths, especially the second one, he announced that he would not seek the presidency after all. But he did finally put forward some of the answers, and they were not popular. The budget could not be balanced without new taxes of some kind. Vast new cuts in spending would seriously affect government programs, particularly entitlement programs, that the majority did not want cut. Deficits could not be reduced without major cuts in military spending. Our nation is too wasteful of valuable energy resources. And so on and on. Thus, Mr. Perot's contribution to American politics. Because he refused to play by the rules laid down by the national political media, rules accepted without question or objection by major candidates in the past, he changed political communication for a brief, shining part of one season and proved in the process that it could and should be the norm. And he confirmed what thoughtful people knew already in the aftermath of the Reagan disaster: there are no simple answers that will also make people happy.

America's strength and greatness far surpass any single campaign or candidacy for high office. Politicians and political leaders come and go. Some leave a legacy of substance, some leave the memory of pleasant personality, and many leave nothing at all. After everything is said that can or ought to be said, the ship of state sails on, and history will make its judgments about who was right and who was wrong. You can't be Irish, a Kennedy or someone associated with them once said, without knowing that life will break your heart.

The hearts of reformers are made to be broken because reformers are on a never-ending quest for the ideal. They seek the better America of memory and of dream. They know that somewhere in the future the grail of humane government and social justice, of fairness and decency, of commonweal and the national good waits to be found. They believe that systems can change even though they seldom do. They trust the hearts of their countrymen—indeed, they trust the hearts of all humanity—to long for the good and not just the acceptable. They battle with conventional systems not because they enjoy the battle but because they know those systems can be better and because they have no choice.

The goal is not to avoid failure—that is the goal of the conventional politician. After inevitable failure, the reformer must always try again. Eventually, his reforms become part of the dialogue, then part of the policy. That is the way reform always succeeds. The goal is to fail better.

In American politics, it is still possible for a reformer to start as a student volunteer and, within the span of a Jeffersonian generation, seek the presidency. That fact alone should be enough to keep the reform ideal alive. It is alive in the world, and it is alive in America. It awaits only a leader who can more clearly show the way and not himself become the issue. Human hearts are made of stuff that breaks and dies. But that does not matter. The ideal of a better America will never break nor ever die.

16

THE AGE OF CLEVERNESS, COURTIERS, AND CAREERISTS

The clever men and women succeed today. They know the right words and phrases, the sentiments that long to be expressed. They strike the right chords. They are quick and bright. They are new and fashionable. At certain stages in every society's evolution, the prize is granted to cleverness. To be clever is to possess a certain charm, a charm that ingratiates and amuses. Native or cultivated cleverness assures a pass to the inner circles.

Today cleverness can secure a job on a newsmagazine or a Sunday-morning talk show. It can open up opportunities in screen writing and successful careers in popular fiction and even book publishing. It is the key virtually to the entire world of television. In any industry or profession requiring facility, trendiness, and modishness, the doors are open to the clever. The slow of tongue, the methodical of thought, the searcher after deeper truths, the stoic, the dreamer, the doubter—all give way to the clever person in an age such as this. Who can compete with the clever quote, the knowing nuance, the succinct and cutting phrase that sums it all up and makes it neat?

Now the speech writer is the new celebrity. Coin a poignant line for a vague political leader, and you have celebrity. Political pundits and advisers themselves are sought after for having placed the telling dart, the quick comeback, the sharp shot on the tongue of the great candidate.

The clever phrase itself is given an independent life. Did you hear what Senator X said about the Gulf War? Did you know how Chairman Y summed up the national deficit? The national dialogue is shaped and framed by the nighttime comedy hosts.

The elevation of cleverness, of verbal facility, is the immutable outcome of the condensation of life, of the need to say and do things quickly. Now, as we are repeatedly told, our politics are dominated by the sound bite, the television edict to say it sharply, quickly, memorably—to say it cleverly. The Teflon president, "Read my lips," "Where's the beef?" Deep Throat, the smoking gun, supply-side economics.

The trick is to load the clever phrase with a world of meaning so that logic, explanation, and discovery are unnecessary. To repeat the magic phrase is to say volumes. A world of meaning—an entire ideology—is packed into a few words. Thus, speeches become strings of clever phrases packed with political explosives and employed like hand grenades. Thought, argument, persuasion become redundant. Why explain when a simple well-turned, meaning-laden phrase will do the trick?

For the clever sophisticates, those who require something more, there is, of course, the aphorism. Pseudointellectual pundits need only employ "quote boys" to cull out the erudite sentence that says it all—

cleverness with a touch of wit, if not of learning. At the feet of recyclers of aphorisms lays the media-political world. After all, to be able to quote De Quincey, Montaigne, Carlyle, one must be outrageously clever, a whole lot smarter than the rest.

Besides condensing and summing up, cleverness also fills the increasing demand for amusement. In a clever age, boredom is the greatest sin. To think, to debate, to consider, to reason—these are the most awful of the social evils. The dinner-party door is closed to the heavy of mind, if not also to the heavy of heart. Question the conventional wisdom, and you send a heavy pall across the table and the room, particularly so if the heresy is direct and sincere. A leader may be skewered, especially if the polls are descending, but not seriously questioned. Seek to debate the consensus policy, and you risk social ostracism.

Cleverness sums up, cleverness amuses, but cleverness also obscures. To insist that the issues of the day be addressed quickly and wittily is to reject the ponderous process of analysis and thought. The cleverness of "Where's the beef?" is that its response is necessarily complex and rational. Minds wander away while the question is being answered. Never mind that the beef is there; to deliver it requires that the truck be unloaded. No wonder throughout history the inevitable response to the school-yard taunt is a frustrated fist in the face. But real reform is as ill served by fistfights as it is by cleverness.

Cleverness is the métier of the courtier. The courtier stands near the ruler and periodically acclaims his wisdom, judgment, and temperance. It is all in all not a bad place to be. It has its social, financial, and political rewards. Rulers like to be told that things are running smoothly; rulers seldom like to hear that things need to change. Courtiers, throughout history, have seldom been reformers.

As the twentieth century comes to its convoluted

close, lines blur and disappear. After considerable personal, as opposed to political, controversy, former White House chiefs of staff, like Mr. Sununu, went from positions of great public responsibility to media positions requiring commentary on the issues of the day in the style of controversy. Other former chiefs of staff, like Mr. Regan, left office after an equally well publicized controversy and received huge book advances negotiated on the condition that the author be as unfaithful to his former employer, the president, as he possibly could be. Courtiers have quickly become clever commentators, willing for a fee to betray loyalties and wittily critique policies that they themselves helped create. At private dinner parties and tennis matches, leading media figures developed social intimacies with political leaders they were called on to "cover" in countless ways that would test even the laxest definition of objectivity. Who would be surprised to know that most Americans saw the whole pack—politicians, media figures, pundits, cabinet officers, and courtiers—as one big, unwholesome conglomerate interested more in its own position and perpetuation than in the national interest?

The position of courtier is especially sought after because it can lead to so much else. By definition, the courtier can represent at court the interests he favors. The courtier's judgment is often sought in the high councils of government. The courtier can introduce and favorably position chosen friends. The courtier passes messages and serves as a conduit of information to and from the court. The courtier has the ear of the king. The courtier has access.

Access to information makes one important to the information industry. Modern-day courtiers often appear on news programs. They help those in the information industry properly define the issues of the day; they often condition the way in which opinion makers and therefore the public "see" things. More and more this is literally true. For what the sound bite is to the ear, the photo op is to the eye, a pictorial synopsis of the truth as the governing elite wants it to be known or perceived.

For many months after the incident, more people would associate the reformer-as-presidential-candidate with a target being hit by an ax in New Hampshire than would ever know about his ideas for economic, military, or energy reforms. And it is but a small step from synoptic image to "gotcha," the phenomenon by which the slight deviation, the slip of the tongue, or the mental error becomes the great story for those who have elected themselves to mediate between political figure and voters and who believe their mission to be the hypermagnification of perceived flaw. Thus for the reformer in 1984, the casual suggestion that the American embassy in Israel might be moved to Jerusalem as part of a comprehensive Middle East peace settlement occasioned screaming headlines totally obscuring the detailed new proposals to obtain the settlement. And later, at a private gathering, the humorous aside that the reformer's wife got to campaign on California's beaches while the candidate campaigned at New Jersey toxic-waste sites was sensationalized as a slur on New Jersey, where—little known to the voters—the reformer had based a whole campaign on New Jersey's miraculous technology-driven economic recovery. Perception becomes reality when it can be manipulated by snapshots and sound bites.

Perception is an important word for a courtier at work in an age of cleverness. Perception is to truth as image is to reality. More important to politics and the information culture than truth and reality are perception and image. What good is truth if the people do not perceive it? What good is reality if it is not presented with the proper image? If perception and image are important to the rulers, the emergence of a subculture of those expert in perception and image is guaranteed. Over thirty years ago, Daniel Boorstin documented the rise of this subculture in a book called *The Image*. "Since the Graphic Revolution," he said, "much of our thinking about human greatness has changed. Two centuries ago when a great man appeared, people looked for God's purpose in him; today we look for his press agent." Continuing to comment on an age that treasures celebrity over true greatness, he wrote, "We can fabricate fame, we can at will (though usually at considerable expense) make a man or woman well known; but we cannot make him great. We can make a celebrity, but we can never make a hero. In a now-almost-forgotten sense, all heroes are self-made."

The closer perception and image approximate truth and reality, the safer things are. The more they diverge, the more dangerous the situation. President Reagan may be taken as an example. His image experts tried, with particular early success, to create an image of a leader structuring the debate, in command of the facts, on top of the ideas, and thoroughly in control of the processes of government. Gradually, however, unfaithful courtiers or simply those seeking to achieve or maintain currency in the great world of news gave it out that the perception offered and the image created were not totally accurate. In truth, the leader was more often than not distracted or abstracted, vague on information, confused as to facts, bewildered by debate, and not at all in command. Clever ways were sought to account for his inadequacies.

President Carter, we were told, was on top of every detail down to the tennis courts, and look where that got him. Great leaders are not supposed to engage themselves in details. Reagan disdained the gritty minutia; he was a bold, big-picture visionary. But even before he was safely out of office, the courtiers' memoirs, those time bombs of history, began to be lobbed over the walls of official Washington. Most were un-kind. The ruler having disappeared or his ear having been closed, courtiers lose their treasured access and with it their currency. They are then free to tell what they believe to be the truth (presuming they could distinguish it after years of neglect), settle old scores, and preserve one more moment of fading glory in the news spotlight. History is then left to sort through the rubble of perception, image, distortions, and half-truths and render some judgment. If history feels tricked, it is seldom kind. Besides, "it is always Judas who writes the biography," said Oscar Wilde.

Cleverness and courtiers are like beauty. They are glorious while they exist, but they are difficult to sus-tain. It is the rare clever person who does not become a bore after a while. Courtiers serve at the sovereign's pleasure. Only the very wise ones preserve their use-fulness, and few are that wise. All great capitals are infested with boring people once thought clever and courtiers who were never wise. They are kept only as relics for display at dinner parties. In an age that values cleverness and courtiers, there are always many court-iers, for they are often replaceable and replaced.

Politicians are under great pressure to succumb to the temptation of perception and image. If a campaign for office is slow in starting or slow to gain the trea-sured momentum, clever courtiers are there, usually for a fee, to change the candidate's image. To succumb is fatal. To create an image that is dissociated from reality requires a very good actor. Most politicians are not good actors. That an actor did indeed become president says all that need be said on the theme. It is much easier to act one's way into office than to use public office as a stage for becoming an actor.

As the twentieth century comes to its complex close, the medium of television has become everyone's Hollywood stage. Through the new technology of home video cameras, everyone can, and many do, become instant television sensations by sending in their own films of themselves behaving oddly. Or persons of at least temporary interest to the public can present themselves for examination on one of the many appalling talk shows to discuss unbelievably intimate aspects of their lives to the horror and delight of vast audiences. It was not only a kind of Gresham's law of entertainment—bad programming driving out good—but also a reflection of the vast number of television hours demanding to be filled. Bruce Springsteen's lyric summarized it best: "57 channels and nothin' on." Politicians are simply in the vanguard of a quickly disappearing distinction between reality and image, actor and authentic person, performer and genuine toiler.

The devices of perception and image are used by society's professional courtiers and clever people to avoid the reality of reform and change. The more desperately a society struggles to avoid reality, the more it is in need of reform. Protectionism is the means used to avoid economic reform. Military buildups are the devices for avoiding military reform. Wars for oil are the tools for avoiding energy reform. Protectionism creates the perception that trade deficits are the fault of others and uses images of evil trading partners. Bellicosity creates the perception of a dangerous threat and employs the image of a nation so under siege that it dare not question its military posture. Invasions create the perception of strong leadership and capitalize on the image of a foreign tyrant out to take over the world unless stopped.

In each case, society is fooling itself and avoiding reality and the truth. Real reform is difficult. It upsets traditional patterns and ways of thinking. It is unkind to conventional leaders and conventional wisdom. It shakes up establishments and established power-sharing arrangements. Reform is painful, and pain is something we all wish to avoid. People who value cleverness and promote courtiers are the enemies of reform. Reform cannot achieve its goals through cleverness; it will not tell the ruling elite what it wants to hear. Military reform has always first required military defeat. The old order comfortable in its traditional ways has to be crushed. Reform is often the product of panic and desperation—thus, the relationship of economic reforms of the New Deal to the Great Depression.

Nations that have not experienced the need for collective sacrifice to achieve modernization and reform have not survived in eras of great change. Nations that have employed distracting imagery to avoid reality simply postpone the day of judgment. Nations that dismiss and scorn the notion of reform in favor of external excuses for their problems are also nations that punish their prophets.

Part of the process of avoiding change and reform is government by consensus. Consensus is a good and necessary thing in a democracy; at the end of the day, it requires general negotiation and agreement by disagreeing parties on major policies. Consensus seeking is a moderating process. All sides have to make concessions, usually of extreme positions. Once consensus is reached, it becomes the policy of the majority, the moderate center.

Consensus building is a necessary part of moving a democracy forward. For a new idea to become a reform policy, there must be a consensus that will adopt it. The issue is over the terms of the debate. If a debate on military policy, for example, is limited to the slight degree of marginal increase or decrease in defense spending each year or to the addition of one or two major new weapons systems, then serious consideration of the overall military posture, political commitments, doctrines and strategies, and ideas and structures is avoided. The reformer seeking debate on larger themes is not included when consensus is sought. The terms of the debate, the arena in which consensus is sought, simply do not include the notion of structural reform.

Consensus government became a device for avoidance of reform in the latter part of the twentieth century. Major changes in direction in the economy, in the military, in energy, and in other important areas were never really considered when policies were adopted. Such change as occurred, occurred on the margin. Even the vaunted Reagan revolution was nothing of the kind. It was simply the wholesale application of Keynesian economics by those who claimed to deplore Keynesianism. Massive tax cuts and massive spending increases, in this case for the military, stimulated economic growth. Lord Keynes and Franklin Roosevelt had demonstrated this very economic principle a half century before. A Democratic president could not adopt this policy because he would have been considered by all to be fiscally irresponsible. Reagan's courtiers simply gave it a new name—supply-side economics—and a new image and made it fashionable in official Washington. Massive deficits, predicted by this reformer, one of the very few to vote against the Reagan tax cuts, were the inevitable outcome of this consensus "revolution." In an antireform age, unhappy reformers are left to oppose only the most outrageous examples of royalism and reaction.

Sifting through the debris of deficit and debt left by the Reagan revolution, a few would wonder how it all happened and, especially, how a consensus managed to be formed around thoroughly unsound and destructive notions. The simplest explanation would be careerism. The Jeffersonian ideal of public service was that of civic obligation. For small compensation, those concerned with the commonweal, with improving the prospects of their communities and their nation, would give some period of time in service to the local board of aldermen, to the state legislature, or to Congress to represent the views of their constituents and help solve the country's problems. Few of the Founders would think of this as other than civic duty; they would have been appalled to think of politics as some kind of profession. Most, like Jefferson, would spend their time in government longing for the respect and the calm of private life and bemoaning the vicissitudes of politics. The phrase *political career* was unknown and would have seemed to Jefferson a confusing oxymoron.

The reformer would have the honor to serve in the Senate with men—and too few women—who had given many years of their lives to government but had done, and were capable of doing, other things. Many of the best retired voluntarily out of fatigue and desire for that Jeffersonian calm. By the time the reformer retired to private life, that same Senate had been largely occupied by political careerists. Some men and women are especially suited to public life and improve in performance with years of service. If they are thus extraordinary and their constituents continually desire their service, they should not be prohibited from representing those constituents. Constitutional term limitations are an unsound idea designed to prevent voters from exercising their will. Voters should not alter the Constitution to prevent themselves from having what they want. Unwanted careerists should simply be voted out of office.

In the main, political careerism is not healthy. It encourages cowardice. The many Democrats in Congress in the early 1980s who voted for Reaganomics did so with the full knowledge that those policies were dangerous. They had been given advance warning of the size of the deficits that could, and most probably would, occur. The dangers were too great to risk experimenting or gambling. But majorities of Democrats in both houses of Congress voted with the new president for a single reason: they were intimidated by his perceived popularity. The Reagan administration skillfully orchestrated large-scale letter-writing campaigns urging Congress to support the president, and otherwise shrewd and even thoughtful Congress members caved in. They were afraid to return to their constituents and explain why supply-side economics was a fraud. They wanted a career in politics, and this was the safest way to achieve it. To get along, you have to go along.

Politicians are not hired simply to do what they are told—thus, the famous admonition of Edmund Burke, that "your representative owes you, not his industry only, but his judgment; and he betrays instead of serving you if he sacrifices it to your opinion." If voters are misinformed, they may demand policies that are ultimately destructive. The politician's job is properly to inform, to educate, and to lead, especially when it is unpopular to do so and even if doing so leads to his defeat. There would be no clearer example of this principle in the 1980s and '90s than the nexus between revenue and debt. Every president and presidential candidate, every senator and congressperson knew in the deepest recesses of his or her soul that public deficits so destructive to economic renewal and opportunity could not be decreased without substantial infusions of new revenues. Since 1980, however, no member of either party could be found to state this simple proposition clearly and explicitly to the American people. It would require a billionaire businessman to do so, and even he had to retire briefly from the political arena to summon both the documentation and the courage to make his case. No other issue before late-twentieth-century America would so immediately illustrate the failure of courage and the triumph of cowardice. And no other issue would so graphically reveal the failure of political leadership and the political system.

But the true political leader is one who refuses to follow the popular course when it is known to be wrong and who is willing to tell the people what they do not want to hear even at the probable cost of an elected position. This requires courage. Political careerism is based on short-term expediency in the pursuit of long-term survival. Survival became an important word in the politics of the eighties. It is a very modest goal for life. Americans periodically wonder why so few great leaders are emerging. Political careerism stresses survival at all cost and compromise when necessary. Great leaders seldom are content with mere survival; true leadership knows that compromise has no end.

All compromise is not bad. Strom Thurmond desperate to have his picture taken on the Senate steps with Afro-American leaders from South Carolina is a definition of good compromise. But one wonders about compromise on the part of the Afro-American leaders.

Careerism seeks the safe course, and safety is usually the enemy of reform. Madison, the moderate, would argue against Jefferson's notion of generational revolution and in favor of the continuity of an elite establishment. Career ministers in the established Danish Church were the most bitter critics of Søren Kierkegaard. A courtier of Czar Nicholas II would seldom be heard in defense of Tolstoy. Career politicians are usually the strongest opponents of political reform. Careerism is based on arrangements. Over time, accommodations are reached with organizations, constituent groups, major contributors, important supporters. The clever careerist discovers the price of support and negotiates its payment. Explicitly or implicitly, understandings are reached concerning the support the group or individual can expect from the careerist, and vice versa. Times change, and bargains are fluid. The negotiating process is an ongoing one for the successful careerist.

The link between special interest political action

committees, intermediating lobbyists, campaign fund-raising, and elected officials would be so obvious to Americans and so overwhelmingly pervasive as not to require still further documentation. This network has dominated the system; indeed it has become the system, a system that has been described and dissected so massively that it has become conventional wisdom and established truth. Its greatest evil, however, is that it produces a "mainstream consensus" that virtually precludes new ideas, thoughts, reforms, or leadership. To step outside the system is to become weird or irrelevant, to be thought of as an exotic unqualified for serious national leadership. The major condition of today's political careerism is not to wander outside the consensus, not to question basic assumptions, not to cross important organizations and their representatives, not even to think about changing the system.

By the mid-1980s, the full extent of the Reagan fiscal disaster was beginning to emerge. The solid consensus that backed the president's policies in the early eighties was fragmenting. Puzzled expressions began to appear with regularity, and formerly happy heads were wagging to and fro. The central question for the opposition party was, What do we do now? What are the alternatives to Reagan and Reaganomics? With a bad taste still lingering from the unhappy late seventies, it did not seem enough to suggest a return to the policies of the previous administration. Waiting for inspiration, Democrats contented themselves with hesitant and qualified criticisms of policies they had voted for and vague suggestions for a confused amalgam of restored funding for human-resource programs, odd microeconomic ideas for the creation of jobs, increased trade protectionism, and occasional minor cuts in defense spending. No one would even think, let alone whisper, the dreaded *T* word, taxes.

The one lasting contribution to conventional political wisdom left by Ronald Reagan would be the certain knowledge that the American people would never pay for the programs they demanded. By the 1980s, it was simply beyond question. No careerist would hazard a fleeting thought of suggesting pay-as-you-go. The reformer had many occasions to remind Senate colleagues and citizens' groups of the policies of Harry Truman, a figure Reagan sought comparison with (to Truman's detriment). When North Korea invaded South Korea in 1950, President Truman, under a United Nations mandate, committed American military forces to South Korea's defense. Within three weeks, he appeared before the Congress, requesting major tax increases to pay for the costs of the operations.

Ronald Reagan, who fancied himself, and was fancied by his courtiers, a similarly courageous leader, of course did just the opposite. He issued dire and frightening warnings about a massive Soviet military buildup, a dark ominous threat to the security of America and its allies (most of whom did not see quite the same threat), and said that the Russians are coming, and they're thirty feet tall! We must spend massive amounts of money to counter this threat if America is to survive. We must make whatever sacrifices are necessary to protect our country, our way of life, our democracy, and our golf courses. Join me, he cried, in this crusade to rid the world of the great Satan. Full stop. By the way, he would say in other venues, we are going to cut your taxes. The government, meaning everything but the monstrously large Pentagon, is too big, et cetera, et cetera. Some threat. Some sacrifice.

By any conceivable definition, taxes, one of the few sacrifices democratic citizens can make, were never to be put on the sacrifice list. They were the most evil institution ever devised by the mind of man, and only the most perfidious, big-spending, big-government, probureaucracy liberal Democrat would ever conceive of asking for a tax dollar to pay for a government service, including this most important one, national security. Ronald Reagan brilliantly eliminated taxes from the national debate. This, and this alone, accounts for the deadlock over the reduction of the federal deficit. For a decade, courageous members of the houses of Congress annually have conducted a charade before the carcass of the federal budget, dancing about and shaking sacred rattles at the evil deficit, never once acknowledging that it would not go away without more revenue. It was the silliest thing in the world because everyone knew it and no one had the courage to say it. The deficit is Reagan's real legacy to America, and there are plenty of political careerists who could, but will not, claim step-parenthood.

The 1992 presidential election claimed to be about change. In any historical sense, however, it was not about fundamental reform of political or economic structures. Real change would mean pay-as-you-go budgeting, which requires taxes to match spending. Change would mean the unprecedented restructuring of American military forces, dismantling the superpower doctrines and force structures designed to meet "commitments" now made obsolete by the demise of the cold war and establishing very different capabilities designed to meet very different threats. Change would mean a policy of true energy independence that could be both environmentally sound and diplomatically liberating. Change would mean conversion of defense production and outdated industrial capacity to a service-oriented, information-based, technologically advanced, modern, competitive economic power. Change would mean affordable health care for all and higher academic standards in the nation's schools.

These and many other reforms will not occur in a society with a political system that rewards cleverness, courtiers, and careerism instead of courage and leadership. Happily, we have built walls of insulation and strong social safety nets to protect us from depression and tragedy. Unhappily, those protections prevent the foundation-rattling political hurricanes that sober us up and require us to rediscover important social values, such as courage, imagination, and vision. In desperate times, America, perhaps out of fear, will experiment, innovate, and reform. Basic assumptions and conventional wisdom go out the window. Careerists and their comfortable arrangements are discarded. Courtiers are banished, and cleverness is disdained. People ask themselves basic questions about the kind of country they have and the kind of country they want.

These are the conditions of reform. And we are largely safe from them now. There is a Faustian element in the bargain, though. For safety, security, and comfort, we trade responsibility, discipline, and creative change. All thoughtful people know we are living in a dreamland, that the end of the cold war just bought us more time before the day of judgment.

Throughout American history, but especially in the late twentieth century, we have found it expedient to blame our capital, Washington, for our problems. Late-night comedians have made careers out of political jokes and jokes out of politicians. But politicians are the people we elect. They are no different from us. They are us. When we lampoon them, we lampoon ourselves. We do get the leadership we deserve. Every member of Congress and every president was elected by a majority of the voters. We should not ask, Who are these politicians? We might ask, Who are these voters? Official Washington has much to answer for, and it should have to answer for everything it does and does not do in the conduct of the public's business. But to believe that the problems of America are confined to Washington is to operate under a delusion.

Cleverness, courtiers, and careerism are rewarded because we permit them to be or even want them to be. We reward them with votes and with acclaim. Perception and image, rather than truth and reality, are the characteristics of the age because we reward them with success. Reform, real change of direction and purpose and value, is not blocked by the culture of Washington but by the culture of America. The culture of Washington is the culture of America.

PART III

Lives of Success in the Good Fight

17

REQUIEM FOR
A HEAVYWEIGHT

The goal of public office may not be reached and opportunities for public service may exist no more, but
the reform impulse does not die. No longer a candidate for national office, a reformer would find himself
at an awkward age: too old to start again and too young
to surrender. He became, instead, increasingly a citizen of the world. If America were not to change its
directions in the 1980s, he would search the world for
real instances of reform and democratic revolution to
prove progressive change is possible and to keep himself alive.

The more this reformer studied his country's challenges in the 1980s, the more he realized how intri-
cately interwoven they were with the affairs of the
world. Silently and swiftly, America had been swallowed up by the greater world around it, like a pig by a
python. Splendid isolation would do no more. If the

cold war were ever to end, and the reformer had some warning that it might, America would be faced with a new and different world, a world of economic competition gathering offshore like a giant tidal wave, for which it was almost totally unprepared. A reformer as private citizen might explore this world like Marco Polo and report on his findings to any who would listen and thus still contribute something worthwhile to his nation's progress.

The first real ray of light suggesting the dawn of a day beyond the cold war came in a trip the reformer would make to the Soviet Union in December 1986 as the guest of a new, younger, and surprising Soviet leader, Mikhail Sergeievich Gorbachev. By then, Gorbachev had been his party's general secretary—and, by virtue of that, head of state—for a year and a half. He had instituted greater freedoms of expression in the form of a policy then strangely called *glasnost*, meaning "openness," and had begun the reform and restructuring of the Communist monolith with a policy not well understood or widely given credibility in the West, called *perestroika*, or "restructuring."

By then, Gorbachev had held his first summit meeting with President Reagan in Geneva and only two months before had concluded a more substantive effort with the American president in Reykjavik, Iceland, to undertake serious reductions of nuclear weapons. The first had been only a get-acquainted, photo-opportunity meeting. The second was widely believed on both sides to have been a qualified disaster. The state of superpower relations was stalemated. The more hawkish Reagan advisers felt they had been given ample evidence to prove the need for a continued nuclear-arms race ad infinitum, evidence they devoured and disseminated with relish. Gorbachev, for his part, was confused and frustrated, facing hawks within his own system who were chanting that Reykjavik proved the Americans were not serious about ending the arms race, and he was looking for any voice of reason or ear of understanding from America. The reformer by then was believed by some to be a serious contender for the presidency in 1988 and was known to the Soviets for having dedicated more than a decade to the arms-control process. Furthermore, in January 1985, he had accepted an invitation from Foreign Minister Andrei Gromyko to visit Moscow with his family for "serious discussions." Gromyko then was de facto head of state and operating a holding operation while awaiting the demise of Chernenko. He would also have a key role in the elevation of the reformer Gorbachev. The Soviets were trying to make fundamental changes of direction and wanted someone in the West to appreciate and respond to their efforts.

Gorbachev arranged to see the reformer on the morning after his arrival in 1986 in what was to have been a short introductory session. The Soviet leader generously invited the reformer's twenty-one-year-old daughter, Andrea, then a student in Soviet-American studies, to join the session; it lasted almost four hours. In style, he was firm, candid, logical, and extremely intelligent; in substance, he was clearly going in a vastly different direction from that of his predecessors, and he was seeking help. Gromyko had told him of the Nixon days, during which the official American line was tough, but positive discussions took place behind the scenes through Secretary of State Kissinger. Gorbachev was searching for this "back channel" into the Reagan administration but could not find it. Sadly, the reformer could not help, although he subsequently informed Kissinger's successor, George Shultz, of this desire.

In sum, Gorbachev was convincing in his determination to reform the Soviet Union, clear in his understanding that the military aspects of the cold war were blocking his way both politically and financially, desirous of better relationships with the West, including those in trade, and determined to do all he could to end the cold war. The following day the reformer would have a similar long meeting with a close Gorbachev ally, Foreign Minister Eduard Shevardnadze, who repeated these strong commitments and proposed undertakings. It was clear they were under great pressure from antireform, hard-line traditionalists, who insisted the United States would never accept friendly relations with the Soviet Union. They were searching for an American interlocutor and a political bridge. They could find neither in the White House of that time.

Gorbachev's reforms unleashed a democratic whirlwind that the Soviet leader successfully rode and channeled for five years. In his efforts to manage a system that was beginning to oscillate wildly and disintegrate, he tacked back and forth between the traditional conservative party and the increasingly demanding democrats. The wonder is not that the coup of August 1991 happened but that it did not happen sooner and with more success. Between 1988 and the present, the reformer made many trips to the former Soviet Union, helped build economic bridges to the West, and wrote a book on *perestroika* fortuitously released on the day of the coup. Based on extensive interviews with a range of leaders across the spectrum, including three key members of the coup plot, the reformer predicted that any effort to reverse this second Russian revolution would fail, and he argued that the Gorbachev reforms offered the best chance for an era of East-West understanding and peace in seventy-five years.

By then, the popular line and the conventional wisdom in the West were that Gorbachev was weak and untrustworthy. It had become fashionable to dismiss and condemn him in favor of trendier factions. Whatever contributions he had made and risks he had taken were condemned as halfhearted by pundits and experts, some of whom knew little, if anything, of the man or the circumstances. In Washington salons, he had become a reactionary against the reforms he himself had instituted and skillfully guided. He was given little or no credit for reform. His eventual demise was practically applauded. The instant historians generally regarded the Gorbachev era as a great failure. To the satisfaction of his many critics inside and outside the former Soviet Union, Mikhail Gorbachev was forcibly retired from public service. At least for now, he is gone from the public stage, but he will most certainly not be forgotten, for he leaves on the globe an indelible impression.

Conventional wisdom now has it that Gorbachev was a halfhearted, reluctant reformer more concerned with saving the Communist party than his nation, that he vacillated and temporized, that he dithered between the conservative and the radical until time and tide finally overtook him. All this presumes certain motives on Gorbachev's part: that he sought only power and its perpetuation; that he identified the dramatic revolution he created with himself; that his principal interest was in remaining on the stage; in short, that he was like all other politicians. But there are occasionally—rarely—personalities larger than the conventional categories. Gorbachev is one such as these. He managed to do what few leaders ever even imagine: he revised the equation; he rewrote the rules; he changed basic terms.

Gorbachev abandoned historic Communist expansionism, thus unilaterally nullifying a century of orthodoxy concerning world revolution. He withdrew support for insurgencies and socialist governments in Latin America, Africa, and Asia. He dictated *perestroika* and "new thinking" for Warsaw Pact satellites in Eastern Europe and granted them self-determination. As a direct result, in 1989 the Berlin Wall fell, and the Warsaw Pact, from Poland to Albania, collapsed. Against the strong admonition of his senior military commanders, he insisted on previously unimagined nuclear-arms reductions and an end to the arms race. He acknowledged his nation's technological backwardness and its lagging standard of living and sought economic cooperation with the West. He granted freedom of speech, assembly, religion, and the press virtually without condition. He allowed emigration and liberated dissidents, including the spiritual leader of the democratic movement, Andrei Sakharov.

Gorbachev was in the process of becoming a true social democrat, the first since Aleksandr Kerensky. For the first time in their long and troubled histories, he institutionalized democracy in Russia and the other Soviet republics. He created a people's parliament and authorized free elections, including the participation of non-Communists. He systematically undermined the authority of the Politburo, the Central Committee, the state security institutions, and the Communist party as a whole. He made war against the corruption that was rampant throughout the traditional party establishment. He empowered a radical opposition movement even as he undercut his own establishment base.

Gorbachev is criticized most harshly for not transferring his flag to the opposition's mast. But this overlooks both pragmatic and philosophical considerations. Had Gorbachev abandoned the Communist party, the party would simply have abandoned him. Until the historic August coup, the party controlled the army and security forces. At any time, it could simply have ousted Gorbachev from premiership and selected an anti-*perestroika* head of state. The center-piece of the drama, so often and so conveniently overlooked by Gorbachev's critics, is the limit of his power and the tenuous hold that his presence gave to *perestroika*. Put simply, Gorbachev did not enjoy unlimited and unilateral power.

More important, Gorbachev is a man of conviction, even if one dislikes the substance of the convictions.

Unlike other Communist leaders in the former Soviet system, he did not find it convenient to abandon the faith of his life. He genuinely seems to believe in the socialist ideal and model. This may signal a lack of pragmatic awareness on his part, but it also suggests a steadfastness of belief that transcends the fashion of the day. By virtue of the party establishment's rejection, Yeltsin was liberated to resign and pursue his own course. Gorbachev was leader of the party. He saw its vast shortcomings and the urgent need for reform and even competition. But until the party's rejection of him during the coup, he did not believe it beyond redemption. By then, of course, it was too late. Short-sighted, ill-advised, even wrong-headed he may have been. But he most certainly was not cynical and self-centered.

There is an authenticity about the man that rises above the modern political norms. His story has about it the quality of grandeur. With the help of very few, he tried to rescue his nation—or group of nations—from accelerating decline, corruption, and backwardness. For his troubles, he suffered the pains of the reformer, always seeing the distance between what is and what ought to be, between the good and the better. There are few other world leaders in the second half of the twentieth century about whom one can imagine, decades, even centuries from now, operas and great novels being written.

His great failing, it is said, was not only his refusal to reject socialism but also his inability to deliver a successful economic revolution, a smooth and productive transition from central management to markets. This he failed to do. In fewer than seven years in office, he put utmost effort into revolutionizing the Soviet Union's foreign policies, restructuring its relations with the West, dissolving the Communist bloc, reorganizing the relationship of the republics to the central Soviet government, and liberating democratic political energies at home. In these efforts, he expended political capital he never had. The formation of a consensus behind privatization, dissolution of state enterprises, termination of subsidies, decontrol of prices, elimination of wage supports, and the vast, wrenching hardships that accompany the substitution of one entire economic system for another eluded him.

But can it honestly be said that anyone else in the Soviet Union could have achieved vast economic reforms within half a dozen years of the starting point in 1985? It is seriously to be doubted. The entire scheme of privatization, so insistently but abstractly urged by Western economists, has never been undertaken on such a scale in such a short period of time in any era. Economists, being by definition theoreticians, are notoriously ignorant of political realities. In the relatively short time that economics has been an academic discipline, few of its practitioners have ever governed a nation, and none springs to mind as a successful peaceful revolutionary. How easy to treat the vast Soviet Union as a giant laboratory on which to conduct a hitherto untried experiment in radical reorganization.

When prices rise and riots begin, when supply takes longer to meet demand than promised, when poverty, crime, monopoly, market manipulation, unemployment, homelessness, and hunger sweep in behind the abstract ideal of capitalism, as they have done, no one truly expects the economic experts to be on hand to deal with these catastrophes. Anyone who has served in public office in any capitalist democracy knows that economists are notoriously diffuse in their judgments, unfamiliar with the realities of daily life and government, and superbly equipped to render explanations in hindsight. It is a wondrous sight to behold quarrelsome tribes of economists blithely espousing clichés about biting the bullet, holding the line, taking the medicine, and so forth when none of them has the responsibility for carrying out painful policies.

One senses Mr. Gorbachev may have instinctively understood the danger in accepting too readily the shibboleths of foreign academicians, especially those in countries still struggling to solve their own serious economic problems. There is something altogether unseemly about Western politicians and economists leaping into the great post-Communist void to peddle theories and systems that still require much refinement in the West. Ideals are wonderful as long as they are dispensed as ideals. Politically and economically, the West has much to be proud of, but the gap between the ideal and the actual should generate some degree of humility in imposing our systems on others.

As the Communist system slips happily into fading memory, it becomes increasingly difficult to recall the bitter rigidity and strangling orthodoxy that made the possibility of a reform leader ever appearing so extraordinarily unlikely. The tenets of the Communist faith preclude reform because by its own definition communism is reform's most extreme manifestation: ongoing revolution. Whatever idea Lenin may have had for a revolutionary machine that would go of itself, Stalin quickly crushed it. The revolution of workers and peasants quickly became a hierarchical monument to the dictator. Never understanding that revolution generally comes from the bottom up and not from the top down (with the exception being the American Revolution), totalitarian Bolshevik discipline throttled evolution in its crib. The revolution became a means of perpetuating party power and not a means of improving the lives of the people it claimed to serve. Gorbachev inherited a system closed to the treachery of reform.

Unlike Gorbachev's many critics and at odds with almost all expert Sovietologists, the reformer, a mere amateur in these matters, would be convinced that Gorbachev knew exactly where he was headed and understood fully the risks of getting there. Although intelligence was never a standard for achieving supreme leadership in the Soviet Union (as it has been in the United States), native wit and shrewdness were. At his age, Gorbachev would not have gotten to the top without shrewdness and intelligence. He had got along by going along, but he also had established a reputation as a dissenter and a crockery breaker. The leadership that elevated him—first Andropov and then a cabal led by Gromyko—did not want a traditional leader. For the first time since Lenin tried to reform his own revolution, the system needed to be shaken up and restructured.

Gorbachev entered office as a reformer, and he disappointed his traditionalist sponsors only in his excesses. It was not long before his sponsor, Gromyko, was gone, too much a part of the old orthodoxy. The actions that followed were not those of a timid temporizer. The two principal unexpected and undesired results of the revolution that he started and directed were the collapse of party dominance and the collapse of the empire. Virtually all else Gorbachev initiated and accepted.

Some would say that the Reagan military buildup was the prime cause of communism's collapse. Unquestionably, the cost of the arms race played heavily on Gorbachev's thinking. He said so to me himself. He knew his reform of the Soviet economy could not take place while vast treasuries of rubles went into weapons systems, and he acknowledged his need for Western technology. But he had reached that decision on his own and was beginning to take unilateral steps to implement it, as evidenced by the later withdrawal of Soviet troops from Eastern Europe. Prior to Gorbachev, the Soviets had repeatedly proved they were prepared to deliver any hardship to their people to avoid military inferiority. Hitler and many before him had taught them that lesson. Under Gorbachev, the Soviets adopted a dramatic new defense doctrine of "military sufficiency"; that is, only the defenses needed to defend Soviet borders and interests. History may prove that the United States bankrupted the Soviet Union, but in the process, it came very close to bankrupting itself.

Though now is not that time, the time will come when Mikhail Gorbachev will be more fairly measured and treated. A failed and unfinished amateur reformer would not, in any case, bear the portfolio to carry out that mission. More unbiased historians are required to do that. At the least, Gorbachev is a lesson in the treatment of reformers whose own goals are far surpassed. The agent of change receives the contempt of those who want no change and those who want even greater change. The best is the enemy of the good. The ideal, by its own definition, will not be reached in a less than ideal world.

In a great ironic drama of history, honors would go to Gorbachev's nemesis, Boris Yeltsin, for defeating the coup de main and administering the coup de grace to communism. The honor would be earned. But the sword used in the ceremony would be one fashioned by Gorbachev himself. Aside from the three martyrs of August '91, the principal victim was the Communist party itself. It committed suicide by hanging, using the rope of reform it could not and would not grasp to pull itself to democracy.

There are few lessons for democratic reform in this stunning collapse of an empire. Gorbachev received his mandate for reform from a system he could escape neither intellectually nor politically. He was the classic case of a reformer in an unreformable system. To save his own soul, he had to abandon the party ship. But by the time he did, the ship had sunk. It would be left to Yeltsin to become the Martin Luther of communism. What lessons there are are but repetitions of age-old commonplaces to all reformers, failed or successful. Orthodoxies resist change; the more dogmatic the orthodoxy, the stronger the resistance. Power is never surrendered without a fight. The wonder of the second Russian revolution was the absence of bloodshed. Extremely rarely, and even then completely unintentionally, do closed systems produce the treachery that destroys them. Orthodoxies permit reform only under great duress and then only to maintain the status quo ante. Once the seed of reform is planted, its roots reach in many unanticipated directions. Reform has a natural force all its own. It is like water flowing downward; once released, it will find a way around, over, or under every barrier.

The reformer's attraction to irony is already well established. But nothing in his lifetime would surpass the irony that the second Russian revolution represented for American politics. For more than four decades, America's central organizing principle was the worldwide containment of communism. Vast resources, energies, and talent went into the enterprise at the cost of much else. Arch-conservatives in America found it convenient to use the Communist threat as a means to deny resources to the government for domestic, human, and infrastructure needs. A nation militant is rarely also a nation humane. There would always be a frightening new aspect to the Soviet threat and a new weapon needed to respond to it. Sorry about the school-lunch program.

Since those same conservatives had never believed Gorbachev to be the genuine article, they were perhaps more shocked than anyone when the system that he had done so much to undermine and that they believed to be immutable and immortal collapsed virtually overnight. The anti-Communist conservatives, as distinct from the economic and political conservatives, had no other raison d'être. Since the second Russian revolution, they have been heard from only rarely. Their sharp deflation had much to do with devaluation of the Republican party's fortunes in 1992 and its defeat in the 1992 national elections. Puff as some might, Saddam Hussein never could be inflated into Stalinesque dimensions. Suddenly, there existed no external threat, no excuse for neglect of the home fires, no argument for avoidance of the crumbling human and physical infrastructure of America. The Russians were not coming, and they had never been thirty feet tall.

One of the reformer's first Soviet acquaintances and one of the best-known Soviet academicians and commentators on America, Georgi Arbatov, made a now-famous statement at the height of the Gorbachev reforms: we are about to do the worst possible thing we can do to you, he said; we are about to take away your enemy. His understanding was keen. A nation with an enemy is a nation with the most basic purpose, survival. Take away the enemy, and a new purpose must be found. The most dramatic outcome of the Gorbachev-inspired revolution, beyond the huge relief from the prospect of nuclear holocaust, was to place America before a mirror. Who are we? What do we now stand for? What is our destiny?

No excuse would now exist to delay an American *perestroika*. American conservatism now found itself abandoned to its traditional arguments against big government. Having been in power for twelve years while government grew, the conservatives would no longer succeed with that argument. Whatever else it may represent, the second Russian revolution has represented a crisis for American conservatism, both in the Republican party and among the neo-conservatives in the Democratic party.

The post–cold war America of the 1990s is an America ripe for reform—reform of its priorities and its purposes and reallocation of its resources. No such time had existed since the New Deal era. But a great depression is not required to mobilize the people. They are ready for change. All that remains in the way is the most important part of the Reagan legacy: huge debts and deficits. That part of the supply-side conspiracy remains to haunt the nation. In the final irony of all, the last barrier to a reform of America for the new century and the new millennium would not be the Soviets' tanks but Ronald Reagan's debts.

18

THE PROPHET
OF A NEW DEMOCRACY

Almost all the heroes of the late twentieth century have spent some time in jail. Democracy triumphant and totalitarianism defeated produced Nelson Mandela, Lech Walesa, and Vaclav Havel, among many others. Each had been imprisoned—in Mandela's case for a quarter century—for his beliefs. Each gained moral authority by this experience. Each was punished for opposing injustice. Each was honored and respected by America and Western democracy for his courage.

The last American so jailed for his beliefs and, following his death, so honored was Martin Luther King, Jr. He had been harassed not only by southern segregationist authorities but also by the highest investigative agency in the land as recently as a few weeks before his death. His hero, it is important to note, was Mahatma Gandhi, who also spent time in the jails of a so-called democratic colonial power. There would be no American heroes of this dimension following King's death. Either America had so approximated democratic utopia that heroes were not required, or ways more sophisticated than imprisonment had been found to quiet its dissidents.

In any case, America is a land without heroes as a century of martyrs and heroes of democracy comes to a close. Is there some association between jail and heroism? Is a jail sentence required for heroism? If so, then a society has merely to eliminate jail sentences to eliminate heroes. To jail a dissident is to create a potential hero. In the postidealistic, materialist republic of the consumer, there could be no heroes, because the dissident is not sent to jail; he is simply ignored. Dissent from materialist values may be contemptible, but it is difficult to label it as criminal behavior in any case. Ignorance of the antimaterialist reformer-dissident eliminates the messiness of heroism created by incarceration.

Heroes are men and women of action, even if the action is passive, nonviolent resistance. In an age of twisted ideology, heroes are often those who simply refuse to go along. But action or resistance in such an age requires belief, and belief is the product of both instinct and thought. Even if the instinct of resistance is present, the republics of consumerism cleverly combat the process of thought with noise, the noise of television sitcoms, action movies featuring superreal "heroes," newer and grander shopping malls, theme parks, professional sports, sensational talk shows, and shouting political pundits. It is difficult to think creatively and critically about the tyranny of materialist social values in the midst of the constant din of noisy amusement. Amusement would become the late-twentieth-century consumer society's substitute for jail: a clever way of silencing the dissident without creating a martyr or a hero. Not accidentally, the most important critique of the noisy televised world of consumerism would be entitled *Amusing Ourselves to Death.*

Arguably, there is some strange connection among jail, thinking, and heroism. Vaclav Havel, the first and last president of the Federation of Czech and Slovak Republics and first president of the Czech Republic, is principally neither politician nor dissident. He is a playwright and an intellectual. His only public office has been as president of his country, a position to which he was unanimously elected following communism's collapse and democracy's triumph in November 1989. His lonely efforts to "live in truth," to resist suffocation by posttotalitarian, repressive bureaucratic society, had earned him several years in communism's prisons. During these periods, in letters to his wife, in drafts of plays, in essays addressed to small circles of dissenting friends, all circulated surreptitiously and illegally in *samizdat* style, Havel created some of the most powerful ideas in the wide political world of the late twentieth century. His moral authority gave the ideas power. His moral authority came from his unwillingness to compromise. Jail was an oppressive state's mindless recourse.

Havel, being an extraordinary man, would have undoubtedly been a hero with or without jail. But the isolation of incarceration, the loneliness of forced internal exile, can help sharpen the mind and spirit of even a hero. Only Havel knows the degree to which his writings then and since gained weight and power from the cold, damp quiet of the prison cell. In the case of his great predecessors, Gandhi, King, and others, the connection would not be in doubt.

The exile of imprisonment visited upon Havel and others like him by the totalitarian regime was punishment for being dissidents. Havel dislikes the word, always putting it in quotes because it suggests the role of professional malcontent. Rather, he believes that "living in truth" and affirming one's own identity is an "existential attitude," and those who share that attitude form a natural movement that "grows out of the principle of equality, founded on the notion that human rights and freedoms are indivisible." "It is truly a cruel paradox," he wrote in opposition to being categorized as dissident, that "the more some citizens stand up in defense of other citizens, the more they are labeled with a word that in effect separates them from those 'other citizens.' " He profoundly disliked being treated like an exotic insect by Western intellectuals seeking to express solidarity or visiting him simply out of curiosity: "Beside the Gothic and Baroque monuments, dissidents are apparently the only thing of interest to a tourist in this uniformly dreary environment," he wrote in 1984. He was particularly distressed by the assumptions of intellectuals who sought to draw him and other dissidents into the East-West ideological struggle. He had long since been operating on a deeper, more humanitarian plane:

> I admit that [the question of socialism and capitalism] gives me a sense of emerging from the depths of the last century. It seems to me that these categories have long since been beside the point. The question is wholly other, deeper and equally relevant to all; whether we shall, by whatever means, succeed in reconstituting the natural world as the true terrain of politics, rehabilitating the personal experience of human beings as the initial measure of things, placing morality above politics and responsibility above our desires, in making human community meaningful, in returning content to human speaking, in reconstituting, as the focus of all social action, the autonomous, integral and dignified I, responsible for ourselves because we are bound to something higher, and capable of sacrificing something . . . for the sake of that which gives life meaning.

As corrupt and corrupting as the "values" of post-totalitarian communism were, Havel did not automatically accept that Western democracy had achieved its ideal. "All of us, East and West," he wrote,

> face one fundamental task from which all else should follow. That task is one of resisting vigilantly, thoughtfully and attentively . . . the irrational momentum of anonymous, impersonal and inhuman power—the power of ideologies, systems, apparat, bureaucracy, artificial language and political slogans. We must resist their complex and wholly alienating pressure, whether it takes the form of consumption, advertising, repression, technology, or cliché—all of which are the blood brothers of fanaticism and the wellspring of totalitarian thought.

A careful man with words, Havel did not rank consumption and advertising with repression accidentally. Instead of consumption manipulated by advertising and the repressive manipulation of political opinion by artificial language, he favored "antipolitical politics"; that is, "politics not as the technology of power and manipulation, of cybernetic rule over humans or as the art of the useful, but politics as one of the ways of seeking and achieving meaningful lives, of protecting them and serving them . . . politics as practical morality, as service to the truth, as essentially human and humanly measured care for our fellow humans." He acknowledged this approach in this world to be "extremely impractical and difficult to apply in daily life"; still, he said, "I know no other alternative."

American politicians do not say or write such things because they do not think such things. Although American citizens might semiseriously wish it for many, jail alone would not encourage this depth of thought for most American politicians. For most, the terror and punishment of imprisonment would not be in the incarceration itself but, rather, in silence's imperative to think and reflect. American politics does not encourage such thinking because it constantly defines its limits too narrowly. It has become too professional and careerist, too anxious to fit the one-dimensional restrictions of television, too uncomfortable with serious thought and ideas, too combative and competitive, too concerned with winning, and not concerned enough with governing. In short, American politics, so long preoccupied with its unfamiliar and negative task of containing communism, may have lost its moral compass and dimension in the process.

In the two years since the velvet revolution restored democracy to Czechoslovakia, Havel has documented a more vivid, but still recognizable, picture of freedom's dark side. "The return of freedom to a society that was morally unhinged," he wrote recently, "has produced . . . an enormous and dazzling explosion of every imaginable human vice." "Society has freed itself," he continues,

> but in some ways it behaves worse than when it was in chains. Criminality has grown rapidly, and the familiar sewage that in times of historical reversal always wells up from the nether regions of the collective psyche has overflowed into the mass media, especially the gutter press. But there are other, more serious and dangerous symptoms: hatred among nationalities, suspicion, racism, even signs of Fascism; politicking, an unrestrained, unheeding struggle for purely particular interests, unadulterated ambition, fanaticism of every conceivable kind, new and unprecedented varieties of robbery, the rise of different mafias; and a prevailing lack of tolerance, understanding, taste, moderation, and reason. There is a new attraction to ideologies, too—as if Marxism had left behind it a great, disturbing void that had to be filled at any cost.

His damning, but uncomfortably familiar, indictment continues: "Partisan considerations still visibly take precedence over pragmatic attempts to arrive at reasonable and useful solutions to problems. Analysis is pushed out of the press by scandalmongering. . . . Anyone can accuse anyone else of intrigue or incompetence, or of having a shady past and shady intentions. Demagogy is rife, and even something as important as the natural longing of a people for autonomy is exploited in power plays, as rivals compete in lying to the public." Predictably, Havel says, "Citizens are becoming more and more disgusted with all this, and their disgust is understandably directed against the democratic government they themselves elected."

To witness the dark sides of capitalism and democracy vividly demonstrating themselves so hard on the heels of cruel communism's collapse would dismay less stalwart and dedicated figures. But moral purpose does not so easily shrivel. "If a handful of friends and I," writes Havel,

> were able to bang our heads against the wall for years by speaking the truth about Communist totalitarianism while surrounded by an ocean of apathy, there is no reason why I shouldn't go on banging my head against the wall by speaking ad nauseam, despite the condescending smiles, about responsibility and morality in the face of our present social marasmus. There is no reason to think that this struggle is a lost cause. The only lost cause is one we give up on before we enter the struggle.

As a reformer in America would be, Havel is motivated to carry on by what he sees as a "huge potential of goodwill slumbering within our society." This dormant goodwill needs to be stirred, he says. "People need to hear that it makes sense to behave decently or to help others, to place common interests above their own, to respect the elementary rules of human coexistence. . . . People want to hear that decency and courage make sense, that something must be risked in the struggle against dirty tricks. They want to know they are not alone, forgotten, written off."

An American citizen could be forgiven for finding these sentiments quaint and unfamiliar. They have not often been heard in late-twentieth-century American politics, the politics of negative television advertising, character attacks, triviality, and scandal. Few pundits, media advisers, or campaign consultants have been heard to recommend the high road, the road that recognizes the politician's duty to appeal to the slumbering potential of citizen goodwill and the better angels of our nature. "They say a nation gets the politicians it deserves," says Havel. "In some senses this is true: politicians are indeed a mirror of their society, and a kind of embodiment of its potential. At the same time —paradoxically—the opposite is also true: society is a mirror of its politicians. It is largely up to the politicians which social forces they choose to liberate and which they choose to suppress, whether they rely on the good in each citizen or on the bad."

American politicians and their professional advisers have increasingly taken the low road; they have chosen to liberate the bad in each citizen and suppress the good while voter participation declines and apathy reaches tidal proportions. There would be little in the political rhetoric of any recent national election to challenge, uplift, or inspire the American people to exercise their civic duties and responsibilities. Candidates and presidents have described the poor and less fortunate as malingerers and social leeches. They have pandered to base prejudice by maligning the very government they seek to lead. They set race against race, class against class, manager against worker, the powerful against the weak. They divide society instead of seeking to unite it. Instead of assuming responsibility, they fix blame for failure on a partisan basis. The press is used, too willingly, as the conduit for every kind of personal character assault. Respecting neither each other nor the people they serve, politicians mourn that they themselves are not respected.

Right-wing attacks on the government's credibility has not been exclusively ideological. It has also been cynical and calculated. To reform society requires citizen confidence in a reformed government. Politicians of the right do not want a reformed government because such a government is both more effective and more widely supported by ordinary citizens. Every effort is made to weaken and discredit government so that people will have no faith in it. If government can be made to seem incompetent and evil, then few will call on or rely on that government to improve or reform society. Politicians of the right, being essentially pessimistic about the nature of man and the improvability of human society and being antagonistic toward all government, are happily willing to destroy faith in political institutions in order to subvert even the ideal of social and economic reforms inspired by government.

How different then, in the dawn of democracy's triumph, to hear not an American reformer but the heroic survivor of Czech Communist jails restate the civic ideal for a democratic society:

Genuine politics—politics worthy of the name, and the only politics I am willing to devote myself to—is simply a matter of serving those around us: serving the community or those who will come after us. Its deepest roots are moral because it is a responsibility, expressed through action, to and for the whole, a responsibility that is what it is—a "higher" responsibility—only because it has metaphysical grounding: that is, it grows out of a conscious or subconscious certainty that our death ends nothing, because everything is forever being recorded and evaluated somewhere else, somewhere "above us," in what I have called "the memory of Being"—an integral aspect of the secret order of the cosmos, of nature, and of life, which believers call God and to whose judgment everything is subject. Genuine conscience and genuine responsibility are always, in the end, explicable only as an expression of the silent assumption that we are observed "from above," that everything is visible, nothing is forgotten, and so earthly time has no power to wipe away the sharp disappointments of earthly failure: our spirit knows that it is not the only entity aware of these failures.

Can it be imagined that Ronald Reagan or George Bush might have uttered these words? When has a national leader described politics as service, especially service to those who will come after? Who today can look us in the collective eye and say that he considers public service a moral responsibility? How many politicians seriously believe that their words or their votes await divine judgment? Most would shudder at the thought that nothing is forgotten, and none would be heard to say, This failure is my responsibility.

Vaclav Havel, the Czech playwright, is the very ideal of democratic reformer. He did not seek to reform the Communist system under which he and his countrymen suffered. He assumes a harder task. He seeks to reform democratic institutions, democratic society, and the democratic ideal. He seeks to restore antique notions of civic duty and responsibility. He believes that society cannot be divorced from the natural world. He believes that politics cannot be divorced from "the culture of everything, the general level of public manners." That includes not simply the relationships of human to human and class to class but also "the quality of people's relationships to nature, to animals, to the atmosphere, to the landscape, to towns, to gardens, to their homes—the culture of housing and architecture, of public catering, of big business and small shops; the culture of work and advertising; the culture of fashion, behavior and entertainment.''

Vaclav Havel, as a reformer of the ideal of democracy itself, in his uniquely humble way undertakes to remind us of the standards to which we hold ourselves and to which we claim God has called us. As with the ancient Israelites, no society likes to be reminded of its shortcomings. Happily for Havel, he is in the faraway Czech republic. A prophet of the democratic ideal would be without honor in the republic of the consumer. He refuses to accept the Western ideal of the economic man, an ideal that lends itself directly and inevitably to the seductive goal of a republic of consumerism and the subtle tyranny of materialism. ''However important it may be to get our economy back on its feet,'' Havel says, echoing the standard political rhetoric but then going far beyond it, ''it is far from being the only task facing us. It is no less important to do everything possible to improve the general cultural level of everyday life.''

His elevated sense of the role of civility and the genuinely civil society extends even beyond the Western goal of the rule of law:

> I am convinced that we will never build a democratic state based on rule of law if we do not at the same time build a state that is—regardless of how unscientific this may sound to the ears of a political scientist—human, moral, intellectual and spiritual, and cultural. The best laws and the best-conceived democratic mechanisms will not in themselves guarantee legality or freedom or human rights—anything, in short, for which they were intended—if they are not underpinned by certain human and social values.

There is something, he says, beyond mere politics: a better economic standard of living. There is something beyond mere economics: a state that recognizes the rule of law. There is something beyond the rule of law: human happiness. There is something beyond mere happiness: a civilized culture, the aim and purpose of which is to elevate moral and spiritual values that give human freedom meaning and content.

Little of this, Havel believes, is possible in a society where the coin of politics is devalued as it is in modern-day America. How unlike Ronald Reagan he sounds when he says, "Despite the political distress I face every day, I am still deeply convinced that politics is not essentially a disreputable business; and to the extent that it is, it is only disreputable people who make it so." "If your heart is in the right place and you have good taste," he continues, "not only will you pass muster in politics, you are destined for it." Good thing that good taste has never been a requirement for politics in America.

Havel, the prophet of a new democracy, rejects the twin plagues of modern-day American politics: partisanship and ideology. Partisanship is simply the hiding place of the worst kind of political careerist. "Power-hungry people," he wrote after more than a year in his presidency, "can use their party membership, their servility to party leaders, their clever concealment behind the party flag, to gain a position and an influence that is out of all proportion to their qualities." Then, in a complaint that has the ring of eerie familiarity, he describes politics in his federation on the brink of disintegration:

> A few months before the elections, electoral politics are already dominating political life. Half the news and commentary in the papers consists of speculations about which parties will ally themselves with which. There are articles about partisan bickering,

bragging and intrigue, predictions about who will join with whom and against whom, who will help (or harm) whose chances in the election, who might eventually shift support to whom, who is beholden to whom or falling out with whom. Politicians seem to be devoting more time to party politics than to their jobs. Not a single law is passed without a debate about how a particular stand might serve a party's popularity. Ideas, no matter how absurd, are touted purely to gain favor with the electorate. Parties formed for reasons of personal ambition compete for free air time. . . . All this displaces a responsible interest in the prosperity and success of the broader community.

While he languished in the Communist prison cell, almost dying of pneumonia and staying alive by willing his country's freedom, it would have been more than cruel for anyone to have told him that what lay in store was very much like late-twentieth-century American politics.

Even worse for the politics of true morality are the politics of ideology. "Systems are there to serve people, not the other way around," Havel wrote. "That is what ideologies always forget." He missed nothing by his absence from the American political scene of the 1980s and '90s. "Right-wing dogmatism, with its sour-faced intolerance and fanatical faith in general precepts, bothers me as much as left-wing prejudices, illusions and utopias." He narrows his aim to focus on rigid economic purists: "The cult of 'systematically pure' market economics can be as dangerous as Marxist ideology, because it comes from the same mental position: that is, from the certainty that operating from theory is essentially smarter than operating from a knowledge of life, and that everything that goes against theoretical precepts, that cannot be made to conform to them, or that goes beyond them, is, by definition, worthy only to be rejected." There would appear no better analysis of the great supply-side experiment of the 1980s, which was so beautiful in theory, so bankrupting in practice. The rigid, ideological cult of the supply-side theory clung ever more tightly to its fraudulent maxims and sang ever more vigorously its dogmatic anthems even as it dragged the nation's economy into the tar pit of debt.

After a decade and a half in the center ring of American politics, this reformer, a disciple of Vaclav Havel's fresh, practical, but principled interpretations of the democratic ideal, would come to deplore the orthodox ideology of the right and to condemn the ideologues of the left when they permitted themselves to become rigid, doctrinaire, and antireformist. Most people do not find comfort in political ideology. They have seen the effects of its worst extremes in foreign dictatorships of the right or left and have been chilled when it occasionally rears its head during troubled times in America. Political extremism offers the momentary thrill of the roller coaster, but its vehicles have no brakes. Almost by definition, ideology is intolerant, and tolerance is a mainstay of American political culture.

Vaclav Havel offers a new paradigm. "I think that the world of ideologies and doctrines is on the way out for good," he says, "along with the entire modern age. We are on the threshold of an era of globality, an era of open society, an era in which ideologies will be replaced by ideas." A state based on ideas is precisely the opposite of the ideological state: "It is meant to extricate human beings from the straightjacket of ideological interpretations, and to rehabilitate them as subjects of individual conscience, of individual thinking backed up by experience, of individual responsibility, and with a love for their neighbors that is anything but abstract." The emergence of right-wing orthodoxy in the 1980s and beyond represents the last gasp of a century of ideology. Its nemesis—communism—gone, its raid on the public treasury in the interest of private wealth exposed, its domestic bogey—liberalism—as toothless as itself, right-wing dogmatism may now retreat to its cave to await another day of economic instability, social unrest, and demand for "strong leadership."

The vacuum created by the retreat of ideology must, however, be filled by ideas—big, new, creative ideas, but most of all, ideas of conscience, thinking, and responsibility. The ideal of democracy has prevailed throughout human history as much as anything because of its ability to survive the efforts of partisanship and ideology to restrict and contain it. If Vaclav Havel is right, if we are bound for a new world of globality, open society, and ideas, "the power of gravity, custom and fear, the dead weight of inertia, of orthodoxy and of complacency" must be overcome by a human spirit that seeks a better world than that which can be had in a republic of consumerism. A republic of conscience, social justice, and moral politics, a republic of higher responsibility, political civility, and a culture of decency and courage can be achieved only if a plurality of citizens feel responsible for serving those who come after them.

To live in truth in today's troubled and fragmented world is to believe in "the principle of equality which is founded on the notion that human rights and freedoms are indivisible." The reform impulse is the natural consequence of the democratic ideal that we are all in this together, that we should never send to know for whom the bell tolls. This is the vision of citizen Vaclav Havel, the prophet of a new democratic ideal.

19

HEROES OF REFORM: JEFFERSON'S NEXT GENERATION

At a time when all else might seem to spiral downward, the inspiration of lives spiraling upward is that much greater. That there are such lives and so few know of them must be a commentary on modern journalism. Plane crashes, not safe landings, are the news we receive. This journalistic hypothesis accounts in part both for the escalation of sensationalism and the decline of genuine inspiration in modern America. Nevertheless, these stories must be known. For as John Kennedy wrote in *Profiles in Courage*,

> To be courageous . . . requires no exceptional qualifications, no magic formula, no special combination of time, place and circumstances. It is an opportunity that sooner or later is presented to us all. Politics merely furnishes one arena which imposes special tests of courage. In whatever arena of life one

may meet the challenge of courage, whatever may be the sacrifices he faces if he follows his conscience —the loss of his friends, his fortune, his contentment, even the esteem of his fellow men—each man must decide for himself the course he will follow. The stories of past courage can define that ingredient—they can teach, they can offer hope, they can provide inspiration. But they cannot supply courage itself. For this each man must look into his own soul.

There can be three responses to social injustice: neglect, collective action, or individual response. Neglect is the policy of the pessimist who accepts injustice and misery as the human condition, and it is the attitude of the selfish who do not care. Collective action is the policy of the reformer and the American liberal, who believe that all society bears a responsibility for the elimination of injustice and that instruments of government must be brought to bear when individual initiative is inadequate or impossible. Individual response, or private charity, is the recourse of the conservative whose social conscience clashes with his antigovernment philosophy. It is also the recourse of reformers frustrated by a coldhearted government.

At issue is an ancient dilemma: are people impoverished by choice or by society's failure? Who, exactly, is responsible for poverty? If it is the individual, then society's only obligation is to create a climate of reasonable opportunity, and the individual has the responsibility to take advantage of it. But if society has failed to open the doors of opportunity to all or, worse, has created conditions conducive to the metastasis of poverty, then a sense of justice requires the society's government to eliminate the conditions of poverty and injustice. Furthermore, if society has permitted injustice to take root and even flourish but has refused to require its government to attack these roots, individuals of conscience and commitment to human decency find themselves compelled to act. These heroes of social justice are inspired but lonely.

For some, their moral sense is so keen and their humanitarianism so great they would wage their own wars on poverty even if the government were the most benign and the most generous. For others, who might have seen public service as the most effective avenue by which to achieve social justice, the coldheartedness of their government toward human ills would bring them to seek their own individual path toward justice.

"I remember exactly when I got the idea to create SOS [Share Our Strength]," says Bill Shore.

> It was late August of 1984 and I was still decompressing from the 1984 presidential campaign and the Democratic convention in San Francisco. I'd been catching up on my sleep, reading the paper more carefully, and actually stopping to think about what I was reading. One morning *The Washington Post* ran a small story deep in the inside pages that was headlined AS MANY AS 200,000 TO DIE OF STARVATION IN ETHIOPIA. This was well before any film footage had conveyed the horror of famine on the evening news; indeed it was one of the very first mentions of a famine that would eventually take on historic proportions. It seemed then—as it seems now—that it should have been a bigger story. As I sat thinking about what it meant and what could be done, my feelings were less those of outrage than of gratitude that for the first time in years I had really *felt* something about world events, beyond the usual calculations of how they could be turned to political advantage.

Begun just eight years ago by Bill Shore, his sister Debbie, and very few others, SOS is now one of the largest hunger-relief organizations in America. In 1991, SOS distributed over $4 million to other groups combating hunger across America. Operating with a very small staff and an army of volunteers, it has one of the lowest rates of overhead of any similar organization. SOS originally sought donations from restaurants, then organized annual Taste of America events, featuring the best chefs in hundreds of cities, and now publishes calendars and books of short stories by well-known writers and pursues an amazingly inventive array of fund-raising activities. Success was not automatic. For almost three years, this band of reformers themselves almost starved, living at times from cash advances from the credit cards of Bonnie Shore, Bill's wife.

During this hard period, lessons were learned, not about organization or fund-raising, according to Shore, but, rather, about "dreams buried deep in the hearts of men and women and the awesome power of unlocking those dreams and bringing them to the surface." The first lesson, says Shore, is that people want to give of themselves: "Talented people want to give of their talents," not just of their pocketbooks. "Paradoxically, our participatory democracy, flooded with handlers, consultants and 'pros,' doesn't really have room for this kind of participation anymore, or at least it doesn't seem to." He notes that the acclaimed writer Anne Tyler would rather take eight weeks to write a story that will earn SOS several thousand dollars than take a few seconds to write a check. "People want to be part of something bigger than themselves," Shore notes. When people attend a Taste of America event in their community, they also know there are ninety-seven other such events happening nationally. To fulfill its theme of a common humanity, SOS is now spreading its net internationally as well.

There is a curious but sympathetic similarity between Bill Shore's motives for starting SOS and those of Alan Khazei, cofounder of City Year in Boston. Together with another young Harvard Law School graduate, Michael Brown, Khazei envisioned a youth service corps as an "action tank," a place where the theory of national service could be tested through experimentation and difficult practical experience on the way to a genuine national service program:

> We asked ourselves what other idea, if implemented, would change the country more for the better? To change America we must change the experience of Americans, in particular young Americans, and then let them loose to change the country. Within the idea of national service is the most powerful theory for democracy and the clearest strategy for long-term social change that we have ever come across. National service is and must be about service, not politics as it is currently understood. Yet, on the level of political theory, national service is profoundly political because it is an institution designed to make democracy work by giving citizens a chance to truly exercise the critical element of self-government in a democracy which is meaningful and direct participation in something larger than oneself.

"Something larger than oneself" echoes the purpose and ideal of SOS and could not represent a starker contrast to the selfish ethos of the 1980s. Indeed, Alan Khazei cites Gandhi as the model for connecting service to democracy. For Gandhi, there were three keys to building democracy: the ballot (political rights), the jail (civil disobedience), and the spinning wheel (what City Year calls the "spade," which represents "the willingness of citizens to do the daily service work or spadework that it takes to create a democratic society"). An important distinction between charity and justice is thus drawn. Acts of charity—a thousand points of light—are individual demonstrations of human compassion. Public service, such as that constituted by City Year, represents the spade, the instrument used to achieve social justice and a truly democratic society. As Khazei says, the thousand points of charitable light are a good first step, but they need to be built upon with the understanding that someone has to "supply the electricity ultimately and that 1000 Points of Light if harnessed, redirected, studied and amplified could become full beacons and lighthouses leading the way for innovation in a host of areas."

In 1992, with new funding from the Commission on National and Community Service, City Year organized more than 220 corps members from all income levels, races, and educational backgrounds, focusing on housing and homelessness, school partnerships, the environment, the enhancement of citizenship, and the building of youth leadership. City Year projects a youth corps of more than 500 members for 1993, which would have a major transforming effect on the greater Boston community and serve as a national demonstration project. As a workshop or "action tank" to demonstrate the viability of public service as a national undertaking—"the missing link in making American democracy work"—City Year has focused on the following:

- Organizing the first youth service corps to be launched entirely through private funds from corporations, foundations, unions, and individuals
- Empowering corps members with the skills and confidence to design and implement their own community-service projects
- Demonstrating that youths from difficult circumstances can succeed in a diverse environment. Over the past two years, fourteen corps members who had dropped out of high school have received a general equivalency diploma or their high school diploma with City Year, and several have received four-year college scholarships.
- Achieving a demand by young people for a year of

service. City Year received more than eight hundred applications for the 1992 program.

- Developing a comprehensive programmatic design for service and education organized around a school-year calendar with semesters, an internship month, and constantly increasing responsibilities, all culminating in a community-celebration graduation
- Successfully developing and spinning off other service ideas and opportunities, including the nation's first Serve-a-thon, which last year attracted more than seven thousand people, who provided fifty thousand hours of service and raised $700,000 for City Year
- Promoting the idea of voluntary national service at the community and national level, City Year has been featured as a model for national service by *The New York Times*, ABC, NBC, CNN national news, *Inc.* magazine, National Public Radio, *The Christian Science Monitor*, and the Progressive Policy Institute.

According to Khazei, City Year has adopted a strategy called public service entrepreneurship, which means taking the same skills, approaches, strategies, and techniques that have traditionally been demonstrated in private-sector entrepreneurship and utilizing them in the public sphere to rearrange resources to a higher public purpose. Noting also the search for a "new paradigm," or a redefined role for government in the post–cold war era, the founders of City Year view national service, properly designed and implemented, as a breakthrough institution that might help define a new role for government and reinvigorate democracy. For example, an innovative national service program, patterned after City Year, could embody a meaningful and significant role for the private and not-for-profit sector in partnership with government; experiment with new ideas such as using a voucher system for service opportunity choice and a new GI Bill for community service. The federal government itself could act more as a strategic venture social capitalist helping to fund programs, evaluate efforts, provide technical assistance to state and local efforts, gather and disseminate information nationally, and pilot some programs but not serve as an administrator of huge federal programs. Thus, says Alan Khazei, "even in the way that national service is developed, implemented and grown it can be a vehicle for reform":

> For City Year, national service has meant *citizenship and inclusiveness*, inviting Americans from all backgrounds to serve equally, and to work on the [needs of] the nation together. It also means inviting people and institutions from all sectors to participate together to create the institutions through which young citizens travel the path of service. To City Year, national service means uniting a nation of immigrants, and giving the most diverse nation on the planet a powerful shared public purpose and sense of community. For us, national service is essentially an institutionalized "meeting place" for our society, using the vehicle of community service as the common ground around which to bring people from all sectors, backgrounds and life experiences together for the common good.

In 1910, William James articulated the need for citizen service in an essay entitled "The Moral Equivalent of War." During the Great Depression, the unemployed were given an opportunity to help themselves while helping the nation through the Civilian Conservation Corps. Asking what could be done for the country, John Kennedy created the Peace Corps and VISTA. From the early 1980s on, this reformer and others have advocated the creation of a voluntary national service corps for the young people of America. He would very much endorse this conclusion by the hero-founders of City Year: "We believe that national service is the next logical step for our democracy and that if we do not come up with a vehicle to develop an ethic of real citizenship and unite our society across sectors and backgrounds, we risk tearing ourselves apart as we continue to become at least two Americas."

Like Bill Shore and Alan Khazei, Trevor Cornwell began public service as a student volunteer in a national political campaign. Later he conceived of a program to provide young people with an opportunity for community service in Central Europe. The National Service League, operating on a very small budget provided by private donations, trains young volunteers in community service programs in the United States and then helps relocate them in Central and Eastern European communities, where they perform similar, much-needed services.

In its first year, NSL sent ten pioneering volunteers to Central and Eastern Europe. Two had begun with the organization by helping a new credit union in the North Bronx establish an accounting system so that it could in turn help finance businesses and homes in the area. One volunteer helped educate Eastern Europeans in ways of solving their serious pollution problems. Another spent eight months in one of the emerging democracies, working on a daily newspaper. And a team of volunteers worked with the United States Department of Energy to learn how to weatherize low-income homes, extremely valuable knowledge in Central and Eastern Europe.

"These volunteers gave up a salary, school, jobs to help people here at home and then in Eastern Europe," states Trevor Cornwell; "they took a risk not only in moving away from home, but in working with a new idea called National Service League." NSL is one of the most cost-effective programs of its kind. Volunteers receive a stipend of only fifty dollars per week, they live in private homes, and they pay half their airfare. The second team of volunteers began service in September 1992, first in domestic community-service programs and then in emerging European democracies. Cornwell says, "This kind of experience is the best kind of investment we can make in young people; they learn, they develop and grow by helping others."

Creatively marrying the values of the 1960s with the values of the 1980s, Cornwell calls his approach "entrepreneurial idealism": "A new generation is tackling social problems by designing entrepreneurial public service ventures to meet these challenges in a quiet —and dramatically—different way. Rather than relying on protest marches or government programs, these entrepreneurial idealists are bringing in corporations and idealistic young people to serve as teachers in the inner city; to help Eastern Europeans make the transition from Communism to capitalism, and to rebuild failed social welfare programs. These are the young idealists of the nineties. From the hope of the Great Society and the laissez-faire of the eighties comes a fresh generation of public servants—people marrying the strategies of the public and private sectors."

Interestingly, Cornwell's logic matches Bill Shore's. The beneficiaries of community service are not only its recipients but also its providers. Official Washington celebrated democracy's triumph in Central and Eastern Europe and then did little else. To build the foundations of democracy in the former Eastern bloc, President Bush did not call on the government of the United States and corporate America; apparently, he simply relied on Trevor Cornwell and his ten pioneering volunteers. There is much to be said for a thousand points of light. But occasionally, a beacon does not hurt.

From late 1989 onward, history will wonder at the meager record of assistance given by the West to the people of the former Communist states. It will find especially confusing the disappearance of the conservative anti-Communist legions, who might have marched to democracy's aid in its hour of infancy. Random ideologues here and there would preach a brand of radical capitalism and conservative, even nationalistic, political orthodoxy. But no corps of teachers and doctors, management experts and business advisers, experts in the conversion of military production lines, engineers, and public administrators would be organized by the United States government. A reformer, himself struggling to draw the attention of American business to this needy market, would endlessly ponder the reasons why the American Republican president refused to lift his voice to his corporate supporters in an appeal to do something—anything—to establish markets and stabilize democracy for the 105 million people from Poland to Albania, not to mention the 300 million who lay beyond. It was nothing but a mystery of the age. At the pinnacle of power, of vision there was none. Indeed, Trevor Cornwell exhibited more vision than did George Bush.

Dennis Walto, from upstate New York, is a young Falstaff; he is up for anything. He is a pure American type. His genius is to organize. He could organize a camel train across the polar ice cap and bring it safely home. Where others see a madcap riot, Dennis Walto sees an army regiment. Had he a tail, it would wag constantly. Yet behind the spaniel-happy eyes, a caring soul grieves for human misery. His heart exudes more warmth than that of official Washington incorporated.

In his few years he has not only helped in three of the reformer's lost-cause campaigns, but he has also organized giant marches on Washington for women's equality and rights, crusades for freedom of speech and expression, the Children's Health Fund for poor children in New York City, and other causes even his own friends are unaware of. At last sighting, Dennis

Walto was one of the first to help organize the effort by the International Medical Corps to relieve the awful siege of starvation gripping millions in Somalia. He is there still.

Unlike many of his generation, Walto was not caught up in the ethos of the Reagan age. One suspects that he could not equate Wall Street's millions with helping to save the life of one Harlem or Somalian child. The abstract theories of supply-side economics could not compete with the concrete realities of day-to-day combat with poverty and misery. The posturing, positioning, and power brokering of national politics were trivial and sterile in comparison with hunger, homelessness, and want. For Dennis Walto and many like him, political campaigns are fun the way a circus is fun but still only the means to a much more important end. Unlike the cranky, angry bison of American reform, Dennis Walto harbors behind a joyful smile his own hopes and ideals for a more humane nation and a more humane world.

Of the Shores, Khazeis, Cornwells, and Waltos, there will always be too few. Cynics would find a society of saints-in-the-making unbearably tedious in any case. Better to keep the focus on human failure than on human mercy and kindness because then we will not be disappointed when a politician lets us down— or gets himself shot. But idealism is like a trick birthday candle: it cannot be blown out. Let the winds of cynicism blow at gale force; it still burns on. It is the hope for the salvation of mankind.

This reformer's frustration with the traditional politics of nominal consensus within the preestablished boundaries of acceptable establishment norms, as well as with the cynical right-wing meanness of the Reagan-Bush era, is more than temporal and partisan; it is deep and philosophical. It is about the search for the heart of the American character. Having gloried in the Reagan years, we critiqued the Reagan years, and now the cry is to move on. Without quoting Santayana for yet one more clichéd time, there are lessons to be learned unless we wish to be endlessly bound like Prometheus to the great rock of our mistakes and endlessly repeat cycles of greed and materialism, social injustice, and cultural meanness. To blame Washington for our troubles, to parody a confused Reagan whom we once praised, and then blithely dismiss the whole destructive era as a political aberration, a cultural frolic, and a detour, is to invite our ennui, our sophisticated boredom, to becloud our minds, to keep us from the lessons that the stern teacher of history insists we learn. Indeed, most people are not poor by choice. Most unemployed people want to work. Few people enjoy sleeping in doorways. Children do not choose poverty.

Years after leaving public service, a reformer would find his blood percolating with anger at even the dimmest recollection of the cruel, insipid, mindless, heartless excuses some fellow citizens and political colleagues would give for the very existence of poverty in America and the futility of taking collective action to combat it. If there were even the vaguest evidence that the nation at large had indeed learned the lesson of the Reagan years, that as a civilized society we were prepared to turn the instruments of government over to the legitimate and necessary cause of social justice in America, this reformer would lay down both his quarrel and the cudgel of reform with utmost happiness and terminate his cranky guerrilla cause.

The evidence of this triumph will be voices in Washington and elsewhere embracing the causes of national and international service, encouraging both young and old, individuals and corporations, to give of themselves to build democracy and combat misery, and appealing once again to American idealism. These chapters make much of the influence of John and Robert Kennedy and Martin Luther King, Jr. This is not simply an exercise in nostalgia; it is by way of contrasting values. In the early 1960s, the Shores, Khazeis, Cornwells, and Waltos would have been celebrated in Washington; they would have been acknowledged with prizes and dinners and invited on talk shows (none of which is their purpose, in any case). Rather than scorned and ignored, idealism would have been applauded and celebrated. Instead, the heroes of our day have been Rambos, Terminators, and Dirty Harrys. We are but the heroes we choose.

Many, many Americans want to give of themselves, to be part of something bigger than themselves and follow large, bold ideas that have a special power of their own. Political leaders cannot meet all these needs. But these needs cannot be met without political leadership. How else to explain the fact that more than three decades later people would still recite, with considerable wistfulness, "Ask what you can do for your country."

For his credo, Bill Shore quotes one little heard of in the 1980s, Albert Schweitzer: "I am convinced that far more idealistic aspiration exists than is ever evident. Just as the rivers we see are far less numerous than the underground streams, so the idealism which is visible is minor compared to what men and women carry in their hearts, unreleased or scarcely released. Mankind is waiting and longing for those who can accomplish the task of untying what is knotted and bringing the underground waters to the surface." Share Our Strength, City Year, the National Service League, and caring individuals like Dennis Walto are "untying what is knotted."

The ideal of political reform is exactly this, to use the instruments and powers of government to untie what is knotted, to release and encourage the vast underground streams of human idealism to come to the surface in the interest of equality and justice. To give a life, or even part of a life, in this cause is to enter the lists of the immortals.

20

THE AMERICAN
FAMILY

A nation living in a state is like a complex family living in a house. The children of a family do not choose where they are born, and the children of a nation are taught to recite the pledge of allegiance before they can possibly understand the implications of the oath. Despite America's persistent difficulties, however, many more are trying to get in than are trying to get out.

The question is what to do about the house and the people in it. After many generations and two centuries, the members of the family still cannot agree among themselves about their purpose. Some, those who are doing quite well, have very fine rooms and wish only to have the house defended from ugly or jealous neighbors; otherwise, they would be left alone. Others, who are not doing well, think their well-heeled relations should do more to help them and to keep up the house. Most of the family members fall in between: they work, have reasonable rooms, and aspire to be like their wealthy relations. When they are feeling secure and optimistic, they are sympathetic to the pleas of their poorer cousins. But when they feel insecure and threatened, they are capable of turning against the less well-off and of blaming them for the family's problems.

Recently, this family tried an experiment that seemed promising. It reduced everyone's obligation to the household account, but it also borrowed a lot of money to build a higher fence around the house and to buy more guns to hold off restless neighbors. The idea was that most of the family would become so wealthy that the household account would automatically grow and long-delayed repairs could be taken care of. The problem is the experiment failed. And the family faces great shortfalls in its account and is confused about its future.

In the meantime, the most dangerous of the family's neighbors collapsed and is totally preoccupied with a messy divorce. All the while other friendlier neighbors were modernizing their houses, concentrating their investments to educate their children, and creating good jobs for themselves, and they have become increasingly stronger and more prosperous. The American house, however, has cracks in its foundation, some windows are broken and the roof leaks, and its basic structure requires major repairs. The fence around the house is in much better shape than the house itself.

The American family is confused, divided, and leaderless. Basically, its members quarrel over whether they should have a strong family council or a weak one. Some think the family will never succeed in the neighborhood until the house is brought in line with modern standards. Others believe each family member should be left to sink or swim on his own. Most family members vacillate between the two arguments and cannot seem to make up their minds as to which is right. The argument began when the ancestors who occupied the house and organized the family were unable to agree among themselves on this question and left the fundamental issue open. While the American family continues to debate, the neighborhood continues to grow, change, and move on.

From the beginning, there have always been a few family members burdened with a reform impulse. They believe that the best way to liberate the independent energies and talents of all members of the family is to keep the house up-to-date and to keep the people in it in the best shape possible. These reformers constantly watch the changes unfolding inside the house and in the neighborhood outside and try to persuade the family to respond to them. They carry no brief for those who say everyone in the house ought to take care of himself and those who constantly attack the very idea of a family council. Likewise, they are impatient with those who want only to quarrel over division of the family wealth and allocation of membership on the council. They are impatient with a debate that seems quaint, anachronistic, and theoretical in the face of a constantly and dramatically changing neighborhood. They see their family in the person of Mr. Rogers, slowly putting on his cardigan and slippers while being mugged by Game Boy.

Mostly, the leadership of the family council, reflecting the dominant argument of the period, goes back and forth between the two old ideological factions, the Hatfields and the McCoys of American politics. If times get bad enough, a genuine reformer will be given leadership, and major improvements will be made. But these leaders do not come along often, and when they do, they are suspect, even considered weird for not belonging to one or the other of the traditional family factions. In the minds of those who take it upon themselves to observe these things, it is better to march to one of the familiar drums than to hear a distant, future beat.

Despite their quarrels, the two old family factions have one thing in common: a respect for power. Since the family rarely trusts one faction with total power, the factions spend more time dividing up the power than they do repairing the house. More and more members of the two factions concentrate on creating careers on the family council than on boldly advancing the family's interests. So many powerful family interests back members of both factions that the council has begun to look like one big, permanent, self-perpetuating establishment. Ordinary family members find that those they counted on to give them a true account of the council's activities have also become part of the establishment, and they are more fascinated by the council members' personalities than they are by their performance. Meanwhile, the house continues to age and crack. Nonpartisan citizens and reformers worry increasingly about the house and the neighborhood in which their children will live.

Do we get the kind of government we deserve, or is it better? Is our government a reflection of ourselves, or is it worse? Is the fault in our stars or in ourselves? Have we met the enemy, and is it us? These are not idle, academic questions in a search for the hidden barriers to the reform of the American house and family.

One faction of the American family, which is called, and calls itself, conservative, is pessimistic about the improvability of society and mankind in general. It dislikes paying taxes not only because it dislikes government but also because it believes that government's benevolent social functions are doomed to fail. Its roots are deep in the American character. If mankind's prospects for improvement are dim, then reform is largely a fool's errand.

Not only are the members of the American family

perpetually divided among themselves over the question of individual versus collective responsibility, but they are also a "people of paradox": they quite often embrace contradictory values. As Professor Michael Kammen has demonstrated, in language sufficiently persuasive to earn a Pulitzer Prize, we want extensive public services, but we want to pay low taxes; we want a strong society but few restrictions on individual freedoms ("collective individualism"); we want freedom of enterprise, but we want government regulations to promote competition and protect public health and safety; we want to retreat from a turbulent world, but we want to retain the right and the power to intervene against those who displease us; we regularly and officially invoke a Judeo-Christian God, but we insist on separation of church and state. Most societies embrace variable sets of values. Few do so as dramatically and innocently as America.

These unresolved paradoxes compound the already complex task of the American reformer. As a public servant, this reformer would constantly find remarkable his constituents' desire for less government while, at the same time, seeking the government's assistance. The only rational resolution of this paradox seemed to be in this: in philosophical principle, we are opposed to government programs, but since a majority of our fellow citizens seem to insist on these programs, we at least want our fair share. As an elected representative, the reformer could recall no instance in which even the most conservative constituent would reject, out of principle, some benefit from the national government for himself or his community. Indeed, some of his most ardently conservative Senate colleagues would fight like tigers for federal boons for their constituencies and states, all the while deploring big government with the most inflammatory rhetoric. Franklin Roosevelt saw the amusing irony of this right away:

For while it has been American doctrine that the government must not go into business in competition with private enterprises, still it has been traditional particularly in Republican administrations for business urgently to ask the government to put at private disposal all kinds of government assistance. The same man who tells you that he does not want to see the government interfere in business—and he means it, and has plenty of good reasons for saying so—is the first to go to Washington and ask the government for a prohibitory tariff on his product.

In the rapidly changing world of the late twentieth century, America would be a nation much in need of fundamental reforms. Impeding change were native conservatism, a fascination with trivia and amusement, the burdensome ballast of gravity, custom, and fear, and shortages of courage and imagination. But no barrier would rise as high as that of unresolved paradoxical values. In recent years, it became popular to blame lobbyists and special interest groups for government stagnation on the one hand and pretzellike contortions on the other. Few paused to examine the membership of the special interest groups that retained the powerful lobbyists. Whether industry or labor, the elderly, environmentalists, banking and transportation interests, health, education, or whatever, each group would include hundreds of thousands, if not millions, of "ordinary Americans"—the same Americans as those put out by the special interest groups. These members paid dues; the dues were used to hire lobbyists; the lobbyists used more of the dues to make contributions to politicians; the politicians enacted a great number of laws and regulations on behalf of the interest groups or refused to do so; more often than not, the members of the interest groups, in their capacity as ordinary citizens, disliked the laws and regulations enacted by the politicians acting under the influence of the lobbyists whose fees were paid with the dues of these same ordinary citizens in their capacity as members of a special interest group. Paradox—hypocrisy, a cynic might say—underlay the whole transaction.

So to the list of barriers to reform—conservatism, trivial distractions, dead custom, caution, and uninventiveness—add cultural paradox. The house of the American family is a more complicated place than most of its residents understand or wish to admit.

As people of paradox, we combine democratic ideals with governing elites, freedom with authority, collectivity with individualism and add it all to a religious secularity or a secular religiosity. Not surprisingly, these contradictory tendencies take their toll. "We have tended to hold contradictory ideas in suspension and ignore the intellectual and behavioral consequences of such 'doublethink,' " concludes Professor Kammen. In his book *An American Dilemma*, Gunnar Myrdal made his famous observation that an American is everywhere recognized as "a practical idealist." Henry Adams called himself "a conservative anarchist" (and, later, "a Unitarian mystic").

Societies as well as individuals can be haunted by unreconciled and unrequited injustices. Near the close of his lifelong struggle, bracketed by Kennedy assassinated and Reagan triumphant, the reformer heard special resonance in Professor Kammen's haunting judgment: "Guilt and insecurity have played a major part in keeping contradictory tendencies inherent in our style. First we wiped out the Indians whose land this was; then we emasculated the Africans brought to work the land. Few cultures in history have had to bear this kind of double collective culpability."

As recently as the 1992 Republican National Convention, an asinine leader of the Republican ultraright would be given access to a prime-time national television audience by a party with neither social conscience nor sense of history's judgment, a party that would claim spiritual responsibility for other people's unborn children but would deny social responsibility for the worst kind of racial injustice. "We are not responsible for [the slaughter of innocent Native Americans at] Wounded Knee, because we were not *at* Wounded Knee!" No, but the soldiers hired by your political ancestors were at Wounded Knee, Mr. Buchanan, and the blood of the original occupants of this land is on their hands—and yours.

If guilt and insecurity, resulting from our failure to satisfy Native and black Americans for the injustices they suffered, permit us to suspend contradictory values, then we shall never be a people capable of unequivocal reform and renewal. We shall remain tentative and cautious, uncertain and confused as to the direction in which we wish to move, and only hesitantly will we adapt to social, economic, and political changes in the world. Less than any other industrialized democracy, America has still to achieve consensus on a basic social welfare policy and assistance for the poor and elderly. Confronted with the dramatically visible increase in homelessness, hunger, and poverty during the 1980s and '90s, many Americans would find themselves shocked and appalled but confused as to the best response. The scope of the problem exceeded even the most callous effort to dismiss the poor as the victims only of their own lassitude. Americans, individually and collectively, are not without social conscience or consciousness. But conscience sublimated is guilt compounded. Issues of race and justice might be dismissed and deferred, but they would not disappear. In a nation that claims for itself a historically high standard of justice, the distance between the ideal and the real, between belief and practice, would remain too great to permit untroubled sleep. Except perhaps in the coldest conservative heart, the specter of injustice would continue to haunt the conscience of the American family.

The barrier of paradox—of contradictory values—is central to the reform dilemma. Major changes of method and direction require some manner of majority consensus. Consensus in a complex culture flows either from security and expansiveness or insecurity and fear. The classic twentieth-century cases of the latter are depression and world war. A close reading of a catastrophe of the Great Depression's magnitude, however, shows there was much less consensus on policies to be pursued than popular recollection suggests. The nation was not quite as united in common cause as Depression nostalgia suggests. Furthermore, it took Pearl Harbor to dissolve stiff isolationist resolve against military involvement in Asia and Europe.

In the postwar era, general consensus resulted from prosperity and the perceived Communist threat. But rather than a consensus for major reforms, it was to the contrary. In the 1950s, even relatively modest improvements in education and transportation were justified as national-defense measures—paradoxical as that was. Cultural paradox continues to confound reform consensus as the twentieth century draws to a close.

Natural conservatism, relative ease (even in the face of unease), and paradoxical values all became reform's subversion. Popular culture, mined for purpose and meaning, produces only fool's gold. Financially successful movies and music would be endlessly repeated and reworked until overtaken by tedium. Unable to imagine even new names, movies, like bored royal families, succumbed to repeating their titles, roman numerals appended. In a vacuum created by cautious leadership and the disappearance of great purpose, single issues such as abortion and gun control assumed almost epic dimensions of social polarization. They increasingly became smoke screens behind which to hide from greater terrors in the jungles of the late twentieth century: crushing public debt, consumption outrunning production, dangerous reliance on unstable foreign energy, a giant military machine whose purpose had evaporated.

Most puzzling of all America's paradoxes of this period was the predominance of gloom and pessimism in the midst of comfort for at least large majorities. Bestselling books bore such titles as *Why America Failed* and *Who Will Tell the People: The Betrayal of American Democracy.* Popular magazines routinely produced cover stories documenting "gloom in America" as well as feature stories concerning rampant psychological depression and teenage suicide. Many people had either found the materialist side of the American dream hollow or were afraid it might turn quickly into a nightmare. In spite of a standard of living far above that of most people in the world, too many Americans have been unable to enjoy prosperity. It could be that these themes of national psychoanalysis were simply novel ways of increasing the sales of periodicals—that is to say, they were cynical warnings of nonexistent social trauma. But even discounting this real possibility, late-twentieth-century America, except for the self-satisfied wealthy, was not a nation savoring its cold war victory and content with its prospects.

Right-wingers, deprived of the Communist demon that had given their lives purpose, sought to create a culture war within the American family, converting that which was merely a trivial, silly, and tasteless episode in popular entertainment into something menacing and evil. At the junction of two eras, when Americans should have been discussing their new, complex future, almost all seemed satisfied instead to have the Republican vice-president debate a fictional television personage on the implications that her fatherless, fictional baby had for "family values." Everyone knew this to be a low point of some sort, a fantastic cultural watershed, but none knew what to call it. At most, it was but the symptom of a new

cultural disease, a disease bred in the dead-calm trop-
ics of reform avoidance. AIDS would kill the body; the
cultural disease of triviality would only kill the mind
and the spirit. A nation unwilling or unable to discuss
seriously the organization of progressive change—let
alone carry it out—cannot be a happy nation.

After a quarter century of political education, the
reformer would still not possess the golden key to the
gate of progressive change for a paradoxical society.
He would come to know that his society was infinitely
more complex than it would permit itself or others to
believe. The myth of the simple, rugged, individualist
cowboy was but a convenient role into which a complicated actor could successfully disappear. The actor
had every night, however, to leave the arena's stage
and return to quarreling children, a leaky roof, and the
routine of an undramatic life that no six-gun could
improve (except in the most dramatic way possible).
The wonder is that the American character actor could
continue to play the cowboy role so well almost a
century after the genuine article had ridden off into
history's sunset, and that he could play it not only to
his own satisfaction but also to the applause of the
world. To mock the myth, Stanley Kubrick, in *Dr.
Strangelove*, had Slim Pickens ride the first nuclear
bomb of World War III on its descent to Russian soil as
if it were the world's greatest (and last) bucking
bronco.

America's paradoxical character, its naïve complexity and sophisticated innocence, its struggle to maintain an idealism that was wrinkling like a fading starlet
made education through reform a precarious occupation. But the impulse toward progress is the product of
both stubbornness and optimism. This stubbornness
scoffs at defeat, and the optimism springs from the
conviction that man will not only endure but will, in
Faulkner's words, prevail. In spite of enough defeats,
frustrations, and setbacks to last a very long lifetime,

this reformer could have no part of the conservative's bleak pessimism about the human condition. Perhaps it was the residue of Wesley's doctrine of spiritual perfection and social renewal. Perhaps it was his own witness to countless acts of human perseverance and resilience in overcoming staggering obstacles. Perhaps it was the universal hope deep in the souls of people in every human tribe that they could make the fortunes of their children even slightly better than their own.

The democratic ideal finds its most profound resonance in the notion of the improvability of the human condition and in each parent's commitment to that notion, at least in the case of his own children. All the barriers of conservatism, triviality, fear, pessimism, and paradox must evaporate before the central reform truth that things can be better for our children. To reject this principle and universal belief is to reject the very purpose of life itself.

God does weigh the sins of the warmhearted and the coldhearted on different scales. To accept injustice, poverty, and human misery as the inevitable fate of mankind is to diminish the promise and the greatness of which the human spirit is capable. Civic virtue and the citizen's duty, moral responsibility and communitarianism—all reflect the sense that we are in this together. America is emerging from an unaccountable era of selfishness and greed. Few felt really good about it at the time; many more are now outraged at its worst excesses. This era represents genuine Darwinian regression only if we refuse to learn from it and resist the appeal some time from now to return to its easy temptation. The collective goodwill must be summoned now to prove that individual freedom is not the enemy of the commonweal and that the surest guarantee of society's security and future is the assurance that all can join in the family's journey forward.

By virtue of its idealistic impulse, reform is always doomed to fail. It can never reach its own impossible standard. There will always be an unrequited cause or an injustice to make right. That is why the implacable American bison of reform will never be satisfied and must always be restless to search. Conditions and circumstances change, and the caravan moves on. But the struggle is always the same. Samuel Beckett summarized the reformer's life and philosophy thus:

All of old. Nothing else ever. Ever tried. Ever failed. No matter. Try again. Fail again. Fail better.

Fail better.

Afterword

THE UNFINISHED SEARCH
FOR NOBILITY

It is a central thesis of this book that egalitarian democracies understand reform to be the price periodically paid in order to avoid revolution and that the
persistent frustration of reform can lead to dangerous
consequences. Reform itself can usually be postponed
as long as economies are expanding and standards of
living are rising. But when institutions and structures
fail to adapt to changing times, when elites become
selfish, when justice is too long deferred, and when
aspirations are constantly frustrated, the sweep and
scope of necessary reforms must expand accordingly
and with greater urgency if more dramatic measures
are not sought by a restless, angry citizenry.

According to Hannah Arendt, failure to remember
that the United States and the foundation of freedom
were born out of revolution "is largely responsible for
the intense fear of revolution in America," and "fear

of revolution has been the hidden leitmotif of postwar American foreign policy in its desperate attempt at stabilization of the status quo." This fear led us to support obsolete and corrupt political regimes that were hated and held in contempt by their own people.

Revolutionary American principles were further distorted when cold war competition came to be seen as a life-or-death clash between antagonistic economic systems rather than as a contest between diametrically opposed political value systems. Thus, instead of focusing the world's attention on America's revolutionary emphasis on individual rights and political freedoms versus a totalitarian Soviet political model, we permitted the contest to be identified as free enterprise capitalism versus the Soviet socialist economic model. The unchained, unbridled private initiative of capitalism—essentially laissez-faire economics—flourished under benign American democratic governments as much as anything because of our nation's enormous natural wealth. Ironically, given time and opportunity, it could well flourish in Russia for the same reason. But preservation of a particular economic philosophy closely associated with preservation of the status quo is not necessarily the same as preservation of a revolutionary political philosophy closely associated with evolutionary reforms.

History will consider it odd, to say the least, that America, victorious without bloodshed in the most prolonged, potentially most dangerous ideological struggle ever, demonstrated adamant insistence on Russia's adoption of a market economic system and seemed apathetic about Russia's adoption of a democratic constitution. Late-twentieth-century America seemed sadly ignorant of, and unconcerned about, its true contribution to world history: revolutionary democratic emphasis on constitutionally guaranteed individual freedoms and human political rights.

This failure to remember our revolutionary heritage

might have its reasons—having to do with insularity, rampant individualism, the privateer-buccaneer entrepreneurial spirit, and most of all, latent awareness and avoidance of the civic duty necessary for the survival of a democratic republic. Americans prefer to see the opportunities and rights that their form of government offers rather than the obligations and responsibilities it requires. No more need be said on this theme than that the political debate of the 1990s has much to do with entitlements and little to do with civic duty. Political candidates cast their campaign rhetoric in the mold of government programs and services but are largely too fearful of their constituents to remind them of their own civic responsibilities. For as Arendt says, "Political freedom, generally speaking, means the right 'to be a participator in government' or it means nothing at all."

The eighteenth-century principles motivating the American revolution were public freedom, public happiness, and public spirit. After the revolutionary spirit was lost in the nineteenth century through the failure of thought and remembrance, these principles gave way to "civil liberties, the individual welfare of the greatest number, and public opinion as the greatest force ruling an egalitarian, democratic society," according to Arendt. By the late twentieth century, these principles had given way to values of rampant private interest, with the government as guarantor-of-last-resort (but otherwise as enemy), and to values of materialism, scorn for the public interest, and disinterest for social justice.

The latest national election focused almost exclusively on economic concerns. George Bush was fired by the voters because his laissez-faire philosophy—largely left over from his predecessor—permitted no government intervention to jump-start an economy that was stuck in a dormant, recessionary cycle. What is a president to do when his belief system is antigovernment and the voters demand government action? President Clinton's victory was attributable not only to the generational contrast his candidacy represented after twelve years of geriatric conservatism but even more to the sense that he represented moderate change by means of a leaner but more active government. The motto on his campaign headquarters' wall —THE ECONOMY, STUPID—seems to have said it all.

Arguably, given the political values of the age, President Clinton will be judged a political success (and the sure winner of a second term in office) if he is able to stimulate—or even simply be fortunate enough to preside over—another cycle of economic growth as well as a stable, if not rising, standard of living for middle America. This would be a suitable and deserved reward for the skillful and increasingly delicate manipulation of the fiscal and monetary levers and gears that is required in treacherous economic currents.

But a more profound measure of leadership lies beyond this. It rests in a new government's willingness to undertake fundamental reforms, reforms deferred for a half century by assassinations, the genuine political scandals of Watergate and Irangate, the fiasco of the savings and loan associations and Bank of Credit and Commerce International, the Vietnam War, and most of all, the seemingly interminable cold war. Major modifications of health-care systems, federal support of and incentives for public education, campaign-financing laws, and job-training programs have succeeded, are under way, or soon will be. The more serious question surrounds our willingness and our ability to restructure national energy policies, reform military institutions, replace consumption with incentives for productivity, rebuild our national communication and transportation infrastructures, convert excess military production to nonmilitary production, clean up nuclear and toxic wastes, reduce deficits, and redirect our foreign policies. All are now possible for one historic reason: the end of the cold war.

But even beyond these huge reform efforts, there remains the challenge to reawaken America's revolutionary spirit, with its principles of public freedom, happiness, and spirit and its commitment to the national interest. The whole idea of reform is based on the notion that virtually all citizens possess within themselves the ideal of a better society. At its furthest extreme, this ideal is utopian. But wars, assassinations, political pragmatism, and repeated violations of the public trust by political leaders have pummeled the dreaminess from the utopian vision as though it were stuffing in a rag doll. Instead, the American people have been left with the belief that there may be no solutions to urban decay, racial disharmony, crime, drug use, and other current maladies. Thus, the challenge for contemporary political leadership, namely the Clinton administration and current Democratic Congress, is to reawaken the belief that progress is not a myth but is indeed possible, that government can be both active and benign, that the public and private sectors are not natural enemies, and that public support for a new round of revolutionary experimentalism —what the urbanologist Jane Jacobs calls "the esthetics of drift"—may be required to solve intractable social problems.

Looking back on this time from the future, we shall come to see how fortuitous—almost divinely so—was the coincidence of the cold war's end with the need for America—and much of the Western world—to manage the transition from a manufacturing to an information-based economy. Indeed, this transition has been dangerously delayed in America by the perceived imperatives of cold war militancy. But that militancy, to the degree it ever was as important as we were told it was, evaporated on the democratic barricades raised against the August 1991 Russian coup, and we are now faced with a host of new, and often harsh, economic realities. The new Democratic leadership has made clear that it is not traditionally New Deal-ish; it claims to have no appetite for larger, more bureaucratic government, increased payroll taxes, programmatic policies, or knee-jerk adherence to interventionist economics.

But that is not to say that reforms in the self-definition of government are out of the question. The New Deal's most exciting contribution to modern government—experimentalism—will lead to policies permitting the private sector to use a wide range of options to meet government-mandated performance standards in environmental quality, health-care protection, worker training and retraining, urban renewal, and a wide variety of other public interest arenas. The nation itself will continue to evolve in terms of pluralism and multiculturalism, thus requiring renewed tolerance and openness in adapting to changing immigration demographics. We will continue to become more Asian, African, Latin, and Caribbean in cultural and ethnic complexion. The national challenge is to absorb the best of all these cultures even as we did with nineteenth-century European immigrants.

But the post–cold war reform of America must also include the careful dismantling and restructuring of the military-industrial complex in ways that protect the lives and prospects of the hundreds of thousands of skilled workers, their families, and the communities in which they live and work. There is clearly work to be done in infrastructure rebuilding, in the invention of new biomedical, environmental, and communications technologies, in information handling, in health-care delivery, and in a great variety of similar activities. Once again the challenge lies in the management of transition. Safe, renewable energy supplies must be developed. Research in new building materials and manufacturing techniques must be carried out. Our military forces must be restructured and reformed. All these demands, so long deferred for national-security reasons, now rise up to be addressed. Consequently, the late twentieth and early twenty-first centuries could become a historic era, one rivaling the revolutionary eighteenth century, but only if great leaders in government, business, and society at large arise to seize the opportunities.

In the end, it is never a question of opportunity but always a question of will and imagination. Great leaders inspire both. It has nothing to do with the tedious ideological quarrels between conservatives and liberals over the size and power of government. It has everything to do with the vision of public leaders for the nation's future and their ability to summon our better instincts in the national service. This is the arena that separates a Washington, a Jefferson, a Jackson, a Lincoln, a Franklin Roosevelt from their more numerous, ordinary predecessors and successors. Almost never in a generation and seldom in a century is a society or a nation given the rare chance at redefinition and reinvention. That is precisely what the post–cold war era offers. But this opportunity will not tarry forever. Either we grasp our destiny, or fate and circumstance will dictate it for us.

Given the still-uncelebrated victory of democracy over communism, why does America seem so hesitant about reawakening its dormant revolutionary spirit? This question is inextricably intertwined with the multitudinous barriers conservative America has erected against reform. From the Founders' insistence on not simply a balance of power but an almost absolute dispersal of power down to today's attempt to exhume and reinstate the mythologically independent Western hero, America constantly finds new ways to escape its revolutionary roots. Liberalism is demonized; government is ridiculed and mocked; activism is made marginal; the idealism of youth is discouraged; and social justice is made a utopian dream. Rewards are granted for cleverness, triviality, and sensationalism. Why is any recollection of a nobler time dismissed as nostalgia for Camelot?

The more attention the reformer gave to the question, the more he would become convinced that late-twentieth-century America is in search of that lost fragment of its own revolution, human nobility. But nobility is inseparable from that equally rare quality, integrity, and a nation whose integrity is hostage to a frantic search for material success, ease, and comfort cannot be a noble nation.

The reformer could not see the country that he deeply loved, his homeland, apart from Jesus' parable of the prodigal son. Seeking its ease, metaphorically, in a foreign land, America forgot its soul, its home, and its family. It desperately needed to return to the home of its Founding Fathers, not those who thought democracy to be but another name for economic determinism and capitalism's most fantastic excess, but a democracy that meant justice, equality, and opportunity for all.

The reformer's historically insignificant efforts at reform, his faults, and his failures were but a single frail human measure of the distance between the real and the ideal, the immeasurable space that represents an instinctive human search for nobility. His mature life was chained by religious belief and family training to the immutable rock called justice. Justice was an unforgiving teacher; she was blind, and she was relentless. She would not let go, and she permitted no compromise.

But this reformer's personal struggles were a trivial matter on the great scale of human injustice and in the context of a unique society's search for its unrealized nobility. If the reformer's belief is correct, that the seeds of injustice were planted by the conquistadors, Pilgrims, and slave traders, then the roots of national discontent go deeper than any late-twentieth-century reformer, or president, could ever hope to reach. The nation's founders, unable to resolve age-old struggles between property rights and human freedoms, markets and social cohesion, capitalism and justice, simply passed those struggles on through each generation down to the present age.

When faced with far-reaching misery, as in the Great Depression, America would seek to deal with these tensions. But occasionally, as in the eighties, the country turned selfish and mean to a sufficient degree to dismay a mature but still idealistic reformer. The values of its popular culture—sensationalism, triviality, and mass exploitation of private lives—would be incompatible with national integrity and any serious sense of true nobility. For his children's and his nation's sake, this reformer would hope with considerable desperation that this represented but a passing phase, a sacrifice to the insatiable gods of amusement and consumption, a temporary detour from a just and moral crusade in search of national integrity and nobility.

No single election, including that of 1992, could immediately alter America's course. But it might represent a point of turning, a creaking shift of the compass point on the great ship of state. Even at two hundred years of age, America is too young to succumb to the erosion, decline, decay, and collapse that have characterized history's many cultures. America is not finished yet. Its reformers and disciples of national nobility will not let it slide beneath the surface of history's turbulent waters without one last struggle to realize a better national destiny. However flickering the candle of justice, the effort has to be made. The prospect of a brighter destiny has to be preserved for yet one more generation.

It is devoutly to be hoped that President Clinton's soul will be stirred by Jefferson's radical notion of generational revolution, by the better angels of our nature so dormant since Lincoln, by Wilson's utopian vision of a family of nations, by Franklin Roosevelt's belief that we are all in this together. Sometimes, even in the crude arena of politics, a leader's soul may be stirred by the mystical chords of a nobler future, a more just nation, a better people. When it happens, it is magic.

May such magic descend on America, at least once more. No president, especially in today's age of leveling and reduction, can ever wish for the hero's mantle, and it should not be expected. But there is still a chance, against great cultural odds, that some spark of inspiration so rare and unexpected as to seem almost divine might visit even the most political of politicians and grant them the courage to seek the grail of national nobility. Only a people with some spark of idealism left after decades of pragmatism, realpolitik, and cynicism could even imagine such a crusade for social justice. More mature peoples, more sophisticated nations had given up such an idealistic quest long ago.

But not the American soul. It is, like Sancho Panza, merely awaiting the quixotic call for one more, perhaps one last, crusade in search of a dream that will never die. And even if we fail to find the dream, we must still fail better.

Index

abortion, 298
Abourezk, James, 153
Adams, Henry, ix-x, 296
advertising, 117, 265
Afghanistan, Soviet invasion of,
 167
Africa, 251
African Americans, 296, 297.
 See also Race relations
AIDS (acquired immune
 deficiency syndrome), 300
Allen, Jim, 118
Alliance for Progress, 80
ambassadorships, 208
America Can Win (Hart; Lind),
 215
American Dilemma, An
 (Myrdal), 296
American Revolutionary War,
 255, 305

amusement, xxxvi, 262–63,
 295
Amusing Ourselves to Death,
 263
Andropov, Yuri, 256
antiwar movement, 77, 95, 98
Arbatov, Georgi, 259
Arendt, Hannah, 14, 303, 305
Armed Services Committee
 (U.S. Senate), 7, 79, 163,
 164, 173
arms: control movement, 83;
 design, 170; procurement,
 164, 170, 192; race, 78,
 83, 184, 248, 252, 256;
 weapons systems, 164,
 169, 175, 192. *See also*
 nuclear arms
Asia, 251

Church Committee (Senate Select Committee on Intelligence Activities), 130–44
Church of Denmark, 20, 21, 23
Church of England, 12, 23, 64
Church of Rome, 18, 23
cities: federal assistance to, 121, 196, 204, 308; decline of, 61, 121, 307; economies of, 180
City Year, 279–84, 289
Civilian Conservation Corps, 283
civil rights: legislation, 72, 73; Senate debates on, 118
Civil Rights Act of 1964, 73
civil rights movement, 36, 65–66, 73, 83, 84
Clayton Antitrust Act, 153
Clinton, William J., xviii, 189; 1992 presidential campaign, 221, 224, 306; promise to stay in touch with the people, xxix
Clinton administration, xvii, 306, 307
coal, 147
Cohen, William, 139
Colby, William, 133, 136, 137
Cold War, 48, 56, 76, 80, 81, 99, 162, 304; end of, 174, 175, 248, 250, 259; and intelligence community, 142
collective action, 277, 288
Commission on National and Community Service, 281
Commission on Party Structure and Delegate Selection (McGovern Commission), 91
communism: collapse of, 255, 256, 257, 263, 274, 284–85, 309; containment of, 78, 79, 94–96, 258; expansionism, 251; red scares and McCarthyism, 104
Communist Party, 252, 257
Congo (Zaire), 133
consensus government, 235–36, 298
conservation, energy, 146, 149, 155, 159, 160. *See also* Energy
conservatism, xviii, xxx, xxxi, xxxii, 213, 309
constitutional rights, 52
consumerism, 262, 263, 265
Cornwell, Trevor, 284–85
corruption, xxxvii, 58–59, 107, 110, 111
crime, 61, 200, 307
Cuba, 78, 79
Cuban Missile Crisis, 62, 67, 75, 76
cultural revolution (1960s and 70s), 83, 103, 104, 105
Culver, John, 7
Czech Republic, 263, 266. *See also* Vaclav, Havel

Davis, Angela, 102
defense. *See* military; U.S. Department of Defense
defense industry, xxxiv, 176, 182, 183; conversion to nonmilitary projects, 184, 242, 306
Defense Intelligence Agency, 131, 143
Deficit spending, 168, 196
democracy, 39–40, 45, 275
Democratic National Convention: 1968 in

global economy, 179, 187, 188
God, 301
Goldwater, Barry, 131–32
Gorbachev, Mikhail, 30, 36,
    215, 218, 248–59;
    departure from office, 251;
    meeting with G. Hart,
    248, 249
Gore, Albert, 197
Gorky, Maxim, 26, 36
government, xxvii;
    participation in, xxix;
    more vs. less, 294–95
Gramm, Phil, 193
Gramm-Latta Bill, 192
Gramm-Rudman Act, 187
Grapes of Wrath, The
    (Steinbeck), 27, 28
grass-roots organization, 88
Great Depression, xviii, xxii,
    27, 180–81, 187, 283,
    298, 311
Great Society period, xxxvi,
    73, 77, 127, 195, 204
Greening of America, The
    (Reich), 83
Gromyko, Andrei, 215, 249,
    256
gross domestic product, 180
gross national product,
    percentage devoted to
    defense, 185
gun control, 298

Haiti, 133
Hart, Andrea, 249
Hart, Gary: campaign and
    election to Senate, 108–
    10, 113–14; campaign
    manager for G. McGovern,
    124; childhood of, 10–11,
    27, 54–55; as
    environmentalist, 114;
    family of, 19, 72, 249;

fiction writing, 139;
    influence of literature on,
    27–28; as junior senator,
    115–29; at law school, 65;
    media invasion of privacy,
    219–22; meeting with M.
    Gorbachev, 248, 249; as
    philosophy student, 17–22;
    presidential campaign of
    1984, 139, 206–14, 216,
    231; on Senate Armed
    Services Committee, 163–
    73; on Senate Select
    Committee of Intelligence
    Activities, 130–44; on
    Senate Subcommittee to
    Investigate the
    Performance of the
    Intelligence Community
    during the Warren
    Commission Investigation,
    135–39; Strategic
    Investment Initiative
    reform plan, 183–85, 215;
    summer clerk in Justice
    Department, 82
Hart, Philip, 115–16, 117, 131,
    153, 190
Hatfield, Mark, 116
Havel, Vaclav, 261, 263–75
health-care, 109, 116, 200,
    215, 218, 242, 306, 308
Hearst, Patty, 102
Helms, Jesse, 118
Hemingway, Ernest, 28
heroes, xxxv, 232, 261–62, 289
hippie culture, 83, 103, 104,
    105
Hitler, Adolf, 66, 256
Hofstadter, Richard, 78, 88,
    89, 90
homelessness, 297
Hoover, J. Edgar, 103
Huddleston, Dee, 131

humanitarianism, 264, 278
human-resources programs, 240
Humphrey, Hubert, 57, 68, 95–97, 110, 122, 212; 1968 presidential campaign, 91, 93
hunger-relief organizations, 278–79
Hussein, Saddam, 6, 259
Hussein I, King of Jordan, 215

idealism, xx, xxi, xxxiv, 59, 63, 107, 287–89
ideology, 265, 273, 274
Image, The (Boorstein), 232
India, 35–36
Indochina, 80
Indonesia, 133
industrialization, and poverty, 32
industry, failures and bailouts, 195–96
inflation, 121
information economy, 111, 230, 307
infrastructures, national, 180, 184, 306, 308
intelligence agencies, 79; invasions of citizen's rights, 139–41; Senate investigations of, 130–44. *See also* Central Intelligence Agency; Federal Bureau of Investigation
interest rates, 182
Internal Revenue Service (IRS), 143
International Medical Corps, 287
International Monetary Fund, 188

international service, 284–85, 288
Iran-Contra scandal (Irangate), 50, 79, 147, 306
Iran hostage crisis, 50, 198
Iraq, 172–73
Israel, 156, 171, 231

Jackson, Henry, 116, 123
Jacobs, Jane, 307
James, William, 283
Japan, 117; 1970s economy, 180, 185
Javits, Jacob, 116, 190
Jefferson, Thomas, xxv, xxx, xxxi, 9, 11, 17–18, 23, 40, 51, 55, 64, 65, 67, 81, 99, 237; and generational revolution, 38–39, 41, 43, 44, 45, 46, 47, 48, 311–12; and government participation, xxix-xxx; and science, xxxiii
Jesus Christ, 18
job-training programs, 183–84, 306
Johnson, J. Prescott, 19–22, 23, 24, 25
Johnson, Lyndon B., 60, 63, 68, 73
Johnson administration, 73, 75; and civil rights legislation, 72, 73; domestic reforms, 75; Great Society period, 127; Kerner Commission, 121; and Vietnam War, 81, 96
Judaism, Lamed Vov (the just), 3–4, 8, 15–16
judges, 88
Just, the (Lamed Vov), 3–4, 8, 15–16
justice, social and legal, 3–16

Kammen, Michael, 105, 294, 296
Kemp, Jack, 193
Kennedy, Edward, 93, 116, 123
Kennedy, John F., 56–67; American University speech of 1963, 67, 77–78; assassination of, and effect on nation, 71–84, 92, 101; assassination connected to CIA plot to assassinate Castro, 134, 136, 137, 138, 139, 143; challenge to public service, 76–77, 111, 283; leadership of, 63; *Profiles in Courage*, 276–77. See also Kennedy administration
Kennedy, Paul, 185
Kennedy, Robert F., 81–82, 85, 212; assassination of, xxxiv–xxv, 83, 84, 92, 101; and Martin Luther King, Jr., 81
Kennedy administration: balanced budget under, 66; defense spending, 185; foreign policy, 78, 79, 80; and intelligence activities, 135
Kerensky, Aleksandr, 252
Kerner Commission, 121
Keynes, John, 236
Keynesian economics, 195, 196, 236
Khazei, Alan, 279–80, 281, 289
Kierkegaard, Søren, 11, 17–22, 23, 24, 25, 55, 64, 239
King, Martin Luther, Jr., 36, 81, 261, 263; assassination

of, 83, 84; and Robert Kennedy, 81
Kissinger, Henry, 128, 249
Kleindienst, Richard, 106
Korean War, 56, 162, 241
Kuwait, 147, 161

labor unions, 89, 105, 123, 124, 212, 214
Last of the Just, The (Schwarz-Bart), 3–4, 15–16
Latin America, 251
Lenin, Vladimir, 33, 255, 256
liberalism, xxxi, 96, 200, 213, 309
Lind, William, 170
literacy, 183
literalism, 275
literature, addressing social issues, 27–28
lobbyists, 240, 295–96. See also special interest groups
Long, Russell B., 116
Lumumba, Patrice, 133–34
Luther, Martin, 18
Lutheranism, 18

Madison, James, 239
mafia, and CIA plot to assassinate Castro, 135, 136, 138
Magnuson, Warren G., 116, 190
Mahan, Alfred Thayer, 174
Mailer, Norman, 23, 104
Malcolm X, 102
Mandela, Nelson, 261
Mansfield, Mike, 116, 117–20, 130, 190; and intelligence reform, 131, 143, 144
manufacturing, and foreign competition, 180
March of Folly, The (Tuchman), 161

political campaigns. *See* campaigns

political parties, 24, 87; two-party system, 87, 88. *See also* Democratic party; Republican party

politics and politicians; advisors, 228; careerism, 48, 236–37, 238–43, 266, 272; image and image-makers, 232, 233, 236; public cynicism toward, 106; seen as corrupt, xxxvii, 58–59, 107, 110, 111

pollution, 49, 50, 180. *See also* environmental issues

popular culture, 298

Populist movement (1880s and 90s), 88–89

poverty, 13, 95, 200, 277, 288; children in, 8, 42, 48, 199, 200, 288; 1960s, 73, 82, 85; Reagan-Bush years, 4, 199, 200, 297; and Tolstoy's 19th century Russia, 31; urbanization of, 32

power, xxxi, xxxiii

presidency, 207

presidential campaigns, 206–26

presidential elections. *See* national elections

press. *See* media

primary elections, 92–93, 95

Profiles in Courage (Kennedy), 276–77

progressivism, xxv, xxxi, 73, 89

protectionism, 186, 234

Protestantism, 18. *See also* religion

protest marches and demonstrations, 83, 105

public service, 58, 76–77, 111, 236–37, 270, 278–82; encouraged by Kennedy, 76–77, 111, 283

Qaddafi, Muammar, 6, 158

Quayle, Dan, 299

race relations, xxvii, 65, 197, 212, 297, 307

radicalism, 77, 95

Reagan, Ronald, 30; leadership of, 63; presidential campaign, 208, 223; public image and popularity of, xxviii, 232–33, 236, 237; re-election campaign, 209, 212

Reagan administration, xxxv–xxxvi; cuts in social programs, 191–92, 196, 203, 204; debt and deficit under, xxi, xxviii, 168, 186–87, 200, 236, 237, 240, 242, 260; defense spending, 167–68, 236, 256; deficit spending, 168, 196; discretionary non-entitlement spending cut, 168; energy policy, xix, 156–59; entitlement programs, 196; and intelligence community, 141; Middle East relations, 158–59; and poverty, 4; and secret arms sales, 79; and Senate, 191–203; summit meeting with Gorbachev, 248; supply-side economics, 42, 43, 44, 159, 182, 203, 205, 215, 238, 260, 274; tax cuts, 25, 43, 44, 182, 193, 194, 195, 236, 241; tax cuts for the wealthy, 199,

Reagan administration *(cont.)*
203; U.S.-Soviet nuclear
arms reduction talks, 248,
252; U.S.-Soviet relations,
241, 248
Reaganomics, 199, 237, 240
recession, 1970s, 121. *See also*
economy
Reformation, 18
Regan, Donald, 230
religion, 10, 12, 18–23, 55, 56,
64, 65
Republican National
Convention, 1992, 296
Republican party: and 1980s,
50–51; as party of the
status quo, 99; post–Civil
War, 88; Senate majority
control in 1980s, 191,
197, 202
research, 122–23, 183, 186
resistance, 262
revenues, from consumption,
183, 185, 187
revolution, 67, 68, 81, 99, 255,
303–5, 307, 309;
generational (Jefferson),
38–39, 41–48, 311–12
Ribicoff, Abraham, 116, 143,
190
riots, urban, xxvii, 102; of
1968, 86; of 1992, 84
Rockefeller, John D., 152
Rockefeller, John D, IV, 197
Rockefeller commission, 131
Roosevelt, Franklin D., xviii,
74, 75, 76, 96, 123, 204,
217, 222, 294–95; and
experimentalism, 110–11;
as reformer, 89–90
Roosevelt, Theodore, xxv, 89
Rosselli, John, 136, 138, 143
Russia, xxxii, coup of August

1991, 250, 252, 307; 19th
century of Tolstoy, 28–35
Russian Orthodox Church, 26,
32, 34
Russian White House, 36

Sakharov, Andrei, 252
Savings and Loan Associations,
bailout of, 200, 306
Schlesinger, Arthur, Jr., xxiii
Schlesinger, James, 132
Schneider, René, 133
Schumpeter, Joseph, 154
Schwarz, Fritz, 139
Schwarz-Bart, André, 3, 4, 16
Schweiker, Richard, 132, 135
Schweitzer, Albert, 289
science, xxxiii-xxxiv, xxxv
security, strategic deterrence,
61
sexual revolution, 83, 102, 105
Sherman Antitrust Act, 153
Shevardnadze, Eduard, 218,
250
Shore, Bill, 278–79, 285, 289
Shore, Bonnie, 279, 289
Shultz, George, 249
Sinatra, Frank, 136
sit-ins, 83
slavery, 13, 49, 296
Smith, Adam, 153
socialism, 253, 264
social justice, 3–16, 277, 278,
288, 305
social programs, 297; cuts in
during Reagan years, 191–
92, 196, 203, 204
Social Security system, 181,
195, 205
Socrates, 19, 20
solar energy, 147, 151, 156
Solar Energy Research
Institute, 160
Somalia, 287

SOS (Share Our Strength), 278–79, 280, 289
Southeast Asia, 72, 77, 78, 81, 82
South Korea, 241
South Vietnam, 61, 133. *See also* Vietnam War
Soviet Union, 304; changes under Gorbachev, 248–59; coup of August 1991, 250, 252, 307; political and economic model, 304; and Nixon administration, 249; and Reagan administration, 241, 248, 249, 252; republics of, 253; and third world, 80; U.S.-Soviet nuclear arms reduction talks, 248, 252; U.S.-Soviet summit meeting, 248
space program, 60
special interest groups, 112, 124, 211, 239–40, 295–96
speeches and speech writers, 228
stagflation, 121
Stalin, Joseph, 255
Star Wars, 43, 182
Stealth bombers, 166, 192
Stein, John, 137
Steinbeck, John, 27, 28
Steiner, George, 29, 30, 36
Stennis, John, 126
Stevenson, Adlai E., 57, 68
Stevenson, Adlai E., III, 190
stock and commodities markets, 181
Stockman, David, 193, 203
Strategic Defense Initiative (Star Wars), 43, 182
Strategic Investment Initiative, A (plan for economic reform), 183–85, 215

student loans, 183–84
students, 91, 95
Sukarno, President of Indonesia, 133
Sununu, John, 230
supply-side economics, 42, 43, 44, 159, 182, 203, 205, 215, 238, 260, 274
Symington, Stuart, 68, 116, 190

tax cuts: Bush years, 182; Reagan years, 25, 43, 44, 182, 193, 194, 195, 199, 203, 236, 241
taxes, 240, 241–42, 294
Teapot Dome scandal, 152
technology, 90, 197, 308; foreign competition in, 180; research, 122–23, 183, 186; superiority in, 60–62
Tehran, American Embassy hostage crisis, 50, 198
television, 233–34; and campaign advertising, 220, 243, 266, 268
Teller, Edward, 43
Tennyson, Alfred Lord, 19, 20
term limitations, 237
terrorism, international, 157, 158
Thurmond, Strom, 118, 239
Tocqueville, Alexis de, xxiv, 28
Tolstoy, Leo, 11, 17, 26–37, 55, 63, 65, 239
totalitarianism, 263, 265, 267, 304
Tower, John, 132
toxic waste, 306
Trafficante, Santos, 136
Trident submarines, 166, 192
Trujillo, Rafael, 133
Truman, Harry S, 241

72, 77–82, 84, 94, 96, 98,
102, 104, 113, 116; and
military strategy, 163, 169;
withdrawal from, 122, 167
VISTA, 283
voter participation, 268
Voting Rights Act of 1965, 73

Walesa, Lech, 261
Walto, Dennis, 286–87, 289
warfare: attrition, 170–71;
maneuver, 171–72
War on Poverty legislation
(1965, 1966), 73
Warren Commission, 135, 136
Warsaw Pact, 251
Washington, George, 78
Watergate affair, 23, 103–4,
106, 107–8, 112, 306
wealthy, the, xxi, xxviii, xxxii,
xxxiii, 4, 199, 203, 299
weapons systems, 164, 169,

175, 192. *See also* arms;
nuclear arms
Weinberger, Caspar, 128
welfare system, 14, 194, 204,
205; reform, 102
Wesley, John, 11–13, 23, 55,
64
White, Theodore, 57
wind energy, 147, 151
women's rights, 83, 91, 95,
105, 286
working classes, 31, 90
World Bank, 188
World War I, military strategy,
170
World War II, 36; military
strategy, 165, 170;
weapons, 175

Yale Divinity School, 56
Yeltsin, Boris, 36, 253, 257
youth national service, 279–83

About the Author

GARY HART, a former senator from Colorado, is a lawyer and strategic adviser, providing counsel to major corporations and negotiating East-West trade projects. He is the author of three nonfiction books and two novels. He lives in Kittredge, Colorado.